SEVENTH CHILD

SEVENTH CHILD:
A FAMILY MEMOIR OF MALCOLM X

RODNELL P. COLLINS

nephew of Malcolm X

with A. PETER BAILEY

KENSINGTON PUBLISHING CORP.
www.kensingtonbooks.com

DAFINA BOOKS are published by

Kensington Publishing Corp.
119 West 40th Street
New York, NY 10018

All Kensington titles, imprints, and distributed lines are available at special quantity discounts for bulk purchases for sales promotions, premiums, fund-raising, educational, or institutional use.

Special book excerpts or customized printings can also be created to fit specific needs. For details, write or phone the office of the Kensington sales manager: Kensington Publishing Corp., 119 West 40th Street, New York, NY 10018, attn: Sales Department; phone 1-800-221-2647.

DAFINA and the Dafina logo are Reg. U.S. Pat. & TM Off.

ISBN: 978-1-4967-4054-0

First Dafina trade paperback printing: January 2002

10 9 8 7 6 5 4 3 2

Printed in the United States of America

To my wife, Annie Cherian-Collins, and our two children, Arjun K.C. and Dayorsha Ella, for their love, patience, and understanding, which have sustained me during the eight years it has taken to write this book.

I also dedicate this work, in loving memory, to my parents, Ella and Kenneth Collins—my mother, the strongest person I ever knew, who never wavered from my corner, and my dad, who always made me smile in our 3:00 A.M. tennis matches.

CONTENTS

"I have sworn upon the altar
of Allah,
Against all tyranny in the minds of men,
FREEDOM BY ANY MEANS NECESSARY."

—El-Hajj Malik El-Shabazz (Malcolm X)

PREFACE

The brilliant, courageous, daring, tenacious, committed, prophetic visionary and revolutionary activist whom most people know as Malcolm X, whom some know also as El-Hajj Malik El-Shabazz, was my uncle; not just an uncle—he was and remains my favorite uncle, my mentor, hero, role model and personal griot. From the time I was old enough to remember, he, third only to my mother and his sister, Ella Little Collins, and my father, Kenneth J. Collins, was the major influence on my life. That influence wasn't terminated on February 21, 1965, the day this extraordinary uncle was assassinated, or on February 27, 1965, the day he was buried (I was a pallbearer at his funeral); it has grown stronger through the years. In reference to that assassination, one of the many revelations contained in this book is that Uncle Malcolm, Martin Luther King Jr., and John F. Kennedy, whose deaths profoundly and forever changed social, political, and racial dynamics in America, were, for a brief period in 1952, all pounding the beat in Boston within a few blocks of each other. This is detailed in the text.

In 1945 Uncle Malcolm was nearing the end of a self-destructive period that resulted in his incarceration. Thus, my first memory of him was sitting on his knees when I visited him in prison. While he and my mother talked, Uncle Malcolm would put me on his knees and, during lulls in their conversation, tell me stories and tease me. I remember his wide-open smile as a source of comfort. Our visits were always a joyous time for me.

After Uncle's release from prison, our relationship grew stronger. I was seven years old and considered Uncle Malcolm a big brother, for Ma always referred to him as her brother. He was very busy with Muhammad's Temple of Islam but visited Boston at least three or four times a year to relax, speak, and confer with Ma. All I knew was that I enjoyed his company. As I grew older, he became Uncle Malcolm, my personal source of knowledge. It was from him that I learned many of the details about African American history. Because of him, I joined the Nation of Islam (N.O.I.) and attended workshops in which he taught us about white supremacy, Africa, Asia, self-defense, and self-determination, among other things. I was impressed with his knowledge, cherished his wisdom, and loved and respected him above all others, except for my parents, Aunt Gracie, and Aunt Sarah. In fact, I saw the world through Uncle Malcolm's prophetic eyes. It's impossible to overemphasize the influence he had on the first twenty years of my life, the time when one develops perspectives and beliefs that last a lifetime. It was a rare day when Uncle Malcolm and his brothers, several of whom were ministers in Muhammad's Temple of Islam, were not the subject of conversation in our home, whose occupants, besides Ma and me, were Aunt Sas, Aunt Gracie, and Kenneth J. Collins, my father. Our beloved, elderly aunts were the sisters of Earl Little Sr., Ma and Uncle Malcolm's father. One of the highlights of my adolescent and early teen years was our annual summer visit with Uncle Malcolm in Harlem, where he was the Minister of Temple Seven. He took Ma and me on fascinating tours of Harlem, which had a mesmerizing effect on me, since I was totally unaccustomed to many of the outrageous sights I saw on its streets.

When Uncle Malcolm traveled, he wrote and called regularly. As I grew older, Ma shared some of the letters and calls with me. She made it very clear that Uncle Malcolm was the person I was to emulate. I was privileged to be an eyewitness to the closeness between them. I would often see them huddled in deep conversation about issues of obvious importance. As I became more responsible, they sometimes included me in their conversations. Mostly, I just listened and learned. The surest sign that I had grown up was when I became old enough to drive my uncle around Boston to meetings and assignments. That meant I was now considered a reliable member of their team.

The last year of Malcolm's productive life was filled with an overt barrage of vicious verbal attacks from several key Nation of Islam officials, including the loquacious Louis X (now Louis Farrakhan), of Temple Eleven in Boston, and equally vicious, more covert attacks from conniving FBI and CIA operatives. I was among those family members and supporters who were frustrated, enraged, and disgusted because of our inability to protect him. As late as the early morning of February 21, 1965, Ma and I were discussing with him possible actions he should take to protect himself. They mostly involved his leaving the country with his family. Uncle Malcolm appeared to listen, but when we last saw him, near sunrise that morning, he still hadn't decided exactly what to do about safety concerns. Our last gesture was to wave goodbye to one another as he drove away. Later that afternoon, now back in Boston, we heard about the assassination.

Ma, whose reluctance to publicly express her grief was legendary among those who knew her best, came closest to doing so in a statement issued not long after Uncle Malcolm's death. She directed it toward those who had believed in and supported him, especially during that last harsh year. Ma wrote: "Nobody could have endured a more painful experience of Malcolm's death than myself; I was not only a sister but a mother to him. . . . To all his friends and acquaintances, his death was a great loss; it was a much greater loss to myself and his family." For Ma that was a passionate statement.

"I already knew what I had to do," Ma told me later. "I had constantly prodded Malcolm to write his autobiography. 'Get something out there for black people to use as a guide and a historical document,' I told him. 'Also, it will help provide for your children. Don't leave them financially strapped like our father did you, your mother, and your brothers and sisters when he was murdered by white supremacists.' Now people used that same argument on me. Because Malcolm's life was cut short, there were important things around his life not included in the autobiography. I had information about many of those things because he confided in me." She felt a responsibility to document them.

Ma began tentatively working on the project in the late 1960s. For the next fifteen years or so, she compiled data, spoke on tape, and kept notes for the proposed book. Initially I wasn't too involved in the project. Having joined the professional tennis circuit in the 1970s, I was on the road six to eight months a year. It was in 1984, after retiring from the circuit, that I actively began working with Ma on the book. In 1980, she was diagnosed with sugar diabetes. By

1984 one of her legs had to be amputated, which lent an urgency to
the book project. By 1988 her other leg was amputated, and my father
had died. Ma, plagued with increasingly bad health but still blessed
with her indomitable will, turned the project completely over to me in
1985. It was then that I realized how difficult and emotionally traumatic
it must have been for her to have to relive Uncle Malcolm's life. Having
to reread the autobiography, listen to recorded speeches on cassette tapes
and albums, watch documentaries, read dozens of newspaper and magazine articles, and speak with dozens of people, including family members, sometimes caused very serious emotional stress and rekindled
many fascinating, albeit sorrowful, memories.

The book's title resulted from the fact that Uncle Malcolm was a
seventh child. In African mythology, and science, it is believed that
the seventh child will emerge as a leader of his people. Malcolm also
considered seven his favorite number. That's why, when he was head
of Temple Seven in Harlem, he named three other temples in New
York City 7A, 7B, and 7C. He also noted in his autobiography that
"among over eight thousand other seats in Miami's Big Convention
Hall [for the 1963 Cassius Clay–Sonny Liston championship fight] I
received seat number seven. Seven has always been my favorite
number. It has followed me throughout my life. I took this to be
Allah's message that Cassius Clay was going to win."

Ma decided, and I fully agree with her, that we should provide new information and deeper insights into three important aspects of Malcolm's
life: his extended family, his unique foreign policy, and his commitment
to orthodox Islam. All three are usually given inadequate attention in
books and documentaries on Uncle Malcolm. Without knowledge of
them, however, one cannot fully know who Uncle was and why.

First, there's the extended family. In every family—and the Littles
are a large clan—there is at least one person who is the connecting link
between various family factions. Ma was that person in the Little family. Our home in Boston was a kind of central headquarters for information about Little family members scattered throughout the country,
especially in Georgia, Michigan, New York, New Jersey, Massachusetts, Florida, Alabama, Texas, and North and South Carolina. Ma,
Aunt Sas, and Aunt Gracie knew better than anyone else about

weddings, births, deaths, graduations, and family feuds. Uncle Malcolm was completely dependent on them for such information. Because Ma had grown up in rural Butler, Georgia, and was raised by her
paternal grandparents, she also had extensive knowledge of the Little
family's oral history. The key person in that area today, however, is
Ma's first cousin, Oscar V. Little, an educator living in Washington,
D.C. Uncle Oscar spent many hours in dusty archives researching the
Little family history. He successfully traced the line as far back as
Uncle Malcolm's great-great-grandfather, an African called Ajar. What
he learned about that rich history will be revealed in this book for the
first time to the general public.

Uncle Oscar's research, and subsequently my own, helped confirm
some of the stories I had heard about the Little family from Ma, Aunt
Sas, and Aunt Gracie. It was those stories that, in the 1970s, initially
led me to seek out Littles in Reynolds, Butler, and Talbotton, Georgia,
while playing professional tennis tournaments in that state. In 1996 I
returned to that area and found more Littles and Little gravesites from
as far back as the late 1800s. This research, plus what I learned from
rereading Malcolm's autobiography, poring over dozens of pieces of
correspondence between him and Ma, listening to his recorded speeches
on cassette tapes and albums, and speaking with many people who knew
him personally, made me even more cognizant of my uncle's greatness
as a person and as a leader of our people.

A second area of immense importance to understanding Malcolm is
his foreign policy. From the late 1950s to the day of his assassination
Malcolm laid the foundation for connecting the struggle against
white supremacy in the United States to the struggle against white
colonialism in Africa and Asia. He wasn't the first to make that connection, but because of his superb communication skills and modern
technological advances in transportation and communications, he
was able to develop the concept more effectively than his predeces-
sors, such as Marcus Garvey and W. E. B. Du Bois. His work paid
off in 1964 when he became the first African American invited to be
an unofficial observer at the Organization of African Unity Conference held in Cairo, Egypt. At that conference Uncle was treated like
an official representative of African Americans by many of the

delegates in attendance and by the African press. He also released an accusatory written statement boldly detailing his position that the struggles against colonialism on the African continent and against white supremacy in the United States were literally connected and should be treated as such by both Africans and African Americans. Presenting his position to hundreds of Africans was a memorable and satisfying experience for Malcolm. His unprecedented accomplishments also clarify why the FBI and the CIA were as much interested in his demise as the corrupt leadership of the Nation of Islam. Three things particularly enraged them: his friendship with world leaders, such as Presidents Kwame Nkrumah and Gamal Abdel Nasser of Ghana and Egypt, respectively; his plan to recruit black Vietnam veterans as advisers to African freedom fighters; and his plan to charge the government of the United States, before the United Nations Commission on Human Rights, with being unable or unwilling to protect the lives and property of African Americans. That may seem rather tame in 1998, but in the early 1960s, at the height of the fervid propaganda battle between the United States and the Soviet Union during the cold war, even talk of such a move by my uncle enraged the CIA.

While traveling on the professional tennis circuit in the 1970s, I saw and experienced evidence of Malcolm's status among foreigners involved in their countries' struggle against colonialism and, later, continued economic exploitation. In Brazil, Guyana, Colombia, and Venezuela I saw his name and image on posters along with those of Che Guevara. I met, among many others, a Middle Eastern journalist, a Muslim imam in Copenhagen, Denmark, and professors in England and Scotland, all of whom had been impressed with, or inspired by, him. The English and Scottish professors had seen him debate the motion "Extremism in the Defense of Liberty Is No Vice, Moderation in the Pursuit of Justice Is No Virtue" in 1964 at Oxford University. Despite the official count against him, they insisted that Malcolm had handily won that debate before Oxford's international student body.

Finally, there's the question of the spiritual Uncle Malcolm, the believer in orthodox Islam. The depth of his religious belief is clearly illustrated in the statement "I do not pretend to be a divine man, but I do believe in divine guidance, divine power and the fulfillment of divine prophecy. I am not educated, nor am I an expert in any particular field. But I am sincere, and my sincerity is my credential." To Malcolm it was just as important to link up religiously with international Islam as it was to do so politically with Pan-Africanism. He eagerly and successfully developed relationships with key Muslims in Africa, Asia, and the Middle East. He considered the religious and political connections vital weapons in the battle for human rights and against white supremacy. One of his concrete accomplishments in this area was to secure twenty scholarships for African-American Muslims to study at the prestigious Al Azhar University in Cairo, Egypt, and another twenty for the non-Muslim African Americans to attend a university in Ghana, West Africa. Because of constant death threats during the last eighteen months before he was assassinated, Malcolm was unable to put his political, economic, and ideological programs into action or to finish the autobiography, which he was writing with Alex Haley. That's why Ma's observations and information in this book are so critically important.

My only regret is that Ella Little Collins, my courageous and indomitable mother, died in August 1996, before the project was completed. For thirty-one years after my uncle's assassination, she tenaciously rejected and challenged those who attempted to involve her in articles, books, documents, and movies that presented a limited, distorted view of the brother she knew so well and loved so deeply. This book accomplishes what she wanted, which was to reveal Uncle Malcolm not just as a leader but as a brother, cousin, nephew, uncle, father, husband, and friend. It includes bitter, haunting memories as well as loving, joyful, precious memories experienced by two people who knew Malcolm as family, brother, and uncle. None of the other forty books about Malcolm (written in eight languages) can honestly make that claim.

RODNELL P. COLLINS'S
ACKNOWLEDGMENTS

Between my mother and me we worked on this book project off and on for nearly twenty years. Many times it seemed a thankless and hopeless task to present a book on Uncle Malcolm that got beyond the stereotypes, half-truths, distortions, and sometime outright lies appearing in too many of the other books on him. That we were finally able to do this is the result not only of our own tenaciousness but also strong support from numerous individuals who provided informational, spiritual, and sometimes financial support because of their belief in the project. Most notable among these are family members such as Oscar V. Little, J. W. Miller, Uncle Malcolm's brothers and sisters, Earl Little Jr., Mary, Wilfred, Philbert, Wesley, Reginald, Hilda, Yvonne, and Robert; persevering members of the Searcey, Miller, Gray, Walker, Saylor, and Mason families, all connected to the resilient Littles by marriage; members of my wife's family, the distinguished and gracious Maj. K. C. and Mary Cherian of India; Lt. Col. Joseph and Maya Samuel; academicians Ors. John Henrik Clark, Leonard Jeffries, Richard Newman, C. Eric Lincoln, Henry Louis Gates, Jr., Gerald O'Grady, Chris Nteta, Teko Manong Ngoye and Professors James Smalls, Eli A. Tubman and Mazizi Kunene; writers James Baldwin, Sonia Sanchez, Louis Lomax, Karl Evanzz, Theresa Perry, Roberto Giammanco, Alex Haley, Dean Archie Epps, Thulani Davis, Art Aveilhe; and other eminent individuals such as Dr. Ahmed Osman, Chuck Moore, Earl Grant, Yuri Kochiyama, the Thomas Wallaces, Ossie Davis, Ruby Dee, Conrad Lynn, A. Peter Bailey, John Eade, Malcolm Jarvis, Rodney Smith, Beverly Wilson, John Taylor (Ike) Williams, Carolyn Goodman, Percy Sutton, Bazeley E. Perry, Iman Heshaam Jaaber, Terrence Collins,

Michael Abdul Malik, Carlos Moore, Victor Prince, Dr. Carol Tandu Smalls, Dr. Alfred and Violet Jarrette, Sid Wellman, Louise C. Jeffers, The Abdoulla N. Shabazzes, the Hue Olivers, Evelyn and Ted Rowe, Gary Page, the Cecil Rousons, Cora Williams, William Hortzeg, Ann Shelton, Toni Adelle, Michael E. Anderson, Calvin Cobbs, the Harold Belfons, Saoud Muhammad, Sheikh Ahmed Hassoun, Congressman Joseph P. Kennedy, James Farmer, Lauren Douglas Boston, Dr. M. T. Medhi, Galdes Fuller, Dorothy Young-Collins, Sidney Ettman, Judge George W. Crockett, Clare Marie Shah, Eugene A. Leahy, Esam A. Modeer, Iman Wallace D. Muhammad, Maphiri Masekela, Malik Addal-Kahalla, the Curtis J. Harrises, the K. M. Josephs of India, Father George Thackekarrh, Richard Newman, Kathy Moody, Governor Endicott (Chubb) Peabody, Dennis and Nancy Brogdon, John Jr. and Joan Walker, the William Starkses, Kwame Toure, Edward S. Spriggs, Clifford Brown, Beatrice Whitnah, Anne Koole, John S. Moshi, Congressman Adam Clayton Powell Jr., Robert E. Williams, Henry (Duck) Miller, Mordecai Ziotnik, Samuel Ibrahim, Helen E. Brown, T. K. Venkatasubramanian, the Anton Tiens, Aubrey and Ruth Barnett, the Fredrik Ensimkiars, the Willie Jameses, Bosnu Nekau, Agatha Gulford; Their majesties King Saud Al Saud and King Faisel Al Saud of Saudi Arabia, also Iman Hasan Maa'moun, Muhammad Ali Salaam, W. W. Perkins, Maya Jacobs, Janice and Bob Petties, Ernest Hamilton, Kabrir Abdul Rahman, Luckson Ejofodomi and Boston Mayor Thomas Menino.

I thank you all.

A. PETER BAILEY'S
ACKNOWLEDGMENTS

As a dedicated Malcolmite, co-writing this book has been an experience of a lifetime. For providing me with that I heartily thank Sister Ella Collins and Rodnell P. Collins.

I also thank Brother Malcolm for introducing me to and anchoring me in black nationalism; Mamoud Boutiba for teaching me propaganda analysis; Harold Cruse for instilling in me the necessity for each generation of black people to document their experiences so future generations won't make the same mistakes; Hoyt Fuller and Charles Sanders for nurturing my journalistic talents; and John H. Johnson for giving me a chance to work in the field.

Finally, I want to thank family and friends without whose moral and financial support I would not have been able to complete this project. These include my father, Upson Bailey Sr.; my sisters, Gloria Spencer, Marian Scott, and Zana Jones; my niece, Sherry Tillman; and righteous friends and colleagues such as William and C. Delores Tucker, Barbara Norris, Walter Stafford, S. Karie Nabinet, Frank Solomon, Angela E. Smith, Bernice Bryant, lshmail Conway, Rev. Tyler

C. Millner, Lewis Duckett, Dr. Billy Jones, Melvin Scott, William Mackey, Earl Grant, Andre Baldwin, Patricia Funderburke Ware, Jerome Gray, James Billups, John Leslie Jr., Bob Law, Rev. Wyatt Tee Walker, Dr. Waltann Belle, Lionel and Frederica Barrow, Djibrill Diallo, Carroll Hardy, Voza Rivers, Percy Sutton, Bess Daniel, and twenty-two righteous others who came through in crunch time.

My Dear Sister,
            I enjoyed my chat with you Friday, tremendously,
and though you weren't able to be out to the meeting that night
yourself, I'm thankful that you were able to get Toni to come.

            She seems to be very wise, and down to earth,
and I think she understood what we were teaching, and enjoyed herself.
It is hard today to get people even to listen to the truth , so
we are always doubly thankful to get some one to listen, accept,
and then act according to what they understand of the Truth. Toni
listened very attentively, and if she continues to go there and
get a more thorough understanding, it will change her entire life.

            I don't know when I'll be back in town, but I would
advise you to attend those meetings as often as possible. Because
as it opens your eyes to different things around you, your past experiences will make everything more easily understandable than it now
is even to the others. YOU YET DON'T REALIZE WHAT TIME IT REALLY IS.
In your spare time, go there and listen to those lectures, and
THEN do whatever you wish....but at least go a few times and listen.
I can't see anyone with your brain passing anything like this up, unless you just aren't allowing yourself to look far enough ahead to see
the VALUE in knowing these things. Today, only the WISE can survive,
ar attain peace of mind. ....

            Concerning the other move you are wondering whether
or not to make: be wise. Use good judgment. Hope to see you soon.

                        your Brother
                        Malcolm

If a man had robbed a bank of a million dollars, and
a traffic cop wanted to argue with him about a minor
traffic violation (not knowing the car actually contains
a million dollars) —— would you blame the
man for taking low — or should he exert his
authority? (smile)

Sunday evening

My Dear Sister,

    I really looked for you today, more so than any other time since I came to prison. Jaci told me someone had been by to see you concerning me but she didn't know the particulars. You could never imagine how extremely important it is that I see you as soon as possible. I know how busy you are, and it's hard for you to get here now, but do please take the taxi and come out alone if the car isn't running .... or else ask Mary if she will dash out. Even Mozelle.

    I've been wanting a private chat with you since last June, but you've always had someone with you when you came out. There are many things you don't know.

    Do give my best to all — especially Aunts Sas & Gracie. Hilda sent me pictures of both of them that she took when she was here. Do be sweet

Your Brother
Malcolm

P.S.
I know I shouldn't expect so much, but I will be looking for you Thursday. OK?

ONE Ajar

It was the summer of 1985. Over one hundred members of the far-flung Little family had gathered together in Memphis, Tennessee, for its first-ever family reunion. A family member who was present described it as an awesome, electrifying, and unforgettable moment when Oscar V. Little, the convener of the reunion and the family's unofficial historian, announced that his extensive research, done at the archives in Washington, D.C., and Virginia, had finally revealed the name of the Little ancestor whom a few of us knew vaguely as an African kidnapped and delivered into slavery in South Carolina in the early 1800s. "His name was Ajar," Uncle Oscar told our stunned family members, "and he was brought to enslavement in South Carolina in 1815." Uncle Oscar told them that he first heard the name Ajar from an elderly Chicago-based relative named Tempie Little. She was the daughter of one of the twenty-two children born to Tony (Ajar's son) and Claire Little, Ma and Uncle Malcolm's great-grandparents. Cousin Tempie Little was a member of the Little family branch that married into the Binon family in the Southwest. She told Uncle Oscar that she had often heard her parents speak of a great-grandfather named Ajar.

The Littles could hardly wait to pass on the incredible revelation to family members who were not present in Memphis. One of those was my mother, Ella Little Collins. Because of illness, she had been unable to attend the reunion. "When I heard about Ajar," Ma later said, "one of my first thoughts was I wish Malcolm was here to share in our joy. We finally had a name for the great-great-grandfather I had mentioned to him but whose name I didn't know. With Malcolm's love of history and his deep awareness of the crucial role of family, he would have enjoyed every minute of it."

Not only did Uncle Oscar do extensive research on the Littles' family history, he has also been the driving force behind family reunions. Following the first one in Memphis in 1985, others were held in Chicago (1986), Los Angeles (1987), Washington, D.C. (1989), Montgomery, Alabama (1991), New York City (1993), Orlando, Florida (1995), and Jackson, Mississippi (1997).

Like thousands of other black folks, Uncle Oscar was inspired to seek out family history after seeing *Roots,* Alex Haley's record-smashing television program, in 1977. "Not too long after seeing *Roots,*" Uncle Oscar explained, "I visited my aunt Florence Scott, in Memphis. While there, I had a long conversation with her and one of my uncles, Elgin Scott, whom I thought was long-since dead. It didn't make sense to believe that a family member was dead because we had lost contact with each other. My commitment to doing research on our family, and later the family reunions, both began with those conversations in the late 1970s."

"It's ironic," noted Ma, "that Oscar was inspired by Alex Haley's *Roots,* because I'm convinced that Haley was at least partially inspired to write *Roots* because of his conversations with Malcolm about the importance of history and family when they were working on the autobiography."

Uncle Malcolm noted in his autobiography that when he joined the Nation of Islam in 1952, "The Muslims' 'X' symbolized the true African family name that he never could know. For me, my 'X' replaced the white slavemaster name of 'Little' which some blue-eyed devil named Little had imposed upon my paternal forebears. . . ." Some people have wrongly interpreted this as Malcolm's rejection of Little family members. "It's extremely important to remember that Malcolm rejected the name dumped on us by slave owners, not our ancestors," Ma said. "Our ancestors were proud black people who, though enslaved physically, were never enslaved mentally."

One of those proud ancestors, the man whose name Uncle Oscar revealed to us that summer evening, was the African called Ajar. "We don't know how he got that name," Uncle Oscar noted, "but after going through many documents, I am convinced that that's the name he was known by." Ma, who by that time was an orthodox Muslim, believed that Ajar may have had a Muslim name, maybe something like Haja, which was then deliberately or unknowingly mispronounced by his enslaver.

Uncle Oscar told us that Ajar possibly came from the Bambara people of Nali, West Africa, the home region for many Africans who ended up enslaved in South Carolina. According to historian Dr. Kennell Jackson in his book *American Is Me,* South Carolina enslavers preferred "Africans from the Gambia region because [they] were useful in rice farming." He wrote that they often advertised for "a Talle [sic] able People."

Ajar's West African beginnings before ending up in South Carolina also conform to an observation made by Frederic Bancroft in his book *Slave Trading in the Old South.* Noted Bancroft, "Cargoes of Africans brought to Charleston, South Carolina, were variously advertised as 'very prime Congo slaves,' or 'prime Mandingo Africans,' or 'Choice Gold Coast Negroes,' or 'prime Windward Coast Africans.'" It's hard to believe that those placing such ads were describing human beings, not livestock. But that was the reality—and the inhumanity—of the times.

Ajar, during the brutal trip across the Atlantic Ocean, must have shared the feelings expressed by Olaudah Equiano, another African kidnapped and enslaved in the United States. Equiano was kidnapped as an adolescent in 1756. In 1789 he wrote a book, *The Interesting Narrative of the Life of Olaudah Equiano, the African,* in which he noted that during the trip across the Atlantic Ocean, "I was now persuaded that I had gotten into a world of bad spirits and that they were going to kill me." When reading this statement, I thought that bad spirits are the same as devils, so the labeling of white supremacists as devils didn't begin with Uncle Malcolm and the Nation of Islam. Brother Olaudah Equiano did so in 1789. It's for certain that Ajar and millions of other Africans enslaved in the misnamed "New World" shared his belief of having gotten into a world of bad spirits that would kill them.

Ajar was delivered into a world of bad spirits in which an enslaver could advertise in a respectable Charleston, South Carolina, newspaper the sale of fifty Africans whom he had "purchased for

stock and breeding Negroes, and to any Planter who particularly
wanted them for that purpose, they are a very choice and desirable
gang." After hearing about Ajar from Ma, I recalled a trip made to
the Goree Islands, off Senegal, West Africa, in 1978. The islands are
one of the sites where African men, women, and children were held
before being put on the ships taking them to America. I met an elderly African caretaker who, at my request (I didn't want to share the
experience with the mostly white tourists), gave me a private tour of
the sites. My most vivid and lasting memory is of the cells where
children were kept. I could see scratches they had made on the walls
with their fingernails while in a state of sheer desperation and fear.
The cells for adults were barely large enough for crawl space and
contained scratches made by horror-stricken Africans. The old man
told me that bones are sometimes still found in the shallower water
where people had drowned themselves rather than board the ships.
Every time I think of that scene, even twenty years later, overwhelming feelings of empathy for our ancestors engulf me. Intense
feelings of anger and loathing emerge for those who put Ajar and
millions of other African men, women, and especially children through
that hell.

Ajar must have found such people the true reincarnation of bad
spirits or devils. Family lore, beginning with the stories told by his
son, Tony, describes Ajar as a rebellious African, one "who was
never anybody's nigger." Tony, to whom Ajar passed on his pride as
an African and his skills as a carpenter, said that one day his father
mysteriously disappeared. "We heard that through family oral history," Ma told me, "that was passed on to us by my grandfather, Papa
John, and reinforced by Oscar's research. He may have run away,
but it is more generally believed that he was sold or traded away by
his enslaver because of his rebellious nature." Sale or threat of sale
was one of the enslavers' most effective and intimidating ways to
control African captives in the United States, according to historian
Dr. Norrece T. Jones, of Virginia Commonwealth University, in his
book *Born a Child of Freedom, Yet a Slave*. Focusing on enslavement in South Carolina, Jones writes that "much emphasis has been
placed on cruel lynchings and executions to the neglect of psychological forces frequently more devastating in their consequences and

more effectual in spurring 'good' behavior. Slaves' fear of being separated from family members and loved ones, for example, made the role of 'miscreant' or 'incorrigible' slaves the most powerful long-term technique of control—short of death—that masters possessed. . . ." Over a century later, words such as "incorrigible" and other similiar invectives would be used by white supremacists to describe Ajar's rebellious great-great-grandson Malcolm Little, who became Malcolm X.

After the disappearance of his father, Tony was sold to the Allen Little family, then based in South Carolina. When the Littles left South Carolina to explore growing economic opportunity in neighboring Georgia, they took Tony and his family with them. Because of his skills as a carpenter, Tony was considered very valuable property by Allen Little as well as by other members of the white Little clan of Talbotton, Georgia. Equally valuable because of her cooking skills was Tony's wife, Clarrie, whose ancestry was a mixture of African and Native American. She is said to have always privately referred to whites as thieves because they had stolen the land of her Native American ancestors. One of the key (and most vicious) figures in that land theft was President Andrew Jackson, who before and during his presidency was famous—or infamous, depending on one's viewpoint—as an "Indian fighter."

In the early and mid-1800s, Georgia was wide open for exploitation by avaricious people, such as Allen Little and his brother Thomas. Native Americans had been driven completely off the land they had lived on and shared for centuries. The state legislature had also passed a law requiring that persons coming into Georgia to purchase land have at least one enslaved African for every fifty acres of land purchased. Land could also be acquired by land grants or lottery.

Allen Little was the first in his family to take advantage of an opportunity to become a kind of feudal lord in Georgia, eventually owning twelve hundred acres in Talbot County, where he built his fortune. In *A Rockaway in Talbot: Travels in an Old Georgia County,* William H. Davidson wrote: "Allen Little, an early settler and wealthy planter of Baldwin County, Georgia, owned a fine plantation in Talbot County. Around Milledgeville, his extensive farms, many slaves, profitable business dealings, country homes and a town house, made him a man of influence during the antebellum era. . . . He began investing in land about three miles north of the town, bought and traded slaves, and owned a hotel in Milledgeville later known as the Wayne Hotel." One of the Africans enslaved by Allen was Ajar's son, Tony.

Thomas Little followed his brother to Georgia, where he also acquired land and enslaved numerous Africans. Davidson mentioned a revealing situation in which Thomas Little's son, Dr. William G. Little, gave "a gift of love and affection for his parents of a certain Negro girl, Charlotte, 15 years of age, and her future increase." In other words, Thomas Little and his wife accepted as "a gift of love and affection" from their son a fifteen-year-old African girl and any children she might have in the future. "No wonder Olaudah Equiano described such people as bad spirits and Malcolm described them as devils," Ma said angrily.

Through the years, the white Littles provided Georgia with numerous public officials, southern belles, Confederate soldiers, lawyers, and other professionals. One of the white Littles helped draft the petition for the Confederate government, and for a period served in that government's legislative body. However, after the Civil War their fortunes declined considerably, having been based so much on the enslavement of African people.

Because of their skills Tony and Clarrie were spared being sold at one of the auctions held periodically by the white Little enslavers. Those skills had made Tony and Clarrie what their great-grandson was to later refer to scornfully as "house Negroes." "They may have worked in the Big House," said Ma, "but from everything I heard from our grandfather, they didn't have the typical house-slave mentality, because most of all they were Ajar's children."

The same skills that enabled them to survive enslavement also served them well after the Civil War. Following emancipation and liberation, Tony and Clarrie remained in Taylor County, mostly in the towns of Reynolds and Butler. Reynolds, according to a history compiled by the Reynolds Women's Club, was "first settled by wealthy Planters, who intended that it should be the Seat of Government for Taylor County, organized in 1852." They took Little as a family name from sheer necessity. When former enslaved Africans wanted to purchase land from the new government, they were asked, "Where did you come from?" Tony and Clarrie's response was "Master Little's plantation." "Your owner was Little, so you are Tony and Clarrie Little," declared the government official. That may help to explain why Malcolm so adamantly rejected the Little name when he joined the Nation of Islam.

Working independently, Tony was able to care for his large family, now grown to twenty-two children, including Uncle Malcolm's grandfather, Pa John. He worked for blacks and whites in the area. One of his main sources of work was building black churches in Taylor and Talbot Counties. He also began the Little tradition of purchasing land whenever possible. "By purchasing land," Ma said, "the Littles were able to avoid the vicious trap of sharecropping. When Malcolm later spoke of the importance of our people owning land, he was reflecting a belief that had long been in our family."

For over 150 years, black Littles have lived in and around the small towns of Butler and Reynolds, Georgia. They married into families named Miller, Sealy, Searcey, and Durham. Few permanently moved away from the familiarity of family and neighbors before the 1920s. However, during that decade, spurred by an increase in white-supremacist violence and a total lack of economic opportunity, many members of the Little family and other relatives moved to the North and West. A sizable number, including Ma, ended up in Boston. Ma never forgot her childhood and teenage years living among the huge Little clan in Taylor and Talbot Counties. "I can say with certainty that my strong sense of pride and connection to my people, like that of my father, Earl Little Sr., was implanted during those years among our people in rural Georgia," Ma said. "Unfortunately, Malcolm didn't have the personal experience of living among our extended family on his father's or mother's side like that, but he got at least a glimpse of what it was like from our father, Aunt Gracie, Aunt Sas, and me when he came to live with us in Boston."

All of Uncle Malcolm's direct ancestors on his father's side are accounted for in Taylor and Talbot Counties. John and Ella Little, his grandparents, are buried together in Reynolds; great-grandparents

Tony and Clarrie are buried near Butler in an area called the Panhandle, near Damascus Baptist Church. Ajar's burial site is unknown. We believe he may have run away to join the Islamic community in South Carolina, or he may have escaped to join up with Native Americans in their fight to hold on to their land. "His burial site may be unknown," declared Ma, "but his legacy of pride and resistance to white supremacy is now an integral part of our history because of his great-great-grandson, Malcolm."

Finally, it must be noted that though this book focuses on the Little family, Louise Helen Norton Little must be acknowledged for her contributions to her son's life. She was as committed to the black liberation struggle as her husband, Earl Lee Little Sr. In February 1997 and 1998, the Caribbean country of Grenada, her birthplace, held memorial services in her honor, services at which she was represented by her oldest son, Wilfred Little.

TWO Omowale: The Son Has Come Home

In August 1940 Malcolm Little received an invitation that would decisively and dramatically change his life. At the time, he was a gangly, troubled fourteen-year-old living in Lansing, Michigan, mostly with foster families; his life had been shattered by the murder of his father, Earl Lee Little Sr., and the institutionalization of his mother, Louise Helen Norton Little, after she suffered a nervous breakdown. Malcolm and his seven siblings were, for all practical purposes, wards of the state of Michigan.

The invitation came in a letter from Ella Lee Little (her maiden name) of Boston, Malcolm's father's child from an earlier marriage. It presented the teenager with a chance for another kind of life. Malcolm Little was my uncle; Ella Lee Little was my mother. Ma, as I called her, related this event to me when I was an adolescent. "From the first time I saw Malcolm on a visit to Lansing after the murder of our father, I knew he was a special child," Ma said. "He was lovable, smart, and quietly assertive." Malcolm's opinion of his big sister is best gained from reading comments about her in his autobiography, in which he wrote:

> I think the major impact of Ella's arrival [in Lansing], at least upon me, was that she was the first really proud black woman I had ever seen in my life. She was plainly proud of her very dark skin. This was unheard of among Negroes in those days, especially in Lansing.
>
> I hadn't been sure just what day she would come. And then one afternoon I got home from school and there she was. She

11

hugged me, stood me away, looked me up and down. A commanding woman, maybe even bigger than Mrs. Swerlin. Ella
wasn't just black, but like our father, she was jet black. The way
she sat, moved, talked, did everything, bespoke somebody who
did and got exactly what she wanted. This was the woman my
father had boasted of so often for having brought so many of
their family out of Georgia to Boston. . . . All that I had heard
was reflected in Ella's appearance and bearing. I had never
been so impressed with anybody. . . .

That initial meeting and several others that followed during Ma's
visits to Lansing eventually led to Uncle Malcolm's first visit to
Boston, in the summer of 1939. During that brief but memorable
homecoming-like visit, Malcolm was smothered with love and attention by Ma and his Aunt Sas and Aunt Gracie, his father's sisters. All
three, who shared a house in Boston, eagerly embraced the son of the
brother they had seen so little of during the last decade of his life.
They were on the East Coast while he was leading a somewhat no-
madic life in the Midwest with his family as an activist in the Marcus
Garvey movement. In fact, my uncle was the first of Earl's seven
children ever seen by Aunt Sas and Aunt Gracie. By the time Uncle
Malcolm's two-week visit was up, the three women had already decided that he should live permanently with them in Boston. "We
didn't want him to return to Michigan," Ma said. "Having him with
us was almost like having my father's spirit with us. We began
planning to have him with us permanently in Boston."

Thus the letter: "Dear Malcolm," Ma wrote in her direct style,
"Sas and Grace is [sic] fine & want you to come back. I would like
for you to come back but under one condition—*your mind is made
up . . .*" [italics hers] In other words, Ma was telling Malcolm: Make
sure your mind is made up to stay permanently with us.

The letter offered Uncle Malcolm an opportunity to leave Lansing, a city with bitter memories for the seven children of Earl and
Louise Little. Their father had been killed in what was officially described as an accident by authorities in Lansing. The Little children
and many other members of Lansing's black community strongly
believed otherwise. They knew that Earl Senior had received threats

from white supremacists in Lansing because of his political beliefs and activism. They were especially aware of the hostility of a group of Ku Klux Klan–like supremacists known ironically as the Black Legion. They firmly believed that this group had strong connections with at least some members of Lansing's police department. So they were very skeptical, Ma said, when told that her father had fallen on the streetcar tracks while in a drunken stupor and been hit by a train. When found, his body was mangled and his skull almost completely crushed on one side. The Littles and others believed that Earl Senior had been brutally beaten by white supremacists, and left on the tracks where he would be run over by a train.

They knew that Earl Senior was a deeply committed supporter of Marcus Garvey, the founder of the New York City–based Universal Negro Improvement Association (UNIA). In the late teens and early 1920s, that was the largest black political organization in the United States. No other black political organization, past or present, ever approached its size of over 1 million members and followers. Because Garvey had such a profound influence on Uncle Malcolm's parents and on Elijah Muhammad and because they, in turn, had such a profound influence on Malcolm, it's important to know some of the positions he advocated that so alarmed white supremacists. Much can be gleaned from statements attributed to Garvey in the book *The Philosophy and Opinions of Marcus Garvey,* compiled by his wife, Amy Jacques Garvey. Garvey, who was eventually deported to his home in Jamaica, declared:

> Men may spurn the idea, they may scoff at it; the metropolitan press of this country may deride us; yes, White men may laugh at the idea of Negroes talking about government but let me tell you there is going to be a government, and let me say to you also that whatsoever you give, in like measure it shall be returned to you. The world is sinful, and therefore man believes in the doctrine of an eye for an eye, a tooth for a tooth. . . . Black men, you were once great; you shall be great again. Lose not courage, lose not faith, go forward. The thing to do is to get organized; keep separated and you will be exploited, you will be robbed, you will be killed. Get organized and you will com-

pel the world to respect you. If the world fails to give you consideration because you are Black men, because you are Negroes,
four hundred million of you shall, through organization, shake
the pillars of the universe and bring down civilization, even as
Samson brought down the temple upon his head and upon the
heads of the Philistines.

Garvey had equally militant, forceful, and provocative positions
on the need of black people to develop their potential power and rely
on self-reliance and respect as tools for liberation in the struggle
against white supremacists. It is therefore not surprising that Earl
and Louise Little, both fervent Garveyites, were reviled for their belief, during a period when white supremacists were much more brutally overt in their behavior than they are today.

Earl and Louise Little met and married in Philadelphia and probably,
Ma believed, could have stayed there and had a reasonably comfortable life. Instead, they involved themselves in the struggle for racial
justice and equal opportunity in the United States. During eleven
years of marriage, they had seven children, five boys and two girls.
The children's places of birth show how often the Littles moved in
order for Earl Senior to find employment or because hostile reaction
to their political activities made it judicious to do so. Uncle Wilfred
was born in Philadelphia (1920); Aunt Hilda (1922), Uncle Philbert
(1923), and Uncle Malcolm (1925) in Omaha, Nebraska; Uncle Reginald (1927) in Milwaukee, Wisconsin; and Uncle Wesley (1928)
and Aunt Yvonne (1929) in Lansing, Michigan. Earl Senior also fathered three other children by his first wife, Daisy Mason: Ma (1914),
Aunt Mary (1915), and Earl Junior (1917). Louise Little gave birth
to Uncle Robert, whose father was a man who befriended her and her
children after Earl Senior's murder. Uncle Malcolm was Earl Senior's seventh child.

Lansing was to be the last stop for Earl Senior. Before Lansing,
there was Omaha and Milwaukee. Omaha was where he began his
involvement with the UNIA. He presided over its public meetings,
presenting its worldview to any black folks who dared to attend.
Louise Little assisted him with her bookkeeping and secretarial

skills and also occasionally wrote articles about activities in Omaha for the UNIA's publication the *Negro World,* which was based in Harlem. It was in Omaha that Earl Senior, a carpenter by trade, built the first home for his family. He wrote his parents that, like all southern black landowners, he and Louise had planted a garden in which to grow vegetables. But it didn't last. Most whites in Omaha were both outraged and alarmed over Earl Senior's Garveyism, and most blacks in the city were nervous that his activities would "bring down the white folks on us." Their fears were not unjustified, since Omaha Klansmen openly harassed those who attended UNIA meetings. The Littles had to move.

Their next stop was Milwaukee. There Earl Senior became president of a black self-help group called the International Industrial Club. Their stay in Milwaukee was brief. There were few economic opportunities for blacks there, and when Earl Senior was told by family members, with whom he was in contact, that jobs were more plentiful in Lansing, Michigan, he decided to move. Especially convincing was his brother Jim, whom everyone called Bud. Uncle Bud worked for the railroad, which made him a social and economic giant in family circles, because that was considered a very prestigious job. Uncle Bud was a great storyteller. Uncle Wesley, Uncle Philbert, and Uncle Malcolm told me that he used to regale them with stories when they were children. He did the same for me when he occasionally came to Boston to visit his sisters, Aunt Sas and Aunt Gracie. He told me dozens of railroad stories and joined me in playing with my large train set. He also let me assist him in making homemade brew from peaches, a skill he learned from a relative back home in Georgia. They insisted the brew had bona-fide medicinal values. To my uncles and me, Bud was like a jolly and wise genie. When he wasn't around, we missed him. When Wilfred, Philbert, and Malcolm spoke of him in later years, there was always a bit of sadness in their voices.

The Littles found that blacks in Lansing were just as fearful of Garveyism as those in Omaha. Many people, Ma said, considered them a bad joke, especially when they spoke about the UNIA's position on going back to Africa and helping to build a powerful black continent. "Go back to Africa?" huffed Lansing blacks, eyebrows

arched. "Why would we want to do that? The people there are unciv-
ilized." Many of those people had escaped from the South, where
their friends, relatives, and neighbors were constantly under the threat
of white supremacist brutality, yet they dismissed Africans as unciv-
ilized. Uncle Malcolm would later describe such people as "parrots"
who only spoke "what the white man says." One of the major "parrots" in Lansing was Walter J. Collins, who was among those ridi-
culed in Uncle Malcolm's autobiography as "Negroes who shined
shoes at the State Capitol and thought they were political bosses." At
one time, Collins was Ma's father-in-law, when she was married to
Kenneth Collins, and he was my grandfather. His basic position
seemed to have been that if black folks worked hard and kept their
mouths shut, everything would be all right. I have come to realize
through the years that Grandfather Collins and the many others who
shared his position lived in the grip of fear. They had seen or heard
about what can happen to those blacks who confront the system, and
to them it was a serious matter.

This is not to say that Earl Senior was an unblemished saint. Like
many people with strong convictions, he probably could, at times,
slip into overbearing self-righteousness. Often functioning under severe stress and strain, there is little doubt that he was sometimes too
harsh and demanding of his wife and children. Ma said that he could
also be hardheaded and impetuous. Earl Senior also had to deal with
a question that confronts committed activists who have families to
care for. Can one effectively fulfill both responsibilities in a hostile
environment, especially if one has very limited financial means?
Earl Senior had to ponder that question; years later, so did his son
Malcolm.

The constant relocations were difficult for Louise Little. After all,
she was pregnant during much of their eleven years together, giving
birth to seven children. Ma said that when the Littles down in Georgia first met Louise, they sensed that she was not really used to hard
work. Back home, in what was then called Grenada, British West In-
dies, she had lived what was generally considered a privileged life,
being both educated and light-skinned, with the latter being a special
plus. The Willie Lynch directive, written in the 1700s, about sowing
division among enslaved Africans, was as effective in the Caribbean

as it was in the United States, South and Central America, and South Africa. Education was more available to the light-skinned children sired by slave-owning fathers than to their dark-skinned siblings and cousins. To Louise Helen Norton's parents, the very dark-skinned, unemployed, politically radical Earl Little Sr. was not a suitable husband for their pretty, intelligent daughter. That he also supported what they considered a "rabble-rouser" like Marcus Garvey doubled his negatives. "They seemed to be totally unaware that their daughter shared her husband's position on Garveyism as the most effective way to combat white supremacy," said Ma.

Though there's no mention of Michigan in the informative book *100 Years of Lynchings,* Ma, like Uncle Malcolm and her siblings, was convinced that there should have been at least one entry for Michigan—that of her father, Earl Senior—whose mangled body was found on Lansing streetcar tracks on September 28, 1931. "Look at history!" she insisted. "Look at the state of race relations in Lansing and most of the rest of the country during that time as exemplified by the frequent lynchings!" Though the official position was that Earl Senior's death was caused by an accident, one of the two insurance companies with which he had policies attempted to label it a suicide so it wouldn't have to pay death benefits to his family.

The killing of Earl Senior was a devastating and lasting blow to his wife and children. Malcolm, only six years old when his father was murdered, cited it in his autobiography as an example of "how the White man thrusts himself into the position of leadership in the world through the use of naked political power."

Eventually the deadly combination of pressure from creditors and from state welfare personnel, and normal pressures brought on by having to nurture and care for seven children under twelve years of age, led to Louise Little's nervous breakdown. She was branded "insane" by the state and institutionalized, and her children were taken away, to be scattered among foster families throughout the area. Aunt Hilda, who was nine years old when her father was murdered, commented on the extreme trauma caused by her father's murder and her mother's institutionalization in the book *Malcolm X: Make It Plain.* "Being torn apart from my family at nine, when we'd always been very tight, was painful, but I don't think I ever shed tears. I put on a strong front. The tears were inside. Because I can remember being petrified. I didn't know how to live around anyone else. I don't think any of my family ever dealt with the others and their own pain. You're suddenly spread apart. I know they have feelings, but to this day we have never gotten together and talked about our pain. I know how strong it was. And I know they had it." Aunt Hilda made that very poignant observation in 1994, sixty-three years after the lynching of her father, fifty-five years after the institutionalization of her mother, and twenty-nine years after the assassination of her brother Malcolm.

Uncle Malcolm wrote forcefully in his autobiography about the treatment of his family after his father's murder. "When the state welfare people began coming to our house, we would come home from school sometimes and find them talking with our mother, asking a thousand questions. . . . We began to go swiftly downhill. The physical downhill wasn't as quick as the psychological. My mother was, above everything else, a proud woman, and it took its toll on her that she was accepting charity. . . . She would get particularly incensed when they [state welfare people] began insisting upon drawing us older children aside, one at a time, out on the porch or somewhere, and asking us questions, or telling us things—against our mother and against each other."

Unfortunately, most blacks in Lansing, including those in a supposedly community organization called the Council of Defense, were of little help to the Little family after Earl Senior's murder. Kenneth Collins, my father, who had been introduced to Ma on one of her trips to Lansing by her brothers Wilfred and Philbert, said that people such as his father, Walter J. Collins, were almost as turned off by Earl Senior's Garveyism ideology as Lansing whites. Their position, he said, was that "the Littles were like aliens from another planet, always claiming to be so independent. Since they were so damn independent, let them get out of their own mess." That, apparently, was their justification for not being more helpful to a grieving, economically strapped widow with seven children under twelve years of age. They were also afraid that supporting the Littles would anger the white community.

"It's painful," Ma told me, "to recall that members of our own family didn't respond to the needs of my father's widow and children in a way that they should have." Some of them, including Ma, tried, but they were up against a system that required the collective muscle of Littles from everywhere. Their apathy left Louise Little basically alone in the struggle against a coldhearted welfare bureaucracy. Malcolm wrote:

I truly believe that if ever a state social agency destroyed a family, it destroyed ours. We wanted and tried to stay together. Our home didn't have to be destroyed. But the welfare, the courts, and the doctor gave us the one-two-three punch. And ours was not the only case of its kind. The state welfare people kept after my mother. By now she didn't make any secret that she hated them and didn't want them in her house. But they exerted their right to come, and I have many, many times reflected upon how, talking to us children, they began to plant seeds of division in our minds. They would ask such things as who was smarter than the other. And they would ask me why I was "so different."

In other words, state welfare authorities schemed to divide the family rather than work to keep it together. Ma, one of the family members who tried to keep the children together, believed that the children were punished because of their parents' political and cultural beliefs. Unfortunately, because of internal disagreements, long distances, and a lack of knowledge about the true evilness of the system, the massive, unified Little family effort needed to help the children did not materialize.

Ma did as much as she could for her brothers and sisters. When she went to Lansing, she was very impressed with the efforts of Uncle Wilfred and Aunt Hilda to keep the children together. "They were mature beyond their years," she said, "and were as serious as can be about taking care of their younger brothers and sisters. Malcolm and Philbert were the hell-raisers who often fought each other and outsiders. When I asked Philbert to do a chore, he responded with back talk. I wasn't about to take such talk from what I considered a child, so I popped him with a frying pan, forgetting that he was also an emerging amateur boxer. He popped me right back. After that neither of us gave the other any trouble."

Ma found Malcolm to be "bright, intelligent, and inquisitive." Though somewhat undisciplined, he had drive and a go-get-it attitude that impressed Ma right away. "I must admit that initially I was taken aback by how much lighter-skinned he was than the other children. He definitely got that from his mother's side of the family. The Littles in Georgia and Boston were overwhelmingly dark skinned."

At first, Ma wanted to bring all seven children to Boston, just as she had brought other family members there to escape the extreme poverty and overt white supremacy in Georgia. There were several major obstacles to her being able to do this, however. One was the inertia of the state welfare bureaucracy. Meddling welfare workers had attempted to cause dissension among the children, and they basically responded the same way to Ma's efforts. An equally potent obstacle was the almost Hatfield-McCoy–like feud between key members of the Little and Mason families, most notably Ma's mother, Daisy Mason. Uncle Malcolm and his siblings were totally unaware of this situation. Some Mason family members in Boston, including Grandma Daisy, and her sister, Aunt Emmy Walker, were still filled with anger over what they considered "the abandonment" of Grandma Daisy by Earl Senior. When he left Reynolds, Georgia, he left her behind with three children (Ma, Mary, and Earl Junior) and no money. Under Georgia law he never officially divorced her before marrying Louise Norton. As far as Grandma Daisy and Aunt Emmy were concerned, Louise Norton had "stolen" Earl Senior, and they had no problem believing that the children must pay for the "sins" of their father. Then there was the added problem of Uncle Robert, Louise Little's eighth child, who was not fathered by Earl Senior. Robert's father was a man who had befriended the family after Earl Senior's death; Ma had no problem with that. "As far as I was concerned, I had eight brothers and sisters in Lansing who needed our help. The rest was irrelevant."

Unfortunately, Aunt Sas and Aunt Gracie, despite their deep Christian beliefs, were not disposed to take into the home they shared with Ma a child who was not their brother's. Since Ma couldn't take all eight children, she focused on Uncle Malcolm. "One major reason for that," she told me, "was his having been sent to live with a white foster family. I was livid when I heard about that. It was absurd and demeaning for Michigan public officials to place Malcolm with a white family. If they had put the same kind of effort and money into getting the children to us in Boston, things might have turned out differently for all of us. I know I could have eventually overcome the internal family obstacles. Often I have thought about what might have been. It's still painful to admit our inability to help the children."

It was in the context of that series of events, some of which he had personally experienced and remembered despite his young age, that Uncle Malcolm read Ma's letter inviting him to live permanently with her in Boston. He loved his brothers and sisters in Lansing and was not happy about leaving them, but, as stated in his autobiography, he had heard his father boast about his daughter in Boston who rescued Little family members from white supremacist–dominated Reynolds and Butler, Georgia. Now that same daughter, who was also his big sister, had reached out to help him escape the hostility and indifference so prevalent in Lansing. He accepted the invitation.

THREE Homecoming

Uncle Malcolm's acceptance of Ma's invitation to move permanently to Boston elicited whoops of joy, excitement, and anticipation from her, Aunt Sas, and Aunt Gracie. "Aunt Sas and Aunt Gracie, in true Christian style, thanked the Lord," Ma said with a smile. "I thanked the spirit of Pa John, our grandfather. I knew Malcolm had some doubts about moving in with us, doubts that were reinforced by meddling social workers and their divisive tactics. There was also the fact that Wilfred, by then twenty years old, and Hilda, then eighteen, were determined to keep all the children together. They were hesitant about one moving away even to live with another family member. I believe that the state's placing of the younger children with white foster families was what finally brought them around to his joining us in Boston."

Ma, Aunt Sas, and Aunt Grace knew that having a teenager, especially a male, in the house was going to require some changes on their part. What they didn't know was how many. Based on Uncle Malcolm's brief visit in the summer of 1939, they thought they were getting a quiet, totally obedient, dutiful, intelligent little brother and nephew whom, with love and attention, they could influence to become what they wanted. During that initial visit they doted on him, treating him like a much-loved, long-lost relative who had finally connected with his extended family. Now that he was to be with them permanently, they planned to pamper him with love and adulation.

That's what they expected. What they got was a very intelligent, restless, curious, searching teenager who, while being respectful to his elders, was by no means prepared to do their bidding simply because they wanted him to. "What we failed to take into consideration," Ma said, "was how dazzling and tempting Boston was to a teenager who had spent all his years in places like Omaha, Milwaukee, and Lansing. We had been in Boston since the 1930s and knew the real truth about the city. We never thought of it as dazzling or even particularly tempting. Our goal was to provide Malcolm with a loving, secure, structured family life and environment where he could develop all the potential we had seen when he visited us in 1939."

Ma thought Uncle Malcolm had the potential to be a lawyer. "I strongly believed that we needed a lawyer in the Little family, and Malcolm struck me as the one with the intelligence and drive to become one. My years in Boston and my having grown up in rural Georgia showed me clearly that the law worked only for those who understood how it works or who had sufficient money to hire someone who understood how it works. That's the bottom line."

Aunt Sas and Aunt Gracie had less specific plans for Uncle Malcolm. "They just wanted him to become a good, churchgoing Baptist, a solid Christian gentleman," Ma said, smiling. "They believed that if he were that, all other good things would automatically follow." Though Uncle Malcolm grew to revere his aunts, he was never to share their commitment to what he came to believe was the white man's religion.

Since Ma didn't believe in wasting time, by Uncle Malcolm's second day in Boston, she was already getting down to business. Because she had as strong a belief in the work ethic as anyone you can imagine, that meant he had to get a job. Therefore, her first task was to take Uncle Malcolm downtown to meet John Walker Sr., her uncle by marriage, who owned Walker's Auto Parks Company, a parking-lot business, located in Boston's Chinatown. Uncle Malcolm and John Senior took an immediate liking to each other, and he hired Uncle Malcolm to begin work the next day. "That caused a serious problem with my mother, Daisy Mason, and my Aunt Emmy, to whom John Senior was married," Ma said, "They were sisters and were still steaming over the fact that they felt that Daddy [Earl Senior] had abandoned my mother with three children when he left

Reynolds, Georgia. Plus, he never officially divorced her by Georgia State law before marrying Louise Helen Norton. It was still an unsettled issue as far as they were concerned. Though all this had happened in the early 1900s, in 1940 both of them were as angry as ever and prepared to take out their anger on Malcolm by denying him a job." Uncle John, who knew all about the feud among some members of the Little and Mason families, was not persuaded, having no intention of letting it affect his business decisions. Ma was also not persuaded. "I loved and respected my mother and aunt," she said, "but saw no reason for Malcolm to suffer because of what our father and my mother's family had endured."

On the evening of Malcolm's second day in Boston, he, Ma, and several other family members celebrated with a dinner at Gordon and Anita Cheu's restaurant in Chinatown. "To us Malcolm's coming to live permanently with us was a kind of special homecoming," Ma said, "so we wanted to celebrate as a family. Cheu's restaurant was the perfect place, since they and the Walkers were good friends. Malcolm got his first taste of Chinese food and greeted several family members whom he hadn't met on his first trip to Boston."

During those first weeks in Boston, Malcolm also got a first taste of the Littles' family history. In his autobiography, he wrote: "Ella told me about other relatives from that branch of the family. A number of them I'd never heard of. . . . our branch of the family was split to pieces; I had just about forgotten about being a Little in any family sense."

Ma wasn't the only one to connect Uncle Malcolm with the Littles' family history. Aunt Sas and Aunt Gracie were equally informative, especially about the early history in Georgia. Aunt Sas and Aunt Gracie, who never strayed far from their deep black southern roots, often related family history to Uncle Malcolm and later to me while sitting on the front porch of our house after Sunday religious services. First, the two of them would dissect the merits or demerits of the sermon delivered that morning by the preacher. That completed, they switched to the latest news they had received from down home in Georgia. The latest news conversation almost invariably led to reminiscences about family figures, especially their father, Pa John, and their mother, Ella, after whom Ma was named. John Little was called Pa John by his children and Big Pa John by an assortment of grandchildren, other relatives, and neighbors.

Pa John and Grandma Ella, Ma said, were the rocks upon which most Little family members stood until he died from a heart attack in 1942. Aunt Sas and Aunt Gracie described him as being tall, over six feet five inches, very dark skinned, lean, muscular, and strong, fearless, hardworking, commanding, and completely devoted to his family. Their description inspired us to think of him as someone like John Henry, the steel-driving man of railroad myth who is part of African-American folklore. Grandma Ella was described as ebony-colored, heavyset, with a head full of braided hair. She was equally fearless, hardworking, and devoted to her family.

According to Little family historian Oscar V. Little, Pa John was one of twenty-two children, eighteen boys and four girls, born to former enslaved Africans Tony and Clarrie Little in the mid- to late 1800s. Most of Pa John's brothers were at least six feet tall, which helps to explain Uncle Malcolm's height. Pa John was the one, according to his two daughters, who inspired them and their brothers, Oscar, Jim, Herbert, and Earl, to have pride in themselves and their people. He, in turn, had been inspired by his parents, Tony and Clarrie. Because they had both been enslaved Africans who worked in the "Big House," they were able to avoid at least some of the severe brutality and family disruptions that often plagued those Africans who were confined to work in the fields. "The pride and spirit possessed by Tony and Clarrie," Ma told me, "has passed down to generations of Littles and has helped to sustain us through some treacherous and traumatic times."

Aunt Sas and Aunt Gracie spoke of Pa John and Grandma Ella with such deep love, respect, and devotion that Uncle Malcolm and anyone else who heard them could almost feel their presence in our Dale Street home in Boston. Photographs and other items brought with them from Georgia to Boston were arranged on Aunt Sas's piano almost like a shrine. "I remember that Malcolm always listened very attentively to the stories from Aunt Sas and Aunt Gracie," Ma noted. "Even as a restless teenager, as he was at that time, he couldn't avoid being impressed and affected by that kind of positive ancestor worship."

Aunt Sas, Aunt Gracie, and Ma also had more negative memories about growing up in early 1900s rural Georgia to relate to Malcolm and later to me. Though legal enslavement had been abolished by President Abraham Lincoln's Emancipation Proclamation followed by the North's victory in the Civil War, white supremacists in Georgia were determined to maintain political and economic control over the freed Africans by all means, legal and illegal, at their disposal. The rural Georgia in which Pa John grew up and raised a family was a dangerous place for a proud black man or woman. In the book *100 Years of Lynchings,* which consists of unedited newspaper articles about lynchings that occurred between 1861 and 1961, three full pages include names of people lynched in Georgia. White supremacists, hooded and unhooded, threatened, intimidated, brutalized, and lynched black folks with impunity. Aunt Sas and Aunt Gracie told us about such atrocities as the "Atlanta Pogrom" of 1906 during which white supremacists enjoyed a three-day orgy of "coon hunting." They spoke of the infamous "Red Summer of 1919," when dozens of black people, including World War I veterans, were lynched or otherwise brutalized by "evil" white supremacists while "good" white supremacists nodded in approval or silently and conveniently looked the other way. Professor Harold Cruse, chairman emeritus of the University of Michigan's Black Studies Department, wrote in his book *Plural but Equal:* "In five and one half months, from April 4 to October 1, 1919, there were race riots in twenty-two cities and towns throughout the nation; seventy-four blacks and at least one white member of the International Workers of the World (IWW) were lynched. This occurred in the immediate aftermath of World War I. After having served overseas in the U.S. military and supported the 'War for Democracy,' blacks, and especially black ex-servicemen, were demonstrating a well-merited racial assertiveness in pursuit of their citizenship rights. . . ."

A particularly horrifying example of the murderous brutality was reported in the April 15, 1919, issue of a prominent black newspaper, the *Chicago Defender.* The paper reported:

When Private William Little, a Negro soldier returning from the war, arrived at the railroad station [in Blakely, Georgia] here several weeks ago, he was encountered by a band of whites. The whites ordered him to take off his Army uniform and walk home in his underwear. Several other whites prevailed upon the hoodlums to leave Little alone and he was permitted to walk home unmolested. Little continued to wear his uniform over the next few weeks, as he had no other clothing. Anonymous notes were sent to him warning him not to wear his Army uniform "too long" and advising him to leave town if he wished to "sport around in khaki." Little ignored the notes. Yesterday Private Little was found dead on the outskirts of this city, apparently beaten by a mob. He was wearing his Army uniform.

Since Blakely is located south of Taylor County, where most of the Littles were based, there's a real possibility that William Little was a relative.

Aunt Sas and Aunt Gracie told Uncle Malcolm about night-riding Ku Klux Klansmen terrorizing any black person they came across on mostly deserted country roads. They would order their victim to stop and tell them where he or she was coming from or going to. If the victim was an attractive woman, rape was always a possibility. Even if they were not ordered to stop, black folks knew it was prudent to do so upon seeing terrorists. Otherwise they might circle back on their charging horses and demand to know "Boy! Nigger! Why didn't you stop?"

Some of those incidents Aunt Sas and Aunt Gracie saw themselves; others were related to them by their parents and other adult relatives and neighbors. Aunt Gracie has a personal horror story about the realities of racism in the Georgia in which she grew up. A howling mob of white supremacists had lynched the young man she planned to marry because they considered him too "uppity," which meant he was not sufficiently servile to members of "the master race." That had such a devastating and lasting psychological effect on her that she never married for fear of losing her husband. Aunt Sas also never married. The two sisters lived together all their lives.

Uncle Malcolm was also told about Little family members in Reynolds who strongly believed in an eye for an eye and a tooth for a tooth when dealing with murderous white supremacists. "Some men in the family always kept shotguns handy," Ma said, "and on occasions used them in self-defense. There were times when bodies of white supremacists known to have been part of a lynch mob were found floating in the river or shot in the woods. There's no doubt in my mind that hearing about those incidents had a great effect on how Malcolm was to later view race relations. They certainly had an effect on how I view them, and our views were similar."

There was a reason why Little family members could be somewhat bolder in their dealings with whites than most of their neighbors. That was their freedom from total economic dependence on white exploiters. Unlike most of their neighbors in turn-of-the-century rural Georgia, the Littles weren't sharecroppers. In sharecropping, black farmers and white landowners contracted to share equally in the division of crops and profits. In reality, sharecropping, as practiced in Georgia and the other southern states in the early 1900s, was a short step up from enslavement. According to Professor Cruse, "Black farmers were seldom given itemized accountings, were seldom allowed to know the price at which the crops they raised were sold by the landlords, were forced to accept the landlords' figures for supplies received, and dared not question the honesty of the accounting. . . . Thus black farmers usually found themselves deeper and deeper in debt every year regardless of how few supplies they used or how high the price of cotton or corn."

The Littles, by slowly and quietly purchasing land of their own, skillfully avoided the sharecropping trap, which Ma said was "as brutal a system of economic exploitation and control as existed anywhere in the world of that time." There were so many Littles that by working together they were able to hold on to their land and grow enough crops to survive. A second trap they avoided was abandoning the land to move to northern cities during the great migrations of the 1920s. During that time, spurred on by lack of opportunity and pie-in-the-sky tales from friends and relatives already in the North, and, most crucially, unrelenting white terrorism, thousands upon thousands of black folks left the South. It was an internal equivalent of European immigrants pouring into major American cities to escape political, economic, or religious oppression. Since surrounding states were just as brutal in their treatment of black folks, they had no safe haven nearby to seek escape from the white supremacists. The attitudes of most southern whites during that time is probably best reflected in a statement made by then U.S. senator Ben Tillman of South Carolina, who, according to Carl Senna in his book *The Black Press and the Struggle for Civil Rights,* loudly boasted that when the whites came to power following Reconstruction, "we took the government away. We stuffed the ballot box. We shot Negroes! We are not ashamed of it." Equally revealing is an observation made by Professor Cruse: "Geographical focus of the most intense racial discrimination and most rigid racial segregation existed, historically, in the southern states. . . . It is merely enough to repeat the blatant assertion by the leading literary southern racist Thomas Dixon, Jr., that if blacks were not checked, they would become *such an economic competitor of the white man that they would have to be massacred. . . .*" Obviously, Dixon disagreed with other of his brethren about the survivability of black folks. A few such scholars were insisting that black folks were so weak and degenerate that they would all expire once freed from enslavement.

It was to escape terrorism exemplified by the many Tillmans and Dixons in the South that several million blacks fled north, including some from Reynolds. Professor Cruse writes:

In 1930 the black population in New York City was estimated at 327,706 (the bulk living in Harlem); in Chicago, 233,903; Philadelphia, 217,593; Detroit, 120,066; Cleveland, 71,899. The rate of increase for these urban populations from 1920 to 1930 was as follows: New York City, 115%; Chicago, 114%; Philadelphia, 64%; Detroit, 194%; Cleveland, 109%. This phenomenal growth was the result of one of the greatest internal mass migrations of any racial or ethnic group in the United States—the movement of southern rural and small-town blacks out of the South into northern and midwestern cities. . . .

The black migrants, having little, if any, knowledge of how the property-tax system worked, too often failed to pay taxes on the land they still owned in the South. State officials gleefully claimed the land and sold it cheaply to whites. Several million acres of land were lost by black folks this way. But the Littles held on. Many members of the family moved north, but many others stayed behind and held on to the land. When Uncle Malcolm later spoke of the critical im portance of land ownership, he was echoing the philosophy of some of his Little ancestors.

Aunt Gracie and Aunt Sas, when speaking about this, made it clear that much of the land was not lost because of negligence on the part of black owners but because of conniving white supremacists who seldom missed a trick that would aid them in their efforts to keep African Americans economically powerless and dependent. One of their most insidious gambits was to illegally intercept mail sent home by blacks who had fled North. Often the mail contained money being sent to relatives for the purchase of food and clothes and to pay property taxes. Being unfamiliar with checks and money orders, the senders had no qualms about putting cash in their letters and packages. Aunt Sas said that white supremacist postal officials and others who knew of this practice would often open the mail and remove the cash. Since they or their allies were in total control and since they knew that most black folks were too intimidated by the terrorists to even complain about their thievery, they had no fear about violating federal laws.

White supremacists not only opened the mail to steal cash; this federal crime also enabled them to spy on the black community. Aunt Sas said that Earl Little Sr., who had moved north, would write to his parents from wherever he was at the time. Among other things, he told them about his involvement with the UNIA, the black nation-alist organization founded by Marcus Garvey that eventually became the largest black mass organization in the country. Mr. Garvey's suc-cess attracted a host of deadly enemies, including Negro integra-tionists and especially J. Edgar Hoover of the FBI. Mr. Garvey was eventually forced into exile. Earl Senior had joined the UNIA and wrote about his commitment to the organization to his parents. Soon white officials in the county would come around and ask Pa John about the whereabouts of Earl Senior and his brother, Uncle Bottoe, who had also left Reynolds. Their questions were so specific that Pa John and Grandma Ella knew they were intercepting and reading mail sent to them by their relatives. Earl Senior was well aware that his involvement with the UNIA was dangerous. I remember once reading a letter Earl Senior wrote home in which he said that his involvement with the UNIA might cost him his life but that he wasn't going to quit because what he was doing was important to his children's future. He emphasized that his wife, Louise, shared his position. This was scary stuff for Little family members in Georgia to deal with. Their stance was to avoid, as much as was humanly possible, any activity that would arouse the violent white supremacists. These fears were not baseless, but founded on the very real threat that white supremacists posed to every black man, woman, and child in rural Georgia. They had no one to turn to for protection, not even the federal government, since major congressional committees were dominated by white supremacists or their allies. Aunt Sas strongly believed that the heart condition that eventually led to Pa John's death was greatly aggravated by his concern over the threat directed toward Earl Senior and his family because of their UNIA activities. Pa John was in his eighties when he died in 1942, on his way to the mailbox to collect letters from members now scattered.

Ma knew that white supremacists opened their mail because of an incident that she witnessed as a nine-year-old, in 1923. Pa John took her along when he went to the post office to pick up a package they were expecting from Daisy Mason, Ma's mother, who had moved north to Boston. When they entered the post office, they saw that the postmaster had already opened the package, which contained a beautiful flowered dress for Ma. When he saw Pa John and Ma, he threw the opened box to Pa John and said, "What that girl need a pretty dress like this for?" Ma remembered being stunned and mad as hell. Years later, when relating the incident to us, she still had fire in her eyes and her heart. "Pa John just stared at the man, calmly took my hand, and slowly walked out of the post office. He didn't say anything to me but I could see the intense hurt and anger he felt, especially since it was done with me there to witness it. Even at age nine I was violently angry at that white man for what he did to my grandfather. There was a consuming thirst for vengeance in my heart. Some sixty years later I have never forgotten that blatant, searing manifestation of white supremacy."

Despite the blood memories unleashed by white supremacists, the

Little women also had precious memories to pass on to Malcolm and to other family members, including me. Little family members, inspired mostly by Pa John and Grandma Ella, were able to outsmart and outmaneuver those who sought to break their spirits. Taking advantage of their large numbers, they jointly harvested their crops, mainly nuts and cotton, and got them to the markets. Their nut crops were so successful that enough was left over to send to family members around the country. When Uncle Malcolm was a teenager and I was much younger, every year we received packages of pecans grown by family members in Georgia. He and I ate pecans by the dozens. Aunt Sas took what was left and made mouthwatering, delicious pecan pies that Uncle Malcolm and I would eat until we dropped.

They told us about family celebrations on major Christian holidays, about church socials, about the fun for the children during harvesting time. Ma remembers wagon rides on dusty country roads with her father and grandfather as they went from small town to small town and tiny church after tiny church preaching about God, family, and pride. Though she later turned away from her grandparents' Christian religion, Ma never forgot the messages they spread about the need to stick together in the never-ending struggle against white supremacy. Uncle Malcolm was a restless teenager anxious to experience the intriguing possibilities of the big city when he first heard these stories from his aunts and his big sister, but they stuck in his subconscious, ready to emerge when he later set out to fulfill his destiny.

My uncle stated in his autobiography that before moving in with Ma, Aunt Sas, and Aunt Gracie, he had never heard of a number of his family members. In Boston he not only met members of the Little family; he also met Grays and Masons, who were related to the Littles by marriage. Grandma Ella was a Gray before she married Pa John, and the first wife of Uncle Malcolm's father, Earl Senior, was Daisy Mason. Ma, Earl Junior, and Mary were the children from that marriage. The Mason and Gray relatives had moved to Boston from Butler and Reynolds, Georgia, mostly during the mass migration of the 1920s and 1930s.

In the passage in his autobiography where Malcolm wrote that "our branch of the family was split to pieces," he was referring to the tragic situation of the splitting up of his mother, brothers, and sisters in the Midwest. He was unaware of another tragic split, that between the Littles and some of the Masons in both Georgia and Massachusetts. Aunt Sas, Aunt Gracie, and Ma shared many stories with him about Pa John, Grandma Ella, and the others, but they made a conscious decision to exclude information about the intense feud between key Little and Mason family members. According to Ma, "We decided that when Malcolm came to Boston, he was already traumatized by serious family problems so painfully described in his autobiography. He didn't need more added onto those. We wanted him to be at peace with all the family members he came to know in Boston. Later, when he was an adult and embarked on a campaign to help liberate our people from racial oppression, we didn't want to distract him with petty family problems." Thus, neither Ma, Aunt Sas, nor Aunt Gracie ever told him the whole truth about why his father, Earl Junior, so hurriedly left Reynolds, Georgia, in 1919.

The whole story was sad and yet so human. The Little–Mason dispute began after Earl Senior married Daisy Mason in 1909. The Masons, like the Littles, were landowners, so they weren't as poor as most of their friends and neighbors. According to Aunt Sas and Aunt Gracie, the Masons were "go along, get along good Negroes" who were always properly servile to whites. They practiced the kind of Baptist religion that justified servility. The Littles, led by Pa John, were also Baptist, but their interpretation of the religion stressed that people of God were not required to pay tribute to a master race, that all people were equal in the eyes of God. It was the kind of liberation theology that had guided historical figures like Nat Turner and Harriet Tubman. It's obvious that those different interpretations of their religion could form a basis for conflict. "That's why we were surprised when Earl Senior told us he was going to marry Daisy," Aunt Sas said. "For some reason the Masons expected a sizable dowry as part of the arrangement. Why they had such an expectation I really don't know. Maybe Earl had made some promise that I am unaware of. Anyway, it didn't get the marriage off to a good start, and it never really recovered. Though they were married almost ten years and had three children, things were never too good between them. Finally, hostility reached such a point that Pa John advised Earl to leave Reynolds. The hostility and threats from some of the Masons, along with those from white supremacists who considered Earl too 'uppity,' caused Pa John to fear for Earl's safety." Though the Littles had extended family in the Carolinas, Alabama, and Florida, Pa John thought it best for his son to leave the South altogether.

Earl Senior didn't stop until he reached Philadelphia, where he met and married Louise Norton without officially divorcing Daisy Mason Little back in Reynolds. Following Earl Senior's departure, things cooled down between the Littles and the Masons, only to heat up again considerably when he had the audacity to visit Reynolds with his very pregnant new wife. "It caused a very touchy situation," said Aunt Sas, "when Earl showed up with a new wife. When he first wrote our parents about her, he described her as being 'educated' and 'light-skinned.' We all wondered if her being educated would make her too citified to properly fit into the Little family and if her being light-skinned meant that she was one of those hincty Negroes who was proud of being related to a white slave owner who presumably had sexually exploited one of her ancestors."

Though there were some Littles who showed signs of having a mixed background, most were dark-skinned. The exception was Gabe, one of Pa John's brothers, who owned a sawmill in Reynolds. Ma said he was a bit lighter than the rest of his brothers and sisters and had slightly straighter hair. Also, Aunt Gracie was light-skinned, with one hazel brown eye and one that was bluish. I remember hearing Uncle Malcolm and Aunt Gracie joke about their light skin. "White slave owners messed up some of us," he said half-jokingly. "They sho-nuf dee-id," Aunt Gracie responded in her Deep South accent. Unlike so many black folks of that time the Littles took no special pride in the fact that some of their ancestors had been sexually exploited by lecherous enslavers.

They found that Louise Little did not have the same attitude as many light-skinned Negroes. "Any doubts we had were resolved as soon as we met her," noted Aunt Gracie. "She fit right in. What we neglected to take into account was the hostile reaction to Earl's return from some of the Masons. When Daisy Mason and several of her relatives heard that Earl was back in town, they were outraged. It was embarrassing enough in that close-knit small town for a woman's husband to leave her, but for him to return home with a new wife, and a pregnant one at that, was too much." In today's usage that would be called big-time "in yo' face."

Aunt Sas said that word spread around that Daisy Mason was determined to physically confront Louise Little. Pa John, whose relationship with the male head of the Mason family was still cordial, once again had to intervene. Pa John told Earl that because of the real possibility of a confrontation with some of the Mason women and because white supremacists still regarded Earl as too uppity for their taste, he must leave Reynolds for the sake of the community at large." Earl Senior left and never again returned home.

Daisy Mason's anger didn't subside when Earl Senior left. She decided that she could no longer live in Reynolds or Talbotton, where her family lived. "What she basically did," said Aunt Sas, "was to abandon Earl Junior, Ella, and Mary." She ended up in Boston, living with her brother, Leonard, and his wife, Lowla. There have been several stories about the relationship between Leonard Mason and Lowla Sissey. "The belief of most family members," said Aunt Sas, "was that Leonard and Lowla Sissey had been childhood sweethearts. She was from a family of poor whites and Native Americans who had come to our area from La Grange, Georgia, northwest of Taylor County. It often happened in the South that poor black and poor white children who lived near each other would become playmates, at least until puberty. After that, white parents usually abruptly called a halt to such friendships. It seems that somehow Leonard and Lowla Sissey secretly continued their friendship and in their teens ran away to the North and married. They stayed together for many years in Duxbury, Massachusetts, until their deaths."

Leonard Mason was a lucky man. In the Georgia of that time a black man who even looked too hard at a white woman, not to mention developing a relationship with her, was a prime candidate for lynching.

When Grandma Daisy left Georgia, Pa John and Grandma Ella assumed responsibility for Ma, Earl Junior, and Mary, a decision that was made by Pa John, not Earl Senior, after consulting with Grandma Daisy's father, Reverend Mason. Pa John decided that his daugh-

ters, Sarah and Gracie, would have the chief responsibility of looking after Ma and Aunt Mary. The four of them formed a tight and
loving bond that was to last throughout the lives of Aunt Sas and
Aunt Gracie. They went north together in 1935 and lived together
until Aunt Sas died in 1962 and Aunt Gracie died in 1978. At Ma's
expense both were returned home to Reynolds, to be buried with
their brother Earl Senior and their parents, Pa John and Ella.

As a child growing up in Boston, I sometimes saw manifestations
of the continuing hostility between feuding family members of the
Little and Mason families. Aunt Sas and Aunt Gracie, who seldom
had harsh words to say about anyone black, especially family members, were unrelenting in their disdain for Grandma Daisy. Sometimes I saw them turn away in disgust when they saw her. Grandma
Daisy seemed to have a guilty look whenever she made eye contact
with either of them. Looking back now, it's hard to believe that an
observant and sensitive man like Uncle Malcolm was unaware of the
tension among his relatives. In fact, in 1954 he asked Ma to host a
gathering to which all family members in the Boston area would be
invited. Uncle Malcolm told Ma he wanted to speak to Little, Mason,
and Gray family members (Grandma Ella was a Gray) in the Boston
area about his new postprison activities with the Nation of Islam. "I
believe that he also wanted to bring the family together and help heal
wounds," Ma said. Unfortunately, Ma was caught squarely in the
middle of the feud between her mother and her father. Her Little
aunts lived with her in Boston on 72 Dale Street, while her mother
and aunt lived close enough that it would be difficult to avoid them.
"It was like walking a tightrope," Ma recalled. "I knew that Daddy
had remarried. I never totally lost contact with him. He wrote me and
his sisters when he could. When Malcolm told me how he boasted
about me to them for helping other family members escape from
Reynolds, I knew I could never feel toward him the way my mother
and Aunt Emmy did. Plus, there was no way I could deny my brothers and sisters. It's just tragic that family events which happened between 1909, when my parents married, and 1920, when my father
was forced to leave Reynolds for the last time, had such a negative
impact on Malcolm and the other children."

As for Uncle Malcolm, after those dinner-table and front-porch conversations with Ma, Aunt Sas, and Aunt Daisy, he could no longer say he had "forgotten about being a Little in the family sense." He not only learned family history, but after settling in following the homecoming celebration, he had an opportunity to meet with, work with, hang out with, and sometime get into trouble with a sizable assortment of Little, Mason, and Gray cousins, aunts, uncles, nephews, and nieces. "By the time Malcolm came," Ma said, "most of our relatives in Boston had settled themselves into city life, a life that was very different from the one they had left behind in Reynolds, Butler, and Talbotton, Georgia. Shoe repair, carpentry, and masonry, trades they had learned from older relatives back home, kept food on the table. Many had gotten married and were building or buying homes. Usually they married folks from back home rather than black Bostonians. One reason for this was that most longtime black Bostonians looked down their haughty noses at the newly arriving, mostly dark skinned country folks; a second was that most of the still deeply religious country folks regarded the city folks as fast-living children of Satan."

Uncle Malcolm's involvement with his recently discovered kin proved to be a sometimes exciting, sometimes exhilarating, sometimes exasperating, sometimes heartbreaking, but seldom a boring expenence.

FOUR Orpheus

One of the relatives whom thirteen-year-old Malcolm Little met in 1939, on his first trip to Boston, one who was to have a great influence over the very impressionable teenager, was Earl Little Jr., his brother. Earl, whose mother was Daisy Mason, was the oldest of Earl Senior's ten children. When Uncle Malcolm came to live in Boston permanently, in 1940, Earl Junior was twenty-nine years old and working as an entertainer under the name of Jimmy Carlton. He was well known to participants in Boston's night-life scene, often being an opening act for better-known singers who performed in the Boston area. Among those for whom he opened was the legendary jazz diva Billie Holiday. "It was rumored," Ma said, "that Earl had a thing going with her when she performed in Boston. One way he really impressed Malcolm was to introduce him to her. Malcolm couldn't stop talking about it. After Earl's death, Malcolm would still go see her when she was in Boston. She sometimes called him 'Little Brother' because he reminded her of Earl."

When Uncle Earl performed, Ma said, he always wore a tuxedo, like his idol, Duke Ellington. Also like his idol, Earl was extremely proud of his chemically induced straight hair. "Earl was very much into being cool and sophisticated," Ma recalled. "The most popular dance among black folks at that time was the lindy hop, but it wasn't Earl's style. He preferred the Fred Astaire dance style. His height, six feet four, his broad shoulders, his dark but not too dark skin, his suave and very charming style and attitude, captivated most women in his audiences."

His hipness, style, and attitude also captivated Uncle Malcolm.

"They hit it off instantly," Ma said, "which somewhat bothered me because, though I loved Earl, I just didn't see being an entertainer as a serious career for an intelligent black man. That was, and to a great deal still is, the way too many whites see us—singing and dancing, mostly for their enjoyment. However, looking back now, it's obvious why Malcolm was so dazzled by Earl's lifestyle. Here he was, fresh from a small city like Lansing, only aware of life in other small-to-medium-sized midwestern cities, meeting a brother who dressed in the latest styles, seemed to know everybody, including Billie Holiday, had money in his pockets, and was the epitome of what was considered hip and cool. It's understandable that he was mighty impressed. In fact, he was so impressed that when he started hanging out in the streets, he patterned himself after Earl."

For Malcolm, a self-described small-town hick, the choice between the course advocated by his sister and his aunts and that exemplified by his brother Earl was no contest. For appearance's sake and because he was still legally a minor, he paid lip service to the dictates of his sister and aunts, but for action he sneaked out of the house to be with his hip brother and friends. Things didn't start out that way, however. As already mentioned, the day after arriving in Boston, John Walker, his uncle by marriage, hired him to work part-time in his auto-park company. His first full-time job was as a soda jerk with the Townsend Drug Store and Soda Fountain, located at the corner of Townsend Street and Humbolt Avenue. "Malcolm strongly disliked being called a soda jerk," Ma said. "He considered it demeaning." The drugstore was a few blocks from Dale Street, where they lived, and across the street from the Townsend Street Baptist Church, where, for a brief period and, ironically, with the encouragement of Uncle Earl, he sang in one of the church's choirs. Of all the images of Uncle Malcolm, the one I have the most difficulty envisioning is his singing in a church choir. It's always tempting to say, "Something is wrong with that picture."

Laura, the girl whom he discusses in his autobiography, also attended Townsend Street Baptist Church and sang in the choir. He was also, briefly, a member of the church's Boy Scout troop. Aunt Sas and Aunt Gracie, as can be expected, were very pleased with his church activities; Ma was equally pleased with the fact that he was working.

She was already planning on how to steer him toward the field of law. "I learned early," she said, "of the role that the courts play in upholding white supremacy. I saw how our people's legal rights were often ignored or violated, especially when we had dealings with whites. If Malcolm became a lawyer, I believed, he would be able to help his family and his people fight legal oppression."

What Ma, Aunt Sas, and Aunt Gracie didn't know, at least at first, was that Uncle Malcolm, who was tall for his age, was already sneaking out of the house to the pool hall or to charm his way into a nightclub or after-hours joint. Ma said, "We found out that besides being intelligent, ambitious, respectful, and lovable, Malcolm was also adventurous and eager to explore what he considered the alluring possibilities available in big-city life. Despite our efforts, Malcolm was not to escape the trap that this society sets for too many young black males. Dazzled by what they think is easy money, even though it was basically chump change, available in a materialistic society, Malcolm and too many young men like him swallowed the bait." Until Uncle Malcolm was eighteen, he was forced to hide his street and nightlife activities from Ma and his other elders, but after that he became bolder with his negative lifestyle and moved slowly but surely down the path that ultimately led to his incarceration.

How this happened is best described by Uncle Malcolm in his autobiography.

Ella couldn't believe how atheistic, how uncouth, I had become. I believed a man should do anything he was slick enough or bad or bold enough to do and that a woman was nothing but another commodity. Every word I spoke was hip or profane. I would bet that my working vocabulary wasn't two hundred words. . . . Ella still liked me. I would go see her once in a while. But Ella had never been able to reconcile herself to the way I had changed. She has since told me that she had a steady foreboding that I was on the way into big trouble. But I had always had the feeling that Ella somehow admired my rebelling against the world because she, who had so much more drive and guts than most men, often felt stymied by having been born female.

Uncle Malcolm was correct in believing that Ma admired his rebellious nature. "I did admire his rebelling against the hypocrisy and racial oppression so prevalent in the United States in the 1940s and 1950s," she explained, "but I didn't admire his using that rebellious streak against himself by using drugs and throwing away his money on zoot suits and conked hair and against his own people by selling them drugs and directing thrill-seeking whites to places where they could indulge in their kinky sexual fantasies with weak, money-mad black folks."

Like Orpheus, Uncle Malcolm had fallen into the netherworld. His descent into criminal life caused serious problems between the two of them. But when he wrote that despite what he had become, "Ella still likes me," he wrote the truth. "As deeply hurt as I felt," Ma said, "I never gave up on him. I wasn't about to help him lead a life of destructive behavior, but the minute I saw he had decided to be the kind of proud black man that we all knew that he could be, one that Pa John and Grandma Ella would be proud of, I was ready to help him by any means necessary."

As he moved in and around Boston, whether going to work or sneaking out for one of his rendezvous, Malcolm had to beware of white ethnic street gangs, who, when not fighting with each other, would join forces to attack any black person they could get their hands on. In the neighborhoods of Roxbury, Dorchester, Hyde Park, South Boston, and Jamaica Plains, Ma said, "blacks had to be wary of being caught alone and unarmed in schoolyards, on public play grounds, and especially outside the white stadium in Roxbury. In the latter, white gangs got really hostile if a black team or predominantly black team defeated one of their teams in football or baseball."

They would also occasionally attack blacks who, by some stroke of luck, had secured apartments in a public housing project. Any who did were lucky because in the 1940s and 1950s in Boston it was extremely difficult for blacks to get into public housing. "The police seldom arrested anyone for such racially motivated crimes even when they involved the raping of black girls by white gang members," Ma noted. "Before the 1940s there were no black gangs in Boston. They emerged only as a response to attacks from white gangs and police indifference toward those attacks. Malcolm was a teenager at that time, but as far as I know, he never belonged to a gang. Later, when he stressed the need for self-defense when confronting white supremacists, I'm sure he remembered those attacks by the violent gangs." According to Clifford Green, one of Uncle Malcolm's teenage friends, "Malcolm was not one to go out seeking fights. He would never put up his dukes, just would not fight." Like many other intelligent people, Uncle Malcolm, whenever possible, sought to outthink and outmaneuver enemies rather than directly confront them.

According to Ma, black Bostonians also had to deal with hostility from many white adults. "Some neighborhoods, including Sugar Hill, where we lived, began to change from being mostly white to being mostly black in the early 1940s. The reason was World War II. Black folks, including Little, Mason, and Gray family members, were now working for companies that had previously denied them equal employment opportunities. Those included the Hood Rubber Company and the federal government's arsenal in Watertown, the Boston Navy Yard, the Quincy Shipyards, the Dominican Sugar Plant, and the booming passenger railroad companies. Many whites didn't want to share that economic prosperity, so they often violently resisted blacks moving into what they considered their neighborhoods."

Uncle Malcolm was aware of those struggles, noted Ma, "but he was too busy sneaking around to the clubs to be overly concerned. After Earl died from tuberculosis in 1941, his role as Malcolm's guide and companion in the Boston street life and nightclub scene was assumed by Malcolm Jarvis. At that time, Malcolm was easily influenced by anyone he considered a friend, which is what he considered Jarvis. However, it is important to remember that Malcolm, even during his worst days, was never a full-time hustler and petty criminal. He usually kept some kind of legitimate job, if only as a front to keep us off his case." From February 1942 to March 1943, Malcolm worked for the New York, New Haven and Hartford Railroad Company. During railroad layoffs, he also worked for Shaw's Jewelry in Lansing for a few weeks and then with A/C Sparkplug Company in Flint, Michigan. He worked the latter two jobs while visiting his siblings in Lansing. From March 1943, when the job ended with the New Haven line, until February 1944 he worked for Seaboard Railroad. After that for one month, until March 1944, he worked for the Atlantic Coast Railroad Company.

Again, during layoff or layover periods, he worked as a dishwasher for the Lobster Pond Restaurant in Manhattan, from July through September 1944, and at Sears, Roebuck in Brookline, Massachusetts, until October 20, 1944. From then until July 1945 he worked for the Capital Bedding Company in Boston. He then joined my father, Kenneth Collins, on another visit to Michigan, where he worked for the Reo Motor Truck Factory in Coral Gables, Michigan, from July to mid-August 1945. Uncle Malcolm returned to Boston in late August 1945 and once again worked at the family-owned Walker Auto Park in downtown Boston. He worked there until he was arrested on burglary charges in January 1946.

It's obvious that Malcolm's job schedule didn't leave enough time for him to become a full-time hustler and petty criminal. "In reality," Ma said, "he was a rank amateur who fortunately was caught and jailed before he advanced to becoming a master criminal on the streets of Harlem and Boston." Also contrary to popular belief, Uncle Malcolm never lived permanently in Harlem. He was there mostly doing short layovers while working with the railroad. He did take advantage of opportunities to "do his thing," however, while on layovers in Harlem, Philadelphia, and other such cities, for it was much more difficult to hang out in Boston, where some fifty relatives lived. In Harlem, for instance, he was free to hit the streets and the clubs anytime he wanted to; in Boston he had to duck and dodge cousins, aunts, and uncles who might alert Ma, Aunt Sas, and Aunt Gracie if they saw him or heard about his being in the wrong places with the wrong people. Uncle Malcolm often had to sneak out of the house with the help, initially, of Uncle Earl and Dad and later with the help of Dad and Jarvis. Uncle Malcolm was well aware that until his twenty-first birthday he had to stay in line both in Boston and in Lansing. He knew the story of how Uncle Earl had once been sent to reform school by his mother, Grandma Daisy, when she refused to care for him after he insisted on pursuing his dream of being a singer rather than a clerk in her store. Ma would never put Uncle Malcolm in reform school, but she most certainly wouldn't support his involvement with the zoot-suited and conked-hair crowd. He needed that support until he was nineteen, so he reluctantly cooled his heels when around her.

Ma said that what finally tripped Uncle Malcolm up was not the petty-hustler behavior he was indulging in but his involvement with the two white women, Sophia (not her real name) and Beatrice Barzanian. "The white cops weren't that concerned about his criminal activities in black neighborhoods," she said. "If he hadn't gotten involved with those two white women, he probably could have and would have continued his petty-hustler activities for quite some time. In a sense, his involvement with them became a mixed blessing, for it got the police involved before he retrogressed to his Harlem street life. Then he might have gotten into really big trouble, since that was the major league of street-life criminal activity."

Uncle Malcolm wrote rather comprehensively about his affair with Sophia in his autobiography. What wasn't covered as thoroughly was the effect that their affair had on members of the family, especially Ma. To describe Ma as being upset about Uncle Malcolm's affair with Sophia is a gross understatement.

"I was thoroughly disgusted with Malcolm's affair with Sophia," Ma declared. "It was bad enough that he had deeply hurt a sweet black woman like Laura [the same young woman who sang with him in the Townsend Street Baptist Church choir], but for him to leave her and get involved with a white woman was outrageous. I made it crystal clear that Sophia was not welcome in our home."

That made things a little difficult for Uncle Malcolm, since he was still living rent-free with Ma, Aunt Sas, and Aunt Gracie on Dale Street. His rent-free status was often a cause of conflict between Ma and Dad. "All we required of Malcolm was that he respect family morality values, which meant no shacking up with girlfriends in the house, and that he do his share of work around the house," she said. "Thus, when Malcolm sneaked Sophia into his apartment on the third floor, he was flagrantly violating a cardinal rule and compounding the violation by doing it with a white girl."

Ma's anger with Uncle Malcolm was not based solely on moral considerations. Her Georgia background made her very conscious of the serious trouble possibly awaiting a black man who cavorted with white women in the North or South. "I knew the danger," she said.

"Malcolm either didn't know or acted as though he didn't know it. He pretended to be surprised when I confronted him about sneaking Sophia into his apartment and about the trouble she could cause him. I am convinced even to this day that Sophia was a white woman driven by sexual fantasies about black men. For women like her, the most devastating way to rebel against their parents and their communities is to flaunt a black man in their faces. Thus, the man becomes a weapon in her struggles with her people. Women like Sophia are also thrill seekers for whom young black men like Malcolm are just another wild adventure. I knew it was only a matter of time before she would get him into some kind of serious trouble."

Though Ma believed she understood Sophia's motivations for the affair, she was less sure about Uncle Malcolm's. "I was extremely disappointed, hurt, and angry that my younger brother, who I knew was very intelligent, with great leadership potential, had fallen into the hoary trap of an affair with a white woman. It meant he had accepted the insidious belief so in vogue for many black people at that time that having a white woman was a much-desired status symbol. The whole situation enraged me so much that once, during an argument, I actually tried to throw both of them down a flight of stairs in the house as they were leaving."

Malcolm Jarvis, who was Uncle Malcolm's colleague in crime, told me that he was more than a black thrill to Sophia. "She was crazy about Malcolm, so crazy that she was once prepared to shoot a detective she thought was going to arrest him. When the detective walked into the room, Sophia was sitting at a table holding a pistol where it couldn't be seen. Malcolm had given it to her to hold, not to shoot anyone but to hold, figuring she wouldn't be searched. Fortunately, the detective was more interested in harassing than arresting."

Ma's premonitions about Sophia's getting Uncle Malcolm into trouble proved to be right on target. Sophia and Beatrice played a pivotal role in the series of burglaries that eventually led to Uncle Malcolm's incarceration. "The people whose homes he, Jarvis, and Brown burglarized in white, upper-middle-class neighborhoods in Belmont, Milton, Winchester, and the Cambridge area around Harvard University were all well known to the two upper-middle-class white women," Ma insisted. "They knew who wasn't at home, whose windows were left unlocked, where special keys were located, and what goodies were available to burglarize."

On January 12, 1946, in Boston, Malcolm, Jarvis, and Brown were arrested by detective Stephen Slack of the Milton, Massachusetts, police department and charged with stealing a $100 watch. "Because of a misguided sense of loyalty," Ma said, "neither of the men ever implicated Sophia and Beatrice in the case, even though one of the women drove the getaway car."

It was obvious from the beginning that the police were mainly interested in getting the men. While awaiting trial in Framingham's Women's Reformatory, twenty miles outside of Boston, the women were allowed open family visits, whereas bail for Uncle Malcolm, Jarvis, and Brown was set at $10,000 each. In court, Ma said, the men were described by one lawyer as "schvartze bastards" and by another as "minor Al Capones." Detective Slack, meanwhile, referred to Sophia and Beatrice as "poor, unfortunate, friendless, scared, lost girls." That's an interesting description of "girls" who, according to Malcolm, "would go to the door and ring the bell and if there was no answer we would go in."

My uncle, along with Jarvis and Brown, was sentenced by the judge to eight to ten years on five counts, to run concurrently. The women, it was found out later, received suspended sentences despite their obvious culpability. Several years ago, Ma and I separately went to the Dedham, Massachusetts, courthouse to investigate the records of Sophia. They were nowhere to be found. A clerk said that the files on the men had been designated for special handling and were kept in a special room in the courthouse called the Red Room. The clerk thought it odd that Dedham County's superior court had handled those records in such a manner. At least they were there. According to Ma, the court documents on Sophia and Beatrice had disappeared altogether when she looked for them. "They had obviously received 'special handling' of another kind," she said sarcastically.

As of 1990, one of the women was still living in Massachusetts and had a business on the North Shore. The other one lives on the West Coast. Both have families, with children, and to date have refused all requests for interviews. In 1995, after reading that the Little, Jarvis, and Brown records, once considered long lost, had been found, I decided to once again visit the Dedham county court to check out the records of Sophia and Beatrice. This time I was told that the women's files were sealed and couldn't be looked at except in very special circumstances. Somehow I knew that I would never be one of those very special circumstances.

When Uncle Malcolm was arrested, Ma said, she could have paid his bond by using her property as collateral. "I refused to do so only after witnessing his rather flippant attitude about the whole situation. At first he really didn't believe that he was actually going to be imprisoned. He showed no remorse about what he had done to himself and to his family. Besides that, he had the nerve to expect me to also post bail for Malcolm Jarvis. I regarded his getting into trouble with those white women and hanging out with Jarvis, whom he knew we regarded as a bad influence on him, as a sign of disrespect that I just couldn't support. As much as I cared for my brother, I wasn't prepared to help him continue on a path to destruction."

Uncle Malcolm found out that even for someone who believed as strongly as Ma did that "we Littles must stick together," there were limits. A young, cocky, hard-headed, self-indulgent, undisciplined Uncle Malcolm had gone beyond those limits. He had become the self-described man "who believed that he should do anything he was slick enough or bad or bold enough to do." Ma and other family members knew they had to find a way to reclaim him.

FIVE Ella

$\mathbf{M}$ost of the journalists, scholars, and others who have written books or articles on Malcolm X during the past thirty years interpret or emphasize his life from various, often warring, perspectives. There is one thing they share, however: a tendency to either completely ignore or debase the pivotal, caring relationship between Malcolm and his sister, Ella Little Collins.

Those who do mention her invariably try to portray her in two distinct ways. During my uncle's hell-raising teenage years, she is often presented as a kind of clever female Fagan leading him astray. Then, when dealing with his later, more public life, she is treated as being irrelevant. To propagate either of these depictions, writers have to deliberately ignore or downplay comments made by Uncle Malcolm about Ma in his much-heralded autobiography. I've already mentioned what he wrote about his first impressions of her during their initial meeting in Lansing. Further along in the same segment he noted that "Ella asked all kinds of questions about how I was doing: she had already heard from Wilfred and Hilda about my election as class president. She asked especially about my grades, and I ran to get my report cards. I was one of the three highest in the class. Ella praised me . . ." and continued praising him for the rest of his life and after he was assassinated.

After moving to Boston to live with Ma and meeting Mary, another sister, he wrote: "It's funny how I seem to think of Mary as Ella's sister, instead of her being, just as Ella is, my half-sister. It's probably because Ella and I were much closer as basic types; *we're dominant people,* and Mary has always been mild and quiet, almost shy."

A teenage Boston friend, Laura, who had a serious crush on Uncle Malcolm, encouraged him to consider being a lawyer, as his sister Ella suggested. She told him she was sure Ma would help him. "She had the idea," related Malcolm, "that Ella would help me as much as she could. And if Ella even thought that she could help any member of the Little family put up any kind of professional shingle—as a teacher, as a foot doctor, as anything—why, you would have to tie her down to keep her from taking in washing."

Later, after Malcolm was imprisoned, he wrote: "My sister Ella had been steadily working to get me transferred to the Norfolk, Massachusetts Penal Colony, which was an experimental rehabilitation jail. In other prisons, convicts often said that if you had the right money, or connections, you could get transferred to this Colony whose penal policies sounded almost too good to be true. Somehow, Ella's efforts in my behalf were successful in late 1948, and I was transferred to Norfolk."

Ma came to his help at another important juncture, in 1964. Malcolm felt a great need to make a pilgrimage to Mecca, but "it would require money I didn't have. I took a plane to Boston. I was turning once again to my sister Ella. . . . She deals in real estate, and *she* was saving up to make the pilgrimage. Nearly all night, we talked in her living room. She told me there was no question about it; it was more important that I go. I thought about Ella the whole flight back to New York. A *strong* woman. . . . had played a very significant role in my life. No other woman ever was strong enough to point me in directions; I pointed women in directions. I had brought Ella into Islam, and now she was financing me to Mecca. Allah always gives you signs, when you are with Him, that He is with you."

In black Baptist churches, Uncle Malcolm's statements about Ma would be called "testifying." When reading them, it becomes clear that there were at least three things about Ma that greatly impressed Uncle Malcolm. She was committed to her family; she was resourceful; she was determined. Those were the elements that enabled her, in the 1930s and 1940s, to personally bring between twenty and thirty Little, Mason, and Gray family members from rural, extremely racist and poverty-stricken Reynolds, Georgia, to Boston, where there was at least the possibility of getting a low-paying job. When they arrived, they always needed help to survive those first few months. Ma worked many different kinds of jobs to help them, but if that wasn't enough, she unashamedly resorted to shoplifting to feed and clothe her family members. "If it was a choice between our being hungry and insufficiently clothed for the cold weather and shoplifting," she told me straighforwardly, "I shoplifted without hesitation as a commonsense response to a desperate situation."

Her response to those who consider this a rationalization for thievery was that "it was better than going on welfare and opening up your whole life to state officials." There was also the reality, she said, that in the 1930s and 1940s it was very difficult for black Bostonians to get public assistance or into public housing "unless you joined the Catholic church, which basically controlled the system, or unless, as a woman, you were prepared to sleep with someone connected with the department. I wasn't about to do either, so I shoplifted so we could eat and be clothed. I still believe that was the right choice." Ma's commitment to her family and her dominant personality strongly contributed to the breakup of her three marriages. When her husbands objected too strenuously to having to share her with her family and forced her to make a choice, family won out. She divorced all three, including my father, Kenneth Collins.

Ma's resourcefulness and determination were strengths that she brought to Boston from Reynolds in the 1930s, strengths that she had gotten from Pa John and Ella Little, her grandparents. Times were hard for black folks; good jobs—in fact, any jobs—were hard to come by in Boston, so she moved to New York City, where she was hired as a floorwalker for a department store. Ma said they looked at her height, five feet nine; weight, 145 pounds, and color, jet black, and decided that she looked evil enough to possibly frighten off potential shoplifters. She was disguised as a cleaning woman, thus enabling her to move throughout the store without attracting too much attention from white and black customers. Ma, never one to underestimate her talents, says she was good at the job but knew that the store owner would never promote her to the official position of store detective, so she quit after six months. The experience did teach her something that would be of value later—that was how to be a successful shoplifter. That skill came in handy later when she had to help feed and clothe relatives with very limited resources. When she quit the job, she also left New York City, having decided that it was "too fast a place for a single black woman."

She moved on to Everett, Massachusetts, outside Boston, to live with her mother, Daisy Mason, and her brother, Earl Little Jr. It should be noted that during the seventeenth, eighteenth, and nineteenth centuries most blacks in the Boston area lived in what are now called the suburbs, not in Boston proper. Those who did live in Boston were located on Beacon Hill, near the state capitol. Crispus Attucks, the former slave who was the first casualty of the Revolutionary War, was a resident of that area. It was also a major stop on the Underground Railroad. When Ma moved to Boston, she became friends with Mrs. Aurora Walker, a member of a family that had owned a home on Beacon Hill since the eighteenth century. Mrs. Walker, for many years, was one of a very few black homeowners left on Beacon Hill. Most of the others had been forced out of the highly desirable neighborhood in the early 1900s in a burst of early-twentieth-century urban removal. Most moved to the lower Roxbury section of Boston. About all that remains from that early black presence on Beacon Hill is the Old African Meeting House, in which Harriet Tubman and Frederick Douglass, among others, used to speak out against the enslavement of African people. It is now a historical site on the Massachusetts Historical Society's Freedom Trail.

From Everett, Ma commuted by bus and train to Boston's lower Roxbury neighborhood to work in a store, owned by Grandma Daisy, on Lenox and Shawmut Avenues. Not surprisingly, since Ma's business acumen was always one of her strong points, it wasn't long before she had sufficient funds to purchase part ownership in the store. It was during that time that Ma met Lloyd Oxley, a physician at Boston City Hospital. Ma said one of his main attractions to her was his support of the political, economic, and cultural positions promoted by Marcus Garvey. Soon he became her first husband. Then trouble erupted. She discovered that Dr. Oxley's bark about his Garveyite position was much louder than his bite. A big problem was her Jamaican mother-in-law, who considered Ma "too aggressive." There was also the question of Dr. Oxley being a control freak as far as his wife was concerned. Ma was most definitely not a woman to be controlled. Complicating all this was Oxley's dismissal from Boston City Hospital, supposedly for doing an unauthorized abortion. His biggest flaw, Ma said, was his strong opposition to her constantly feeding and clothing family members and sending money back south—money that often came from her husband's pocket in those early years. On June 28, 1934, Dr. Oxley and Ma divorced. On February 16, 1945, Dr. Oxley, along with Dr. Frank Butler, delivered me. By that time, Ma was married to her third husband, Kenneth J. Collins.

The store owned by the Mason women prospered. In fact, it was doing so well that envious, white-owned Folsom's Supermarket felt the heat of competition. The owners pressured white suppliers about doing business with the Mason women. Besides the store, Ma, Grandma Daisy, and Aunt Emmy also owned two hundred acres of land on Boston's South Shore; each owned one-third. Everything appeared to be operating smoothly and profitably until the dormant feud between some Little and Mason family members erupted once again. Grandma Daisy, who was still resentful of the way she had been treated many years ago by Earl Little Sr. and Aunt Emmy, knew that Ma was using much of the money she earned in their business ventures to help Little relatives in Reynolds, Georgia, and Earl Senior's children in Lansing, Michigan. That enraged them. They didn't want one dime of Ma's money earned in their store to be used to help Earl Senior's children. Ma says that in order to limit the amount of money she would have for this assistance, Aunt Emmy began double-dealing her share of the store's profits by showing more loss than profit in the bookkeeping. An angry Ma decided that it was best to leave the business and asked them to buy her out. Grandma Daisy and Aunt Emmy, knowing that Ma would use much of any money she received to help Earl Senior's children, used stalling tactics to keep from paying her all she was due. "If I had gotten all that money when it was owed me," she insisted, "I might have been able to bring a couple more of my younger brothers and sisters to Boston. My mother's and my aunt's obstinacy strengthened my resolve." She waited for an opening through which she could collect the full amount they owed her. It took a while, but Aunt Emmy finally provided Ma the opening gambit she had been waiting for when she asked Ma for a loan—not for her husband's business but for personal use. Ma would agree to the loan if Aunt Emmy signed over her third of the land as collateral. When Aunt Emmy, as Ma expected, failed to repay the loan, Ma won an out-of-court settlement which stipulated that Aunt Emmy had to turn over to her the disputed third of the land. A furious Aunt Emmy never spoke to her again.

Ma credits her business acumen to Grandma Daisy. "When my mother left Reynolds for Boston, she had absolutely nothing but her will and determination. When she died in 1972, she had money in the bank and a third share of two hundred acres of valuable land."

There were some prices to be paid for Grandma Daisy's success. The education of her children was of secondary importance. Operating the store came first. Earl Junior and Mary began working in the store in their early teens; Ma was a little older when she started. Though she shared her mother's feel for business, Uncle Earl and Aunt Mary didn't. All he wanted to be was an entertainer, so he worked all day in the store and then worked half the night singing in various clubs. It was a very strenuous existence and may have increased his susceptibility to the tuberculosis that killed him in 1941.

Aunt Mary's way of handling a situation which displeased her was to just avoid it. Ma said she was as much a master at avoiding her chores in the store as she had been on the farm in Georgia. "Earl and I had to do extra work to cover for her." Ma knew that Grandma Daisy was not paying them sufficiently for all the work they were doing, but she didn't complain. "I just watched everything Ma did— how she dealt with customers, how she handled suppliers, how she dealt with competitors, and how she maneuvered around city officials. I soaked up everything." Ma said she also saw firsthand how upset some whites were when blacks successfully competed with them for black business. "They acted as if they had some kind of divine right to black consumer dollars. We couldn't even own stores in their neighborhoods, but they could come to ours, open up stores, grab as many dollars as they could, and spend those black-earned dollars among their own people. When we successfully competed with them for those dollars, they conspired in attempts to put us out of business."

Ma's resourcefulness and determination were also exhibited when

she outsmarted a bigoted white family who didn't want to sell her
the property at 72 Dale Street. She didn't run to a civil-rights organization seeking help. "I always kept an ace in the hole for such people," she said. She checked at the bank and found that all the family
wanted for the property was five hundred dollars cash and payment
of overdue real estate taxes. After checking with Mr. Gordon, a Jewish realtor who had schooled her in the process of purchasing property threatened with bank foreclosure, and Mr. Charlie Roundtree, a
black realtor whom she trusted, Ma once again approached the family and offered them six hundred dollars cash and payment of the
overdue taxes. They wouldn't even show her the house.

Then Ma made her move. By now the owners had raised the price
to nine hundred dollars. What they didn't know was that Ma was
prepared to pay twelve hundred dollars, a fact she made known to
the bank. The bank, interested only in getting their money, pressured
the bigoted family to sell to her. They still balked; almost a year went
by. Finally, a persistent Ma approached them again with an agreement paper and nine hundred dollars in hand. Now they wanted
twelve hundred dollars. "I didn't blink," Ma said. "I told them that if
they signed the agreement paper immediately for twelve hundred
dollars, I would leave a nine hundred dollar deposit and pay the bal-
ance in twenty-four hours. If I didn't, they could keep the nine hundred dollar deposit. That offer convinced them they were dealing
with a dumb Negro, so they quickly signed the agreement." She then
called the bank and told them that she had both a signed agreement
and the twelve hundred dollars in hand. The bank, now drooling with
eagerness to close the deal, called the family and told them they
wanted their money that day. The property owners were shocked to
find Ma sitting there when they came to the bank. "They were sure
that they were going to have both my nine hundred dollars and the
house," Ma said. The bank insisted that they stick to the signed
agreement and sell for the twelve hundred dollars agreed upon. By
the time they paid the five hundred dollar mortgage to the bank and
six hundred dollars' worth of overdue real-estate taxes, they had exactly one hundred dollars in cash." That's what they got for messing
with Ma.

Later, she bought other property from white folks with foreclosure problems. "They hated dealing with a black woman," Ma noted, "but I never pressured them to deal with me. They put the pressure on themselves by letting their problems get out of hand. Once I purchased a building, many white tenants moved because they couldn't stand having a black landlord."

Later, when he was a member of the Nation of Islam, Uncle Malcolm, who carefully watched Ma in action as a realtor, applied much of what he learned from her when purchasing property for the Nation. In fact, Ma said proudly, "it was the Little brothers, Wilfred, Philbert, and Malcolm, who pushed the Nation into buying land. Elijah Muhammad and the others were satisfied with just the way things were going."

Ma didn't just battle with bigoted whites solely for her own benefit. She was equally tenacious when looking out for the interests of her family and members of her community. I remember when she went to war with the Boston public school system. "I was determined that it wasn't going to cheat you out of an education as it had done to so many other black children," she told me. It all began with a flashy-dressing elementary-school teacher named Frances O'Toole, who showed very little concern for the black children in her class. Our problem was ignited by an American history assignment to do an essay on George Washington. Ma strongly believed that American history as taught by white teachers in Boston's public school system was at best incomplete and at worst deliberate miseducation. When she heard about my assignment, she told me, "I want you to do an essay on the famous black scientist George Washington Carver, along with one on Washington. Turn them in to your teacher." It must be noted that Ma didn't tell me to disrespect my white teachers but to treat them like human beings if they treated me like one.

When I turned my history assignment in to Miss O'Toole, she ignored the one on George Washington Carver and gave me a very low grade on the one on George Washington. Like any other white teachers during that time, she dismissed George Washington Carver as "the peanut man." Finally, I told Ma what was going on. She went to Julia Ward Howe Elementary School to confront Miss O'Toole and the principal. When no satisfaction was forthcoming from them, she proceeded to confront the Boston School Board. As far as I know,

Ma was the first black person in history to confront the Boston public school system about its failure to teach black history. Prominent on the school board at that time was the very pompous Louise Day Hicks, who was famous, or infamous, depending on one's point of view, for being a vociferous opponent of busing to achieve school desegregation in the 1960s. The day Ma and I arrived for the school-board hearings, Mrs. Hicks sat there in all her glory. The stony looks she gave Ma practically screamed out, How dare you challenge us? Ma could be just as pompous as Hicks if the situation demanded it. She returned the stony looks with one of her own. Hicks declared that so-called Negro history had no place in Boston public schools. Ma and Hicks were almost toe to toe and nose to nose. The next thing I saw was the two of them scuffling. The question as to who grabbed who first is still officially unanswered. Ma said Hicks, who had the reputation of being an instigator, grabbed first because she couldn't stand Ma being right in her face and not backing down. As the two hefty women prepared to duke it out, my money was on Ma. Unfortunately, the scuffle was stopped before the grabbing became slugging, but both Hicks and other board members had learned that Ma was not to be messed with. After making that point, Ma decided to transfer me to Davis A. Ellis Elementary School, where I had a gracious, intelligent, wonderful black teacher, Miss Agatha Guilford. Ma explained to her what happened with Miss O'Toole and the board. Miss Guilford, a truly great teacher, taught children of all races and worked educational wonders with all of us. Mrs. Hicks later became a U.S. congresswoman from Massachusetts; Ms. Agatha Guilford today is retired and living in Cape Cod, Massachusetts.

Ma's direction about my American history papers wasn't simply a weapon with which to antagonize Miss O'Toole. She had always insisted that I learn black history.

If asked which person in black history most symbolizes Ma, I would say the great abolitionist Harriet Tubman. Of her it's said that when a former enslaved African whom she had helped escape on the Underground Railroad got weary and wanted to return to the slave owner from whom he had been rescued, Miss Tubman pulled out a pistol, pointed it at him, and said he would "be free or die." I believe Harriet Tubman would consider Ma a soul sister.

Since black history was not taught in the Boston public schools in the early 1950s, she actually hired a private tutor, Forrest Scott, to teach me. He was succeeded by another tutor, A. Jarrett, with whom Ma became close friends. Mr. Jarrett later helped us with the Organization of Afro-American Unity (OAAU), which was founded by Uncle Malcolm when he left the Nation of Islam.

Ma's run-in with Louise Day Hicks was not an isolated incident. She also had several confrontations with the Boston police department over their often hostile and disrespectful treatment of black people. One that I remember most vividly occurred over bicycles. Ma and I were working with twenty disadvantaged children from Boston's South End. Of those, the one we particularly loved was Jackie Barrows, who, at ten years of age, helped his mother sell newspapers in Boston neighborhoods, such as Back Bay, Downtown, and the South End, from sunup until late at night. Since they had no transportation, they walked some thirty miles daily to complete their route. That was a lot of work for so young a child who also had to attend school. Ma decided that we could help Jackie by providing him with a bicycle. If he continued to sell papers, the bike would then be his free of charge. This worked so well that we decided to provide bikes for other children for working and recreational purposes. This enabled us to take them on bike trips and feed them wholesome food. We also fed them in our home at 486 Massachusetts Avenue. Ma, who purchased the bikes with her own money, believed that children would be more appreciative of what they were receiving if they had to pay a small fee for the bike trip, so they were asked to pay one dollar for a bike and all they could eat. We provided everything else. As often happens, some parents began grumbling and accused us of scheming to get portions of their welfare checks. Members of the Boston police department, especially Division 4 and its detectives, with whom we had often locked horns, believed that "that nigger woman" was up to something. They got a search warrant to raid 486 Massachusetts Avenue, the apartment building in which we lived and which Ma owned at the time. Early one morning, without first knocking, they broke down the front doors of many apartments in the building, including ours. They confiscated all the bikes we had for the children, claiming they were stolen property. We went to court, and Ma whipped them every way possible. They had no proof that we had done anything criminal. Not only did the judge find in Ma's favor; he ordered the police to personally return the bikes to our building. It was the first time in history that a black person had won a court case against the Boston police department, the oldest such police force in the country.

Ma's lawyer urged her to sue the city, but Ma, who was basically her own lawyer, was not interested in the money. She just wanted to stop the police from treating black people so contemptuously. The police department, which had been embarrassed by the judge's decision, defiantly refused his order to personally return the bikes. Unaware of her position on filing a lawsuit, the police finally told Ma that if she didn't sue the city, they would return the bikes. She played their little game, telling them she wouldn't sue. Very late one night we heard a knock on our living-room window. We looked out and saw some police officers unloading our bikes from the paddy wagon and putting them into the yard. They kept their word; Ma kept hers. Another Boston institution had learned that Ma was not one to passively accept abuse.

Ma also moved against exploitative and abusive fellow blacks. This was best illustrated in her move against a black doctor who had a reputation for exploiting female patients. Ma got involved when she heard that he was holding a young woman against her will in his expensive home. The woman was the sister of Rodney Smith, a captain in the Nation of Islam (N.O.I.). Rodney's wife, Lt. Beverly Smith, was the head of Muslim Girls Training. (Ma was opposed to the Nation's not having female captains and was always after Uncle Malcolm about that.) Both were members in Temple Eleven. Rodney's sister, who was not in the Nation, had been "kidnapped" by Dr. Baron B. Denniston and held in his home at 679 Massachusetts Avenue for a year under the influence of drugs. Ma and Dr. Denniston, who had been my outpatient doctor at Massachusetts General Hospital in 1954, once had a business relationship. They had a fiftyfifty partnership in the five-story building at 679 Massachusetts Avenue in which his office and his home were located. Denniston was considered one of Boston's premier physicians, but he also had a Mr. Hyde side. He was rumored to use drugs to control female patients, causing them to fall under his spell. Ma said that he had once attempted to make her sister, Mary, one of his victims. She also had to take him to court for not living up to their agreement on the building. The doctor, aware of Ma's reluctance to take a black person before a white-controlled court, basically ignored her. She eventually lost $10,000 because of his conniving.

When Rodney Smith first learned of his sister's plight, he didn't notify the Boston police department because he didn't believe they cared about what blacks did to other blacks in Boston. He was also aware of the department's great hostility toward the N.O.I. Rodney sought help from his Muslim brothers in Temple Eleven. Minister Louis X (now Louis Farrakhan) was head of the temple. Rodney knew that the N.O.I. had a strict hands-off policy about helping what they called "lost-found Negroes," which was their label for any black who was not a member of the Nation. However, considering his position and his wife's in the organization and the seriousness of the situation, Rodney thought an exception would be made. He was heartbroken when Minister Louis X, citing official policy, refused their request for help.

Rodney's mother, who was also a member of the Nation, had received a call from her kidnapped daughter begging for help in getting away from Denniston. Despite Rodney's hesitancy, she went to the police. Rodney, Beverly, and I accompanied her to Division 4 headquarters, where she was told that there was nothing they could do, that her daughter was a grown woman who could do as she wished. She must have chosen to be with Dr. Denniston.

A devastated Mrs. Smith then turned to Ma for help. She knew that Ma had influence with Uncle Malcolm, who was the head of Temple Seven in Harlem and the N.O.I.'s most visible leader. When Ma asked Malcolm for help, she was livid when he also refused, citing the N.O.I.'s policy against assisting "lost-found Negroes." It was the first time I had seen her really angry with him. "I should cut your head off," she said vehemently. "You don't own it. The Messenger [Elijah Muhammad] does. Here I am, a mere woman, ready to act and you so-called black men, you so-called Muslims, and your Mr. Muhammad are boys acting like men."

Uncle Malcolm attempted to soothe her. "Ella, they are lost-found

Negroes, not Muslims," he argued. "[Helping them] is not what we're about."

"Mr. Muhammad is not doing anything," Ma countered, "but for himself and his own. What are you doing for yourself and your family? You don't have a pot to piss in or a window to throw it out of." Ma knew that such outbursts bothered Malcolm, because afterward he wouldn't call or come by, sometimes for a whole month. Ma made similar charges about Mr. Muhammad to Wilfred and Philbert. They believed that she didn't know what she was talking about, that she would cause trouble for them in the N.O.I. Ma says she based her charges on what she had seen on a visit to N.O.I. headquarters in Chicago. "What I saw," she told me, "was Mr. Muhammad's enrichment of members of his family claiming all the glory for himself." She had also heard rumors of Mr. Muhammad's impregnating Evelyn and other secretaries. Finally, she resented the N.O.I.'s treatment of her brother, Reginald, the first Little to join the Nation.

When the N.O.I. and the police refused to help the Smith family rescue their sister and daughter, Ma put together a plan of action by which she, Rodney, Beverly, Mrs. Smith, and I would rescue the young woman. Without going into detail, I'll just say that we raided the building and successfully rescued her. It took all of five minutes. Minister Louis X was not pleased that the Smiths and others turned to Ma for help. He considered her insubordinate. Hesitant to move against Ma himself, he reported her "insubordination" to Uncle Malcolm. Since the N.O.I. had a very strict, military-like chain-of-command system, Malcolm believed he had no choice but to suspend Ma for ninety days. Despite his urgings, she never returned to the Nation. Rodney and Beverly Smith also left the organization permanently. When speaking of the rescue and its aftermath, Ma said, "We tried to go through the chain of command in Boston but received no assistance. It was a critical situation that had to be dealt with, so we did so. I was not prepared to blindly follow anyone, not my husbands, not Minister Louis X, not Elijah Muhammad, not even my beloved brother Malcolm."

One of the husbands Ma refused to "follow blindly" was my father, Kenneth Collins, whom she first met in the 1930s when visiting her siblings in Lansing, Michigan. Dad attended public school with

Wilfred and Philbert and played playground basketball with them while Malcolm, several years younger, looked on. My father and his brother Buster had the reputation of being "cool cats," "swinging cats," and "cool daddies" who captivated local girls, black and white, with their looks, attitudes, and dancing style. "We considered the Little brothers impossibly square cats," Dad said, "because they were so serious all the time due to their family situation." The Collins brothers were especially impressive to the girls for their dancing to a popular song during the 1930s and 1940s called "Flatfoot Floogie and a Floy Floy" (words and music by Slam Stewart, Bud Green and Slim Gaillard; this song and music was one of the theme songs used in the 1997 motion picture *The English Patient*). In his auto-biography, Malcolm wrote of "Negroes going crazy at dances to get those white chicks." The Collins brothers were prominent among those "Negroes going crazy."

When he was twenty-four years old, Dad left Lansing for Boston, mainly to be with his mother, who had divorced his father, Walter J. Collins, and his grandmother, a full-blooded Lakota Indian who, as a teenager, had been raped by some of the American reinforcement troops of Civil War general George Armstrong Custer. They also killed her father. The result of the rape was the birth of Dad's mother, Delores.

Despite having married Ma in 1941, Dad spent hours after work on weekends hanging out with Uncle Earl in the clubs and dance halls of black Boston. When Uncle Malcolm came to Boston, he was very impressed with the two "swinging cats" and before too long was sneaking out of the house to hang out with them. Sometimes Ma, frustrated and angry, would actually search through the clubs looking for him. If she found him, she would drag him home, only to have him sneak out again at the first opportunity. "I was really angry with Earl and Ken," she said. "They knew he was a minor, but they acted like two irresponsible teenagers themselves."

The "wiry, brown-skinned, conked shoe-shine boy Freddie," whom Uncle Malcolm wrote about as working in the Roseland State Ballroom, the one who could "make the shine rag pop like a fire-cracker," was Dad. The same "Freddie" helped Malcolm get a job at the shoeshine parlor and taught him "how to hustle white patrons for larger tips." The "Shorty" who took Malcolm to the shoeshine parlor was actually Malcolm Jarvis, who later became his partner in crime.

One of the reasons Uncle Malcolm didn't use my father's real name in the book, Dad told me, was "because he didn't want to jeopardize my job with Harvard's Department of Athletics." Beginning in the early 1970s, after I began playing professional tennis, Dad and I used to play tennis on the department's courts, sometimes at 3:00 A.M. Dad also introduced me to Harvard's squash and tennis coach, Jack Barnaby, my instructor for some time on prospective tennis coaching. Mr. Barnaby was a cofounder of the U.S. Professional Tennis Teachers Association.

The reality is that I began playing tennis in the first place to escape Ma's constant pressure to become a scientist and to avoid confronting a promise I had made to Uncle Malcolm years earlier on one of his trips to Boston. As always when he visited, my room became his room; my favorite lounge chair, his chair. The two of us were sitting in a room in our home, which was then 486 Massachusetts Avenue. At the time Uncle Malcolm was under severe pressure from both the FBI and members of the Nation. I watched as he sat quietly in a rocking lounge chair, looking out the window as if in deep thought. Finally, he spoke to me about the number of times throughout his life when he wished he had listened to Ma. "Rodnell," he said, "promise me that you'll always listen to your mother. Always listen to Ella and you'll be all right. I wish I had." Though I said yes to Uncle Malcolm's request that day, I really didn't mean it. His words tore at my heart on the day of his funeral when I acted as one of his pallbearers. At the gravesite, after the casket had been lowered, I asked Ma and Betty, his widow, if I could stay behind after everyone else left. While I knelt in prayer, the white grave diggers began covering his casket with dirt. That struck me all wrong. "I'll do that," I told them. Other brothers, Muslim and non-Muslim alike, who were preparing to leave, saw what I was doing and rushed to help. It seemed right that we cover Malcolm's casket. After the brothers left, I stayed behind to continue praying, asking Allah to help me keep the promise I had made so casually to Malcolm. The day after the funeral, Ma asked me about my future plans. I knew she still wanted me to be a scientist, but despite what Uncle Malcolm had said to me, I was determined to pursue my own goal. I mumbled a vague response to Ma and proceeded to continue traveling thousands of miles annually, playing the professional tennis circuit. I was also a part-time computer program analyst. Both activities kept me away from Ma's pressures for months at a time.

My tennis sessions with Dad at Harvard in the early 1970s ended our estrangement that began when he and Ma were divorced in 1960. I was thirteen years old at the time. During the first few years, Dad was extremely bitter and said some pretty negative things about Ma to writers who were interviewing him for books on Malcolm. I remember one particularly bitter confrontation and low point after which Dad had Ma arrested for assault. Dad had come to our home to take me and a friend to the circus. Unfortunately, he didn't come alone. Sitting proudly in his car was Miss Velvet (not her real name), one of the current women in his life. Dad told the judge that when he reached down to pick up my friend, who had polio and who had fallen, "she [Ma] hit me upside my head with something." Miss Velvet, he continued, was a witness to the "unprovoked assault." Ma was unrepentant. "He had some nerve coming up to my home with the neighborhood whore in the front seat planning to pick up my child and have him riding with them around the city. That was too much, totally disrespectful." The judge found her guilty and sentenced her to ninety days of psychiatric observation. As she so often did, Ma found something positive in a negative situation. While under observation, she met and befriended a wealthy Jewish woman whose husband was attempting to have her declared insane and a young black man whom authorities thought needed a psychiatric observation because he was pimping a stable of white women. When the Jewish woman was released, she lived with us for a month until she was rid of her husband. The young man, under Ma's guidance, cleaned himself up, joined the Nation of Islam, and got married. When I met him years later, he told me that Ma saved his life.

As I grew older, I realized that Dad's major problem with Ma was his "me Tarzan, you Jane" attitude when discussing anything with her. Dad actually spoke in this manner. He found out that she was no compliant Jane. Dad, like Uncle Malcolm and me, was spoiled by Ma, Aunt Sas, and Aunt Gracie. Ma would darn our socks, have dinner ready promptly between 5:00 and 6:00 P.M. no matter how busy she had been that day, clean up behind us, and help with homework and all such wifely and motherly things. Despite her tough veneer, Ma was very traditional when it came to her men—in her family, that is, as long as they took care of what she expected them to do. If we shucked and jived, Ma could move from being a black Donna Reed to a very angry feline in a moment. She gave much to her men, but she also demanded much from them in return. Dad never quite understood that while they were married. It took a while for Uncle Malcolm and me to understand it.

Even though he didn't understand everything Ma did, Malcolm was impressed with her resourcefulness and determination in getting things done. That was clear when he wrote: "Then there was my sister Ella herself. I couldn't get over what she had done. I've said before, this is a strong, big, black, Georgia-born woman. Her domineering ways had gotten her put out of the Nation of Islam's Boston Mosque Eleven; they took her back, then she left on her own. Ella had started studying under Boston orthodox Muslims. Then she founded a school where Arabic was taught. *She* didn't speak it; she hired teachers who did. That's Ella. . . ."

There were times, however, when Malcolm didn't appreciate Ma's "domineering ways," especially during his teenage years. Ma wanted to control everything, from what he would do for a career to who his friends would be and whom he would marry. Ma was one happy big sister when Uncle Malcolm began seeing Laura, the beautiful, churchgoing daughter of a Sugar Hill family. Besides her intelligence and beauty, her dark skin was another plus as far as Ma was concerned. "I get so tired of black men," she said scornfully, "who chase after women *solely* because they have light skin and straight hair." She was even more scornful of those men who chase after white women. "They make fools of themselves over women who seek to live out some sexual fantasy about black men that, ironically, was drilled into them by their white supremacist fathers and grandfathers." Uncle Malcolm's abandonment of Laura for Sophia, a white woman, put the first serious strain on their relationship.

The next woman whom Ma favored for Malcolm was Evelyn (called Heather in his autobiography), who was the foster daughter of Dorothy Young, one of Ma's closest friends. Aunt Dot, as I called her, was also my godmother. Their friendship ended in the 1960s when Aunt Dot married Kenneth Collins, my Dad and Ma's third and last ex-husband. To Ma's great pleasure, Malcolm and Evelyn dated for a couple of years, dates that were properly chaperoned by either Ma or Aunt Dot. Ma, having failed in efforts to hook Uncle Malcolm up with Laura, got fervently behind Evelyn, whose grandparents, the Bonapartes (parents of Dorothy), had raised their children in the kind of secure, structured environment that Ma wanted for her favorite brother. What Ma failed to realize was that the Bonaparte children got one message from a mother-and-father team with very similar ideas about what was best for their children. Malcolm, on the other hand, when living with Ma, Aunt Sas, and Aunt Gracie, was given different messages on the best way to become a responsible black adult. Aunt Sas and Aunt Gracie, both pious Christians, emphasized Jesus as the guide to a successful life; Ma, being more practical, promoted education and hard work and commitment to black empowerment as the way to go. (Ella L. Collins and the late Reverend, U.S. Congressman Adam Clayton Powell Jr., D-New York, are the founding mother and father of degreed Black Studies programs at colleges and universities across North America; *West's Encyclopedia of American Law,* vol. 7, 1999.) Uncle Earl Senior, in the short time they had together, offered Uncle Malcolm the excitement of the entertainment world. Less lofty folks promoted the street life and easy money. These competing messages, coming from people he loved or looked up to, inevitably confused a sensitive teenager about the direction to take with his life.

Ma said that Laura and Evelyn were the only two women Malcolm dated in Boston of whom she and his aunts approved. They had absolutely no use for any of the other women who chased after Uncle Malcolm, especially Sophia and Jackie Massey, a middle-aged black woman whom they considered an older woman on the make for a hot young teenager. I was old enough at the time to remember Miss Massey. She was five feet eight in high heels, and her 125 pounds were all in the right places. She used to strut down Dale Street in tight, flashy dresses and skirts, her arms loaded with noisy, dangling bracelets that announced that she was in the vicinity before we even saw her. Any breathing male couldn't help being impressed with the body and the walk, but she had one major problem. Her face looked like it had been the site of several major battles. Fortunately for her, her other attributes were so pronounced that they caused many men to ignore the face. Miss Massey was the recurring nightmare of every housewife in the general area despite the unsustained rumor that she didn't mess with married men.

"Jackie Massey was the most aggressive of all the women who pursued Uncle Malcolm during his Boston days," Ma said. "She frequently turned up at our home asking about something or the other. What she really wanted was Malcolm. When he was in prison, she often visited him, bringing along the kind of home-cooked food she knew he craved for. She had concrete plans to marry Malcolm when he was released from prison and was making arrangements to do so." Ma's position was "I don't think so! I bluntly told Malcolm that if he married Jackie Massey, he should expect no help from me in prison or out." As determined as she was to block his marrying Miss Massey, she was equally determined that he would marry Evelyn. What she found out was that Uncle Malcolm had no intention of marrying either one of them. Caught up in the fervor of his newfound commitment to Elijah Muhammad and the Nation of Islam, he had little time for anything else, including a hasty marriage.

When Mr. Elijah Muhammad transferred Uncle from Boston's Temple Eleven to Harlem's Temple Seven, Evelyn switched her membership to the Harlem mosque. Malcolm, knowing how Evelyn felt about him and knowing that he was not ready for marriage, thought it would be better for both of them if she transferred to another mosque. Mr. Muhammad, who knew of the situation because Malcolm had confided in him, agreed to hire Evelyn as one of his secretaries. It seemed a perfect solution to an extremely uncomfortable situation. As it turned out, Evelyn became one of the young women impregnated by Mr. Muhammad, a fact that caused my uncle much grief because he felt responsible for her being in Chicago.

When Ma wasn't trying to dictate whom Malcolm would marry, she was trying to select his career. She wanted him to be a lawyer who would use his skills not only for himself and his family but also to help black people in the ongoing struggle against white supremacy. What Ma failed to say but which Malcolm realized was that she also wanted him to practice law to impress Boston's black "society." Malcolm knew there was something wrong with that rationale. Ma had strong cultural pride, but at the same time, she and Uncle Earl were eager to be accepted by those "Negro Bostonians" who themselves desperately wanted to be accepted by the white "aristocrats" of Boston. Despite her will, strength, and confidence, Ma, deep down, wanted the "wannabees" to respect her and her family. She also believed that she could turn at least some of them into "proud black people." Uncle Malcolm was to be a major instrument for accomplishing this goal. He was intelligent, articulate, attractive, and most important to that community, light-skinned. Ma said that the latter was crucial if one was to appeal to most of Boston's so-called Negro society. No matter how committed and able a dark-skinned person was, he or she would find it extremely difficult, if not impossible, to appeal to most color-obsessed Boston Negroes.

Ma's plan was to surround Malcolm with black people who were focused and had a productive outlook on life. She used her extensive connections to provide him with jobs. It was Ma who got him a job as a fourth cook in the dining department of the New York, New Haven and Hartford Railroad. That may not seem to be a very impressive position today, but black men with railroad jobs in those days had great prestige among their black neighbors. Ma knew Charlie Roundtree, who was a leader in the Brotherhood of Sleeping Car Porters, the union that represented porters, attendants, and maids who worked for the Pullman Company of the United States and Canada. That company, in the 1920s, 1930s, and 1940s, was one of the largest employers of black labor in North America. Pullman hired white men as conductors and waiters, but for the low-paying jobs, they hired black men and women. Right after the Civil War, former enslaved Africans, desperate for work, flocked to the Pullman Company for jobs. Many of those hired in Boston first lived in the Beacon Hill state capitol area of the city. When Uncle Malcolm began working with Pullman, the tradition of keeping blacks in low-paying jobs was still intact. But conditions had been bettered somewhat because of the Brotherhood of Sleeping Car Porters, which had been founded by Ashley Totten in the 1920s. Totten, a native of

St. Croix, had worked as a porter on the New York Central Railroad until he was fired for attempting to organize black men and women who were being exploited and discriminated against by the Pullman Company. Totten asked A. Phillip Randolph, who later was to become a noted civil-rights leaders of the 1960s, to join the Brotherhood and become its chief organizer. The brotherhood was officially organized on August 25, 1925, three months after Malcolm Little's birth.

Fidel S. Barboz, a Pullman porter who was secretary-treasurer of the brotherhood in Boston, said that "the union was always trying to see if they could get us shorter hours. When we first started in the 1920s, we worked 365 days a year. We had no time off, no relief. If we got sick, they wanted us to die and prove it! You talk about injustice! The Pullman went from Boston to California, and we didn't have a rest period." Pullman porters like Mr. Roundtree and Mr. Barboz were important people in the black communities of Roxbury and the South End. Though they weren't haughty professionals, Ma was proud of them as black folks who had fought for what was right and who didn't back down from the white man even if it meant losing a job. She wanted Malcolm to be a part of something like that. After he began working, she would make sure that he went to Charlie Roundtree's real estate office on Humbolt Avenue to pay his monthly dues. If there was any problem with Malcolm, she, Aunt Sas, and Aunt Gracie would try to correct it at home. "We wanted him to be a giver, not a person who abused himself or his community."

That may be what Ma, Aunt Sas, and Aunt Gracie wanted, but based on what he wrote in his autobiography, we know that Uncle Malcolm, fresh to the big city, wanted something else. That something was to have as good a time as humanly possible. Instead of being impressed with hardworking, dedicated people like Charlie Roundtree and A. Phillip Randolph, and even like Ma and some of his other Little, Gray, and Mason relatives, Malcolm was dazzled by the flashy style of the zoot-suited, conked-hair men who lit up Harlem's nightlife. His job with the railroad provided plenty of opportunities to pursue a hedonistic lifestyle with his street buddies in Harlem during train layovers in New York City while at the same time living a semi-respectable life with his sister and his aunts when home in Boston. In Harlem, he could bop with the hoodlums and the whores with impunity, but in Boston he had to cool his heels somewhat because a relative lived around practically every corner of his neighborhood.

At one point in 1945, Ma went to New York City to rescue Uncle Malcolm from those "Harlem Nights." But since he was then twenty years old and officially an adult, he wasn't compelled to listen to her. Anyway, he felt no need to be rescued. Ma said that between 1940, when he moved to Boston, and 1945, when he was arrested, Malcolm basically lived two lives. In one life he enthusiastically participated in family picnics and family dinners. I've heard relatives and others say that he was caring, thoughtful, kind, and available when people needed help. He was very solicitous of his aunts and Ma. He saved some of his money to send to his brothers and sisters in Lansing. It was that side of Uncle Malcolm that Ma believed would ultimately triumph over the "Detroit Red" side. She admired all of her brothers, especially Wilfred, but "it was Malcolm in whom I saw the spirit of Pa John, our grandfather. Besides his spunk and spirit, I was also impressed with his willingness to listen and to decisively make up his mind about things. Even I couldn't move him in a direction he seriously didn't want to go."

The feeling was mutual. Malcolm respected his sister's opinion and often turned to her for both advice and assistance. "He would talk to me about anything pertaining to himself except the Nation of Islam's business," she said. "After 1960, when he had to face the reality that all wasn't well in the Nation, he began conferring with me about that." Through the years, her loyalty was such that she always remained very diplomatic in any commentary about him. Uncle Malcolm recognized and paid tribute to that loyalty when he wrote in his autobiography: "Though at times I'd make Ella angry at me, beneath it all, since I had first come to her as a teenage hick from Michigan, Ella never once really wavered from my corner."

Not even when his hedonistic lifestyle landed him in prison.

SIX Brothers and Sisters

When Uncle Malcolm was sentenced to serve ten years in prison, in February 1946, Ma and Uncle Reginald, one of his younger brothers, were in the courtroom. "I was still angry with him," she said, "for the situation he had gotten himself into. The first time he got arrested, in March 1945, I bailed him out by using our house as collateral. This time I refused to bail him out because of his attitude. In fact, I told him that since he refused to listen to me and other family members, maybe you want the white man to teach you."

Despite her frustration and anger, Ma was Malcolm's first visitor after he was sent to prison. Of it he wrote: "I remember seeing her catch herself, then try to smile at me, now in the faded dungarees stenciled with my number. Neither of us could find much to say, until I wished she hadn't come at all."

Ma's recollections were slightly different. "It was not a very pleasant visit. Malcolm was as jive-talking, cocky, and unrepentant as ever. He showed no remorse or concern about family anxiety and seemed to believe that his only problem was being caught, that the next time he would be a smarter hustler. When I left after that visit, I was as upset as I had ever been with him."

Ma wasn't the only one upset with Uncle Malcolm's attitude and actions, which included getting high on drugs bought from prison guards. His siblings in Lansing were equally concerned and upset. They wrote him letters of support and encouragement daily and were disturbed by his seemingly cavalier attitude toward the situation he was in. When Aunt Hilda came to stay with us in Boston, she went to see Uncle Malcolm in prison. After a couple of visits, she was so dis-

gusted with his attitude that during her next trip to Boston, she refused to see him. When he heard about that, Malcolm wrote, in a letter to Ma, "It really hurt to hear that Hilda had gone all the way back
to Detroit before she came to see me. . . ." He seemed to have no
clue that his attitude was the problem.

A four-page letter he wrote to Ma, dated September 10, 1946,
shows just how insensitive he was during his first year or so in
prison. It included the following: "The person that you said called
me is a very good friend of mine. He's only worth some fourteen
million dollars. If you read the society pages you'd know who he is.
He knows where I am now because I've written and told him, but I
didn't say what for. He may call and ask you. Whatever answer you
give him will have to do with my entire future but I still depend on
you. . . ."

Ma said the friend never called again, but "I was outraged that
Malcolm had given my number to such a person and actually expected me to be a kind of courier between them. I assumed that that
'friend' was one of those decadent whites whom he had been hus-
tling."

The one sensitive note he struck in that same letter was about photographs she had sent to him. "I want to thank you for sending me
the pictures. . . . They offer more consolation than anything else,
Ella. They keep my mind diverted from my troubles, so please don't
stop sending them. I have received what money you've left for me
always. I just don't like to mention it. Maybe you can understand; I
can't. All I know is when I mention it I feel ashamed." Maybe Uncle
did feel ashamed for he wrote in his autobiography: "With some
money sent by Ella, I was finally able to buy stuff for better highs
from guards in the prison. . . ."

When Ma visited Uncle Malcolm in prison, she often took me
along. I remember his putting me on his knee while they talked.
Sometimes he would tell me stories, which became parables as I got
older. I thought of Uncle Malcolm as a big brother who gave me a
small table and chair that he made in the prison workshop. He also
made musical jewelry boxes, which he gave to a few family members. At least one of them, given to his cousin, Clara Little, is still in
existence, owned by her son, John Walker Jr.

Ma said it seemingly didn't occur to Uncle Malcolm that while his brothers and sisters loved him dearly, they were not prepared to support his irresponsible behavior and attitude. She was especially outraged by his treatment of Aunt Sas and Aunt Gracie. Uncle Malcolm loved his two elderly aunts, but he resented their constantly pushing Christianity on him. To Aunt Sas and Aunt Gracie, accepting Jesus was the solution to everything. As a teenager living with them and Ma, Uncle Malcolm at least paid lip service to their prodding, even going so far as to be baptized in Townsend Street Baptist Church and singing in one of the church's choirs. He did this out of love and respect for his aunts. However, the reefer-smoking, hip Malcolm who was in Charlestown prison was in no mood to accept his aunts' pious Christianity. His knowledge of the way his father had been killed by so-called white Christians, of how many of the so called black Christians in Lansing had refused to help his mother and siblings because of their hostility toward the Garveyite political beliefs and actions of his slain father, and of how many so-called religious white men in Boston and New York had paid him to help them find black women to fulfill their sexual fantasies undergirded his resistance to the urgings of his aunts. Malcolm later wrote in his autobiography: "I just couldn't believe in the Christian concept of Jesus as someone divine. And no religious person, until I was a man in my late twenties—and then in prison—could tell me anything. I have very little respect for people who represented religion."

In a letter to Ma dated April 12, 1946, Uncle Malcolm sharply expressed his feelings about his aunts' religion. "I got a letter from Sas preaching to me. I appreciated the letter but she can have her gospel. For the past month I've been praying like mad and if there was any sign of someone up there I asked for proof of it by some justice when I appeared before the Appellate Court. Heretofore you can have my share of religion. They refused to cut my sentence because of the racial mixture. Well if that's the Bible way of justice, it's not for me. . . ."

Though Ma shared Uncle Malcolm's reservations about Aunt Sas and Aunt Gracie's Christianity, she was very upset by his request that she never again bring them to visit him. "I reminded him how much they loved him, how to them he was a connection to their dead brother, how sincerely concerned they were about his future. They expressed fear to me that 'the devil' was trying to take control of their beloved nephew." Aunt Sas and Aunt Gracie weren't too far off target with that observation. Uncle Malcolm, in a chapter called "Satan," said his cellmates called him "Satan" because of his anti-religious attitude.

Because of that attitude and because I suffered from asthma as a child, Ma said she seldom visited Uncle Malcolm during his first year in prison. That upset him; despite what he had done to himself and his family by hooking up with Sophia, he fully expected Ma to back him all the way without questions or doubts, as she had done so often in the past. "I decided to be cool until he came to his senses," Ma said. "I never believed for a moment that my brother was a confirmed criminal."

Neither did his brothers and sisters and other family members. Despite his nonchalant attitude, his siblings sent him a steady supply of letters of encouragement. Other family members and friends visited as often as possible. His most frequent family visitors during that time were his brother Reginald and his sister Mary. Family and friends were shocked to discover that he could get high smoking marijuana while locked up. This doesn't shock us in 1998, but in the 1940s it was news to most everyone that prisoners had relatively easy access to drugs. "We were concerned but didn't know what to do about it, since Malcolm seemed determined to smoke as much reefer as he could get his hands on," Ma noted.

It was the reefer smoking that especially angered Aunt Hilda and caused her to stop visiting him on trips to Boston. But she, Ma, and all the others continued writing, convinced that Uncle Malcolm would come around. They knew their brother, knew that his bark was greater than his bite. The observation made by his brother Philbert in the book *Malcolm X: Make It Plain* probably best sums up his siblings' feelings about their then misguided brother.

He didn't have the temerity, I suppose you'd call it, to be bad. Malcolm was good. Everybody who knew Malcolm would tell you he was a good man. And this is before he came into Islam. He was not vulgar. And he wasn't disrespectful of your rights.

He was a braggadocio. He would brag about what he had done and this and that, but it hadn't been that bad. He just knew how to tell it so it sounded as though he was a gang leader. But he didn't have no gang. . . . I learned that he was a hell-raiser (initially) in prison because he was trying to organize people as though he was going to break out and all that kind of stuff.

Uncle Malcolm's visitors also included his cousin Mary Ann Saylor (from the Little side of family), and her husband, Sleepy Williams. They were the couple who had once gone to Harlem to rescue Uncle Malcolm when he was being sought by West Indian Archie, a major player in Harlem's illegal numbers racket. Malcolm was in hiding, since he was too small-time a hustler to tangle with a big-timer like West Indian Archie. Malcolm Jarvis, Mary Ann, and Sleepy went from dive to dive looking for Malcolm. When they finally found him, they rushed him back to Boston.

Two of Uncle Malcolm's most frequent visitors during his early prison years were Evelyn, to whom he had once been engaged, and Jackie Massey, who had every intention of marrying him. Ma cared deeply for Evelyn and was very angry when Malcolm broke their engagement. Despite the broken engagement, she urged Evelyn to hang in there until Malcolm saw the light. It was only a few years ago that I found out why Malcolm broke the engagement. He never talked about it to anyone as far as I know, not even to Ma. But Evelyn told her best friend since childhood, Beverly Wilson, who is now one of my close friends, and Beverly told me. Uncle Malcolm was afraid that both of them had people suffering from mental illness in their families. He had heard unconfirmed rumors of mental illness in Evelyn's family, and he had also been convinced by public officials in Michigan that his mother was afflicted with mental illness. He and Evelyn might pass such traits on to their children, so it was impossible for them to marry. Ma was very upset when she later heard about Uncle Malcolm's fears. "It's a tragedy that he believed that," she said. "As far as I know, and I've known Evelyn's family for many, many years, there was no mental illness in her family, at least not the kind that is passed on by genes. As for Malcolm's mother, I still believe that all she suffered was a nervous breakdown brought on by the pressures of her husband's violent death at the hands of white supremacists and of having to deal with the hostility and indifference shown by the state of Michigan and many blacks in Lansing towards her and her children. I don't think she was mentally ill. She thought that if she went along with the state's position, they would see that her children were taken care of." The idea that Uncle Malcolm broke his engagement with Evelyn because he had been misled about mental illness in their families caused Ma great pain.

Ma said that things got a little complicated when Uncle Wesley, another Little brother, fell in love with Evelyn, whom he had met at a dinner hosted by a Muslim family in Boston. Wesley knew that Evelyn had once been engaged to Malcolm, so he told him how he felt about her. Malcolm said it was over between them and that Wesley should go for it. Which poses an interesting question: If Malcolm had real concerns about mental illness in the two families' history, why would he urge his blood brother to go ahead without sharing his concerns?

Ma said that Evelyn, who never stopped loving Malcolm, unintentionally broke Wesley's heart. A broken-hearted Wesley eventually left Boston and ended up never marrying. Even after Malcolm's death by assassination, Evelyn continued to love him. We have been told by cemetery officials that from 1965 at least until 1989, an attractive black woman would visit Uncle Malcolm's grave. From their descriptions we are convinced that Evelyn was that woman. She now lives on the West Coast. One of her two daughters, Maria, is now married to Joshua Farrakhan, the son of Minister Louis Farrakhan, leader of the Nation of Islam. They have two children.

Uncle Malcolm's second frequent female visitor was Jackie Massey, who lived across the street from us on Dale Street. Ma, like most women in the neighborhood, regarded Miss Massey as a "common street woman" and disliked her as intensely as she liked Evelyn. A few years ago Dad told me that Uncle Malcolm revealed to him that Miss Massey had seduced him not too long after he came to Boston. Dad said he came home early one day from work and found Uncle Malcolm and Miss Massey indulging in some serious carrying on. He never told Ma about this, fearing that she might explode. Ma said, "I didn't know all the details, but I was well aware of how much havoc an older, experienced, predatory woman could wreak on a teenaged, adventurous, highly impressionable wannabe city slicker like Malcolm was at that time."

Besides, she had heard other interesting things about Miss Massey from Uncle Malcolm himself. According to Ma, during her prison visits, Malcolm, for the first time, filled her in on some aspects of his street life in Boston and Harlem, including a business deal he and Malcolm Jarvis had with an elderly, wealthy white millionaire named Paul Lennon, who would pay them to rub powder over his body. He was the wealthy man Uncle Malcolm referred to in a previously mentioned letter to Ma. Lennon's current powderer was Frank Cooper, who had sometimes visited him with Uncle Malcolm and Jarvis. Since Cooper was ostensibly Miss Massey's lover, Ma wondered what was the deal with her and Malcolm. When Malcolm told Ma that he was now trying to convert Jackie Massey to Islam, she said, "That may be your goal, but hers is to marry you. I can't support such action."

If Ma had had her way, Miss Massey wouldn't have been allowed to visit Uncle Malcolm at all. But she didn't, and Miss Massey, loaded down with the kind of home-cooked food she knew Uncle Malcolm loved, visited him probably more than anyone else. She rode up to Norfolk Prison Colony with members of Jarvis's family, which solidified Ma's hostility toward a man she considered a bad influence on her brother. Ma was so concerned about what she scathingly referred to as "the Jackie Massey mess" that she told Malcolm, "I'd rather see you stay in jail than get out and be with Jackie Massey." Her concerns were such that she refused to sponsor his parole. Uncle Wilfred and Aunt Ruth, his wife, became his sponsors.

Malcolm, Ma said, wasn't in prison long before the realization set in that prison authorities were trying to do a number on him, not so much because of the burglary as because of his relationship with Sophia. He told her that prison caseworkers John Rockett and Pete Donahue asked him many questions about the sexual relationship between him and Sophia and about the death of his father, Earl Little Sr. In addition, there was a detective who told Malcolm and Malcolm Jarvis that if they were down South they would be lynched for messing around with Sophia and Beatrice. Finally, they got word from the two women that the same detective had been pressuring them to testify that they had been sexually assaulted by the two prisoners. "It was those things," Ma said, "that helped him to see the seriousness and the danger of the situation he was in. In that sense that detective and those caseworkers did him and us a favor."

From the moment Uncle Malcolm was imprisoned and despite their disgust with his attitude, the Little brothers and sisters began developing a strategy both for securing his release and for making sure that he would never find himself in that situation again. After hearing about the caseworkers' questions about the killing of his father, Ma and Wilfred told Malcolm that the less he said the better. "Our first priority was getting him out of prison," Ma explained. "If that meant telling white supremacist officials and caseworkers what they wanted to hear, so be it. Once we got him out, he could tell the truth. We also urged him to stop complicating matters by pretending to be a big-time criminal. He knew better, and we knew better."

Not too long after Malcolm's imprisonment, his brother Wilfred joined the Nation of Islam. "I came into the Muslim movement in 1947," Wilfred said, "and started bringing my brothers and sisters in. We already had been indoctrinated with Marcus Garvey's philosophy, so that was just a good place for us. They didn't have to convince us we were black and should be proud or anything like that. We had learned that from our Garveyite parents." Soon Reginald, Philbert, Hilda, and Wesley joined their older brother in the Nation of Islam. The Little siblings didn't just join the Nation; they became some of its most dedicated members and effective proselytizers, especially Wilfred. With the support of his siblings and his wife, Ruth, he set up temples in Michigan, Ohio, and Indiana. Wilfred also became head of Temple One in Detroit.

Ma was proud of her brothers and sisters and how they were continuing their grandfather and father's fight against white supremacy. One of her most prized possessions is a photograph taken during that period of Wilfred, Philbert, Wesley, and Reginald. They are standing tall, looking like four strong and determined black men. I was a child in the late 1940s and early 1950s and remember Ma telling me how proud I should be of my uncles. When we visited our Collins relatives in Lansing, we always spent time with my uncles Wilfred and Philbert in their homes. We also went to the N.O.I. temple where they spoke and taught in Detroit. Hearing Wilfred and Philbert speak always captivated me. I thought my uncles were special because Ma often told me they were. Though Ma was not then a Muslim, she loved bragging about her brothers to members of the Collins family and often tried to get those staunch Christians to join us on a visit to the Muslim temple.

Wilfred, Ma said, was the kind of organizer that Malcolm would later become when he joined the Nation. "My brothers put their time, skill, money, and tenacity to work building up the Nation of Islam. They would use their own money, if necessary, to carry out its objectives. If it hadn't been for them, the Nation of Islam wouldn't have grown so fast and so large. They really believed that what they were doing was carrying out the legacy left them by their parents."

My uncles influenced me toward Islam. When I joined the Nation in 1958, it kept me from becoming like so many of my directionless peers on Sugar Hill. Many years earlier, they and their sisters had influenced my uncle to finally begin taking control of his life. They began writing him about a new religion, a new organization with which they were involved that offered an alternative to Christianity, which they dismissed as "the white man's religion." In 1948, Philbert wrote him that he had discovered the "natural religion for the black man." Malcolm, still possessing a cavalier attitude about the whole situation, was not impressed. He wrote that "my brothers and sisters in Detroit and Chicago had all become converted to what they were being taught was the 'natural religion for the black man' of which Philbert had written to me. They all prayed for me to become converted while I was in prison. But after Philbert reported my vicious reply, they discussed what was the best thing to do. They decided that Reginald, the latest convert, the one to whom I felt the closest, would best know how to approach me "

Slowly, Uncle Malcolm began to respond positively to the urgings of his brothers and sisters. Ma said that initially she was not sure what the Nation of Islam could do for Uncle Malcolm, but "I trusted the judgment of Wilfred, Hilda, and Philbert. If they believed that the organization could rescue our brother from those people and

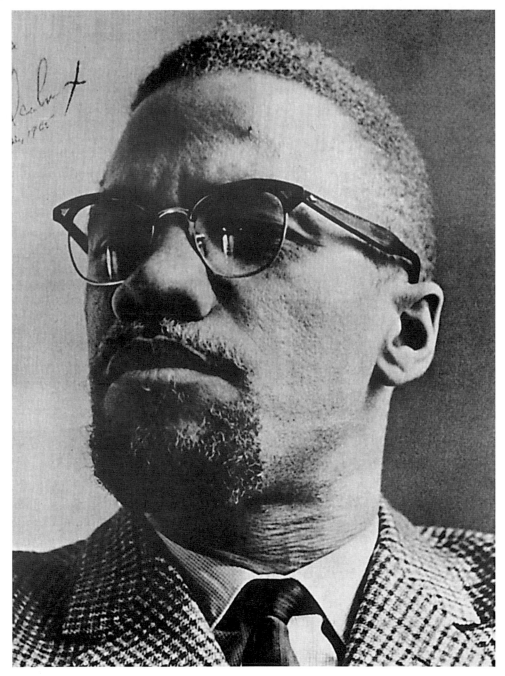

Photo taken two days before Malcolm X's assassination. Photo courtesy of Robert L. Haggins

Malcolm's parents, Louise Helen Norton-Little and Earl Little Sr.

Malcolm's paternal grandparents, John and Ella Little, circa 1890

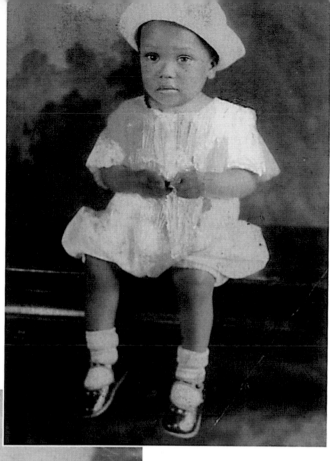

Malcolm at nine
months, Omaha,
Nebraska

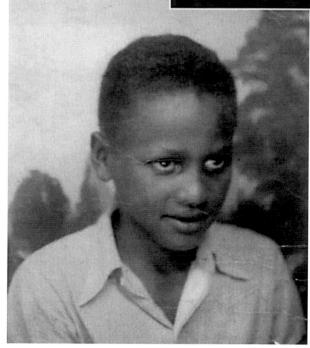

Malcolm at age nine

Malcolm, in Boston, age eighteen

Ella and Malcolm (ax in hand) in Halifax, Nova Scotia

Malcolm, age fifteen, with Ella and friends, 1941

Hilda Little, 1941, high
school graduation

Malcolm in the driveway at 72 Dale Street, Boston, 1941

Ella and Malcolm at 72 Dale Street, 1941

Malcolm's brothers (left to right): Philbert, Wesley, Wilfred, and Reginald, 1949.
Not pictured are Earl Little Jr. and Robert.

Sas, Bud, and Emma Little, 1953

Malcolm about to
appear at a conference
in 1963, not long after
he left the Nation of
Islam

Malcolm X sitting with
his daughters Qubilah
and Ilyasah in the
office of the
Organization of Afro-
American Unity, at the
Hotel Theresa,
Harlem, 1964

Malcolm at an OAAU rally in 1963 with a security force that included Leon Amer (top left)

Malcolm at the home o[f]
Mrs. W. E. B. Du Bois,
Ghana, Africa, 1964

Malcolm and
Sheik Hassoun of
Sudan, Africa,
1964

Malcolm on return
from Africa, 1964.
Photo courtesy of Earl
Grant

Malcolm in a radio interview, Boston, 1964

Malcolm and Prince Faisal (before his coronation), 1964

Rodnell Collins with Malcolm's children at the World's Fair in New York, August 1964

Betty Shabazz and Malcolm with two of their children at OAAU headquarters in New York, February 1965

The night before Malcolm's assassination. Left to right: Tom Wallace Sr., Rodnell Collins, Tom Wallace Jr., Malcolm. Front row: Mrs. Wallace and daughter Gail. February 21, 1965

Rodnell Collins, at far right,
covering Malcolm's grave.
AP/Wide World Photos

Ella in 1967

Ella in her later years, and son Rodnell Collins

Document from the Railroad Retirement Board in which Malcolm designated Ella his beneficiary. Note that he lied about his date of birth.

Form AA-11
Revised March 1938
(DUPLICATE)

IMPORTANT.—Read Instructions on Back of This Page Before Filling In This Form

376-16-3429
(Social Security Account number)

DESIGNATION OR CHANGE OF BENEFICIARY

(Railroad Retirement Board A-No. if you have filed application)

TO THE RAILROAD RETIREMENT BOARD,
Washington, D. C.

SECTION 1. I, **Malcolm** (First) **(none)** (Middle) **Little** (Last) born on **May** (Month)
19, (Day) **1921** (Year) hereby designate the person or persons named below in this section to receive any death benefits payable under section 5 of the Railroad Retirement Act of 1937 and any accrued annuities due at my death under the Railroad Retirement Act of 1937 or 1935: (If more than one person is named, the benefits will be distributed in equal shares unless you indicate the percentage to be received by each.)

NAME OF BENEFICIARY (If a beneficiary be a minor, also give date of birth; if a married woman, state her full maiden name and her husband's last name)	ADDRESS	RELATIONSHIP
Ella Little Johnson	89 Harrishof St., Roxbury	Sister

SEC. 2. In the event no person or persons named in section 1 are living at my death, or at the time the death benefits become payable, if later than my death, I designate the following as beneficiaries in their place:

NAME	ADDRESS	RELATIONSHIP
Louis Norton Little	4111 Logan St., Lansing, Michigan	Mother

SEC. 3. I direct that, if more than one beneficiary is named, the share of any beneficiary or beneficiaries who die before me or before the death benefits become payable, if later than my death, shall be paid in equal shares to the survivors, or entirely to the survivor if only one survives.

SEC. 4. By this designation I revoke all previous designations, if any, and I reserve the right to change or revoke any or all of the above designations at any time in the manner and form prescribed by the Railroad Retirement Board and without the knowledge or consent of the above beneficiaries.

NOTE.—No person listed above as a beneficiary may be a witness.

(Signature) *Malcolm Little*

WITNESSES: We, the undersigned witnesses, hereby certify that we saw _**Malcolm Little**_ (sign this) designation on the **27th** day of **June**, 19**41** and he (she) declared it to be his (her) free act and deed.

First witness Name _____ Address _____
Second witness Name _James W. Murphy_ Address _163 Dorchester Ave, Boston_

Full name of present employer **New York, New Haven & Hartford RR**
My occupation **Fourth Cook** Department **Dining Car** Division **Boston**
(Print or type your name and address below to insure return of this copy:) Location **163 Dorchester Ave.**

Name **Malcolm Little**
Address **89 Harrishof St.** (Number and street)
Roxbury, Mass. (City and State)

Boston, Mass.

Copy Returned for your Records
Railroad Retirement Board

(Fill out both original and duplicate completely and forward without separation to the Railroad Retirement Board, Washington, D. C., through your employer, if agreeable.)

CITY OF OMAHA
EXECUTIVE OFFICE
EUGENE A. LEAHY, MAYOR

PROCLAMATION

WHEREAS, during the past 16 years, America has witnessed a valiant struggle on the part of black people, concerned whites, and other minorities for equality under the law; and

WHEREAS, evolving out of this struggle for basic human rights America has had to come face-to-face with the fact that lack of fair treatment of minorities has created a domestic crisis in our country; and

WHEREAS, many men and women have contributed their knowledge, and in some cases, their lives to the awakening of America on this problem; and

WHEREAS, one of these men was a native Omahan, born Malcolm Little, at 34th and Pinkney Streets, and later known as Malcolm X, a man who dedicated his brief life to teaching men to strive for self-dignity and to mold their own destinies; and

WHEREAS, no American more exemplified this essential link in our national creed than the late Malcolm X,

NOW, LET IT BE RESOLVED that we acknowledge the contributions of Omaha-born MALCOLM X on the occasion of his 46th birthday, MAY 19, 1971, not as a gesture to a certain segment of the community, but rather as a genuine indication that the City of Omaha can be proud that a man of this temperament arose from within our midst.

THEREFORE, as Mayor of the City of Omaha, I do hereby proclaim the period May 16 – 22, 1971, as MALCOLM X WEEK throughout the City of Omaha.

EUGENE A. LEAHY
Mayor

William G. Milliken

Governor of the State of Michigan

presents this

Executive Declaration

in Observance of

October 12, 1975

as

MALCOLM X DAY

Malcolm X, born Malcolm Little in 1925, symbolized the Black Revolution of the 1960's. He was an advocate of "Black Power," which to him meant the building of black business, the cooperative improvement of black communities, and the growth and encouragement of race pride and self-help. He called attention to the problems of unemployment and poverty in the ghettoes, and demanded action of himself and of the government in a "War on Poverty."

Malcolm X was a stern, intense, self-disciplined man who underwent a religious conversion while in prison. He became a devotee of the Black Muslim faith, and after his discharge from prison, swiftly rose to national prominence with his sometimes shocking oratory on the Black man's struggles and the racial injustices in America. He believed that Afro-Americans had a basic right to an equitable share of the food, clothing, shelter, education, jobs and power that had been a birthright of other Americans, and he encouraged them to defend these basic rights.

Malcolm X related the struggle of blacks in this country to the situation of non-whites throughout the world, and his expose on the great resistance to social change marked the first significant attempt in the post-independence era to link the African and African-American struggles.

In recognition of his efforts for human dignity and racial justice in our country, I, William G. Milliken, Governor of the State of Michigan, do hereby declare October 12, 1975, as Malcolm X Day.

Given under my hand this ninth day of October in the year of Our Lord one thousand nine hundred seventy-five and of the Commonwealth one hundred thirty-ninth.

William G. Milliken
GOVERNOR

Proclamations from Omaha, Nebraska, and the State of Michigan honoring Malcolm those influences that had encouraged him to run the streets of Boston and Harlem, I was prepared to strongly support their efforts. After they began working on him, I could see a real change in his attitude. There was also a practical aspect to Malcolm's new attitude. He wanted to be transferred to the Norfolk Prison Colony and began to understand that unfocused belligerence resulting from a misguided, ineffective street attitude was not the best way to secure a transfer and possible parole."

Malcolm had heard via the prison grapevine that the Norfolk Prison Colony was as close to paradise as any prison could be. According to Professor Robert James Branham of Bates College, "Norfolk placed particular emphasis on prisoner education, including evening academic and vocational courses with instructors drawn from Harvard, Boston University, Emerson College and other nearby institutions. . . . Colony officials were convinced that debate and discussion groups were an effective tool in prisoner rehabilitation."

Malcolm, who had already been transferred from Charlestown prison to Concord, knew that one had to be a model prisoner to be considered for transfer to Norfolk. He also knew, from rumors circulating among the inmates, that money and connections were also needed to facilitate such a transfer. Once he found out about Norfolk, and encouraged by his brothers and sisters, Malcolm's drive and go-get-it attitude, along with his discipline, came into play. He would take care of the model-prisoner requirement; he depended on Ma for the money and connection requirements. Now that he was getting serious about his future, Ma was ready to assist in any way she could. She arranged the transfer with the help of a local black political operative and white judge, both of whom she knew. Of course, there were some funds involved. There was then, and probably is now, such a man in practically every black community in this country. He was the person whom white politicians, police, and public officials choose to use as their "man" in black communities. Thus, he was the person to whom many black people turned when in need of a favor from downtown. What that person provided those white folks for doing the favor was probably different in every city. In Boston's Lower Roxbury section he owned a popular and illegal after-hours club which could only stay open if one had a "you

scratch my back, I scratch yours" arrangement with white politicians, police, and other public officials. It was rumored that he provided them with whiskey and wild Negro women. That's what they
got. What this man wanted from those he helped, it is rumored, was
cold cash. Since he was not known for his benevolence, cash was
what he got from Ma for himself and the judge. How much has never
been revealed.

Years later, in the 1960s, I met the judge for the first time when
Ma approached him for assistance in a land problem (land taken by
the town by eminent domain for conservation) she had with the town
of Duxbury, located outside of Boston. The judge was five feet
seven, heavy set, and very pleasant. He and Ma laughed about Malcolm's transfer without revealing any of the details to me. This was
Ma's first contact with him in years, but I wasn't surprised that she
was able to locate him. Whenever Ma got involved in a problem involving the courts, she did her homework and was always well prepared. Back when she had that problem with members of the Boston
police department who illegally raided our home and took many
bikes that we had been making available to disadvantaged children,
Ma shocked everyone by having in her possession the names, ad-
dresses, phone numbers, and dates of birth of every policeman who
had participated in the raid. She got all that information by hiring a
private investigator. People still believed it was a major contributing
factor to her winning the case.

Ma's determination and relentless maneuvering finally resulted in
Uncle Malcolm's transfer to Norfolk in late 1948. The ahead-of-its-
time prison colony, as Malcolm noted extensively in his autobiography, was everything he had heard about. It was a place where he
could do serious studying, develop his oratory skills, and have an
impact on prison life. Malcolm was especially fond of the William J.
Parkhurst Collection of books in the prison library. It consisted of
twelve hundred to fifteen hundred books, mainly on European and
American literature, which had been donated by William J. Parkhurst, a wealthy Boston publisher. None of the books dealt with the
history and culture of Africans, Asians, and Native Americans, except as minor appendages of European history and culture. In his six
years in Norfolk, Uncle Malcolm read most of the books in the col-

lection. Parkhurst had donated the books to the prison when one of his male relatives was incarcerated there on a murder conviction. It says something that a convicted murderer was in a model prison like Norfolk and causes one to wonder whether there was any connection between his incarceration there and the presence of the collection.

Malcolm didn't limit himself to reading books in the Parkhurst collection, however. Ma received frequent requests for books. Often, to her great pleasure, he wanted law books. He had to request those books from Ma, she said, because books in the Parkhurst Collection that dealt with the subject disappeared when Malcolm began studying them and using what he learned to challenge prison authorities on legal issues. Ma enthusiastically supported his newfound interest in the law and his willingness to confront abuses, but, like Uncle Wilfred, she didn't want him to force the issue enough to affect his being paroled.

Ma had two ways of getting the requested books to Malcolm. Initially, she had help from a guard whom she had befriended. In return for delicious home-cooked food, Ma would leave the book with him, and he would get it to Malcolm once we left. After a while, the guard began to get nervous about the arrangement, so Ma would put the requested book into my pants. Malcolm would retrieve it while I sat on his knees during the visit.

In 1951, Malcolm was denied parole. Malcolm Jarvis, on the other hand, was not. It was obvious, Ma declared, that Malcolm was being punished for such activities as attempting to convert other inmates to Islam, for refusing to eat pork, and for being at the scene of a riot, though not directly involved. Prison authorities were especially alarmed by his ability to garner support from white inmates around various reform initiatives. It is indicative of their attitude that his refusal to eat pork became a major issue. They actually threatened to put him in the hole for refusing to eat a staple prison food. When this didn't work, they threatened to transfer him to a mental hospital, having found out about his mother's so-called mental illness. They finally transferred him from the coveted Norfolk Prison Colony back to the more traditional Charlestown prison. While there, Malcolm continued to proselytize for Islam. Osborne Thaxton, one of his recruits, later became a minister in the temple in

Springfield, Massachusetts. His brothers and sisters were aware of, and alarmed by, Malcolm's problems with prison authorities. In a letter dated June 5, 1951, Aunt Hilda told Ma: "We heard from Malcolm. He was denied parole for another year and Malcolm Jarvis got his. I guess you know that by now I think they are trying to break him down."

"Hilda was right on target," Ma said. "They were trying to break Malcolm down, to goad him into doing something rash and stupid. But the Malcolm they were dealing with in 1951 and 1952 was quite different from the hedonistic, misguided, street-influenced Malcolm they had dealt with in 1946. Due to the encouragement and support of his brothers and sisters and his own focused direction, he was not going to fall into their trap. Once Malcolm decided on a goal, he went for it. And he wanted to get out of prison so he could join his brothers and sisters in their efforts to carry on the legacy of their parents."

SEVEN Muhammad's Temple of Islam

The strategy developed by the Little brothers and sisters paid off, leading to Malcolm's parole in August 1952. Wilfred signed his parole-sponsorship papers and procured from his employer a promise to hire Malcolm for a permanent job upon his release from prison. That meant he had to relocate to Detroit. "We all agreed that Boston would not be the best place for him," Ma said, "because the police there would use any excuse to constantly harass him. They knew him as an undisciplined, jive-talking, conk-haired, zoot-suit-wearing petty criminal and, we were sure, wouldn't accept the fact that he had become a disciplined, self-respecting, focused black man who had diligently used his time in prison to vastly expand his knowledge of history and current affairs. I am convinced they would much prefer to deal with the former Malcolm Little rather than with the person he had become."

It wasn't just a few white police officers who Ma thought had it in for her brother. She said, "There was also a black detective named Wade, one of whose daughters was crazy about Malcolm before he was imprisoned. Wade considered Malcolm a common criminal who wasn't good enough for his daughter. Since that daughter now lived across the street from us and was still very much interested in Malcolm, I was afraid her father would cause him trouble."

Another reason Ma thought Boston wasn't the place for Malcolm to begin a new life was the presence of the tenacious Jackie Massey. "Aunt Sas, Aunt Gracie, and I were convinced," Ma explained, "that she would attempt to sweet-talk or trick Malcolm into marrying her.

We didn't put it past her to get pregnant by someone else and claim it was Malcolm's child."

The day after being released from prison, Malcolm left Boston for Detroit, where he became an active member of Detroit's Temple One, the religious home of his brothers and sisters. Upon arrival in Detroit, he began working as a salesman in a furniture store managed by Wilfred, the job that had been promised to secure his parole. Next he worked for a Lincoln-Mercury assembly plant in Wayne, Michigan; later, he worked at the Garwood Truck Factory. It was while employed there that Uncle Malcolm, then twenty-eight years old, was questioned by FBI agents about his failure to register with the Selective Service Board. He noted that their questions showed they were more interested in his involvement with the Nation of Islam than in his failure to register with the board.

When Malcolm wasn't working, the bulk of his time was spent increasing his knowledge of the Nation. He soon realized that Aunt Hilda had been right when she wrote him "that although I felt I understood Elijah Muhammad's teachings, I had much to learn and I ought to come to Detroit and become a member of a Temple of Practicing Muslims."

It was in Detroit that he gained a deeper knowledge of what the Nation was really about. He was impressed with the skillful way his brothers and sisters ran the temple and "fished" for new members. He watched closely and listened carefully to lectures and sermons about history, economics, and the legal system. Watching Wilfred, Philbert, Hilda, and Wesley in action prepared him to eventually head Temple Eleven in Boston and later the extremely important Temple Seven in Harlem.

What is so often overlooked by scholars and biographers in their efforts to complicate the relationship between the Littles and Mr. Muhammad is that it was a mutually beneficial one in which the Littles needed Mr. Muhammad's platform and he needed a united family such as the Littles had in Detroit. The biographers, by focusing solely on Malcolm, ignored the importance of other Little family members in the development of the N.O.I. They base their books and theories too heavily on government reports issued by J. Edgar Hoover's FBI. Thus, they consistently ignore the human factor of the Little children's using the Nation as a means to advance some of the racial goals of their slain father and their hospitalized mother. The older Little siblings had burning memories of the role played by white supremacists in the murder of their father and the harassing role played by the system in causing unbearable stress that led to their mother's hospitalization. They had equally burning memories of attempts to scatter them among numerous foster families after the removal of their parents. They were rightfully proud that despite all this they had stuck together and were now part of a program that might enable them to carry on where their parents left off. They had confidence in their ability as a family unit to do some serious fishing among "lost-found Negroes," first in Detroit, then around the country. Ma, though not yet a member of the Nation, strongly believed in the abilities of her brothers and sisters. "After all, they are Pa John's grandchildren and Earl Senior's children," she said proudly, recalling her much-loved grandfather and father.

While with Temple One in Detroit, Malcolm also went to Chicago several times to meet Elijah Muhammad. The meetings, described so thoroughly in his autobiography, convinced Malcolm that Mr. Muhammad was indeed the "Savior" whom he had heard so much about while in prison. Before those meetings they knew each other mainly through correspondence. After several months of intense preparation and studying directly with Mr. Muhammad, Malcolm was very proud, in early 1954, when the messenger, as Mr. Muhammad was called by his followers, asked him to return to Boston and help spread his message at Temple Eleven. When Malcolm moved to Boston, the Temple's membership was so small that they used to meet in Brother Lloyd X's living room. About three months after Malcolm's arrival, his oratorical, organizational, and fishing skills had increased membership enough that they were able to open a small temple.

Ma said that was when she first heard him speak, an event that Uncle Malcolm noted in his autobiography. "She sat, staring as though she couldn't believe it was me. Ella never moved, even when I had only asked all who believed what they had heard to stand up. She contributed when our collection was held. It didn't bother or challenge me at all about Ella. I never even thought about converting her. As tough-minded and cautious about joining anything as I personally knew her to be, I wouldn't have expected anyone short of Allah Himself to have been able to convert Ella."

"I had a serious problem with some aspects of the group's program," Ma explained. "Their Garvey-influenced positions on black political, economic, and cultural issues I could fully support, but their treatment of Elijah Muhammad as a divine being was too cult-like for me. It was the same problem with people like Father Divine, Daddy Grace, and a host of Christian ministers. Though I admired their feeding hungry people in hard times, I wasn't prepared to consider them divine beings." Ma added that she had heard vaguely about the Nation even before her brothers and sisters got involved with the organization. "In the early 1940s some of my Collins in-laws in Lansing and Detroit spoke scornfully of it as a kind of Garveyite group that they feared would 'needlessly rile up white people.'"

Malcolm was well aware of Ma's doubts about Elijah Muhammad. Even after she made the decision to join the N.O.I., he knew she believed not in Muhammad himself but in the platform as presented by her brothers. In fact, I joined the N.O.I. before Ma did as the result of a deal between me and my uncle. Concerned that I would fall into the same trap Malcolm had as an adolescent in Boston, Ma wanted to send me away to a military school. I didn't want to go; Dad, Aunt Sas, and Aunt Gracie didn't want me to go, either, but Ma was adamant. Malcolm saved me when he visited us and Ma asked him about it. After their conversation Malcolm asked me what I wanted to do, and I said, "Stay home." That's when he and I made a secret deal. "If you help me get your mother to join the Nation of Islam," he offered, "I will suggest that she allow you to join the Nation and become a member of the Fruit of Islam (their military-like program for boys and men). That will provide you with a better education and more discipline than any military school in the country. It will strengthen you as a black adolescent and as a black man. If you become an exemplary member of the Nation, it might influence Ella and even Aunt Sas and Aunt Gracie to change their minds about us."

Ma may change her mind, I agreed, but Aunt Sas and Aunt Gracie, never. "They are too hooked on Jesus." At the time, neither Ma nor I was an active member of any church. Uncle Malcolm and I agreed on the plan; Ma went along with his suggestion despite still having doubts about Mr. Muhammad. Sure enough, not long after I joined the Nation, Ma joined, leading Malcolm and me to believe that our plan had worked. That is, until Ma told us that she had always been on to our little scheme. "I wasn't fooled one bit," she told us, "but I figured that since my two favorite men were working so hard to convert me, I would go along up to a point. However, I'll leave without hesitation if the N.O.I. doesn't live up to its promises."

Ma reminded Malcolm that she was joining the N.O.I. solely because of him, adding that along with her other reservation, she was still upset with the way it had treated their brother, Reginald. Reginald, who had played a major role in fishing Malcolm into the Nation, had begun expressing doubts about the divinity of Elijah Muhammad. Reginald also charged, after he was excommunicated from the N.O.I. for committing adultery, that Muhammad was breaking the same rules for which he was excommunicating him. "I told Malcolm that I would never forgive Mr. Muhammad for what he did to Reginald," Ma declared. "His excommunication nearly drove him crazy. I was angry then and even angrier years later when Reginald's charges about Elijah Muhammad, first made in 1949, were confirmed. In 1954 or 1955, Reginald also told me somewhat sketchily about the disappearance of W. D. Fard. I suspect that Reginald either knew something or suspected something about Fard's disappearance that he never told me. I believed that something about it has remained on his conscience all these years."

By the time Malcolm returned to Boston to shore up Temple Eleven, he had become more keenly aware of black history in particular and American history in general. The many hours he had spent reading and listening to lectures by N.O.I. ministers, including his brothers Wilfred and Philbert, had prepared him for a return to the city to which he first came as a fourteen-year-old.

When walking through Boston's streets as an adolescent and as a young adult, he had seen some of Boston's historical landmarks without knowing much about, or even caring about, the history behind them. For instance, there was the statehouse with its Latin

motto *"Ense Petit Placidam Sub Libertate Quietem"* (By the Sword
We Seek Peace, but Peace Only Under Liberty). The history he
learned while at Temple One in Detroit and Temple Two in Chicago
enlightened him to the fact that many of the same men who piously
spouted that and other slogans had amassed enormous family fortunes as builders of ships that transported millions of Africans into
slavery in North and South America and the Caribbean. He now
knew that Ruggles Square was named after Edward Ruggles, an
owner of enslaved Africans, and that the statue of Revolutionary War
hero Dr. Joseph Warren honored a man who, in 1770, paid thirty dollars for an African boy. The statue was right in the middle of the
black neighborhood in which Uncle Malcolm had lived with Ma,
Aunt Sas, and Aunt Gracie. In the 1960s, some black Bostonians
successfully pressured city officials to remove that statue from now
heavily black Roxbury. Uncle was also aware that Dudley Square
was named after a famous Massachusetts governor who once proposed a four-dollar-per-head tax on Africans as a way of encouraging the importation of white indentured servants rather than Africans
into his state. I guess that made him somewhat of a white liberal. It
was this part of Boston's role in American history that probably inspired Malcolm's biting observation that "we didn't land on Plymouth Rock; Plymouth Rock landed on us."

Now, because of his studies, Malcolm knew more about the statue
built in honor of the 54th Regiment's Negro Civil War soldiers
whose exploits were later popularized in the movie *Glory.* He was
also aware that thousands of Africans had fought with the colonists
against the British in the Revolutionary War in a mostly vain attempt
to secure their own freedom. No one taught him that in school. The
only black person paid any tribute, at least in the 1940s, was Crispus
Attucks, cited as the first casualty of the Revolutionary War. Malcolm, as the following statement indicated, was not impressed with
Attucks. "Crispus Attucks laid down his life for America, but would
he have laid down his life to stop the white man in America from
enslaving black people? So when you select heroes about which
black people ought to be taught, let them be black heroes who have
died fighting for the benefit of black people. We were never taught
about [Henri] Christophe or [Jean-Jacques] Dessalines. It was the

slave revolt in Haiti when slaves, black slaves, had the soldiers of Napoleon tied down and forced him to sell one-half of the American Continent to the Americans. They don't teach us that. That is the kind of history we want to learn." That's just the kind of history Malcolm skillfully taught at Temple Eleven, a history he taught so well that soon dozens and then several hundred people began to listen. Word of his oratorical and teaching skills soon spread throughout the Boston metropolitan area; growth was such that they were now able to purchase a small building in which to move the temple.

That was a significant accomplishment in Boston, a city whose black community was usually led by the kind of people described in Willard B. Gatewood's book *Aristocrats of Color.* He wrote that "Boston's aristocrats of color had a reputation for exclusiveness that went even beyond that of those in Washington or Philadelphia. . . . The old upper class in Boston thought of themselves as special, as far superior to other blacks, especially those who migrated to the city from the South in increasing numbers after the beginning of the twentieth century, and to most dark-skinned Negroes everywhere." Malcolm's Little, Mason, and Gray relatives were among the migrants and dark-skinned Negroes to whom the "aristocrats" of color felt superior. To Uncle Malcolm those same migrants and dark-skinned Negroes provided a great source for fishing new members into the Nation. They were the main ones who came to hear him speak about the need to study history; the importance of economic development; the need for self-respect, self-determination, and discipline; and the need to leave Christianity, "the white man's religion," and return to Islam as taught by Elijah Muhammad.

Malcolm's success in Boston impressed the Messenger of Allah so much that in March 1954 he decided to send him to establish Temple Twelve in Philadelphia. By the end of May, that temple was established solidly enough that the Messenger once again moved Malcolm, this time to energize Harlem's Temple Seven in what Malcolm called "vital New York City."

New York City was vital, Ma said, "because practically anything successful or controversial that happened there got national and often international attention. It was a major move for Malcolm."

By now Malcolm was on a roll. Even before leaving prison, he had decided to be an evangelist for Islam as taught by Elijah Muhammad. Now, after nearly two years in the field, he was more energized than ever. "The N.O.I. had given him a platform to structure for his life's battles and a black perspective to take to the country and the world," Ma said. "I still had my doubts. I believed that the N.O.I.'s growth was due more to the organizing and oratorical skills and commitment of Wilfred, Philbert, and Malcolm than to anything else done by Elijah Muhammad. It was the Little brothers who were establishing or energizing many of the new temples." When she made such observations to her brothers, they were mortified. "It's due to the Honorable Elijah Muhammad," they would say with some annoyance.

Malcolm fervently believed that what the N.O.I. had done for him, it could do for thousands, if not millions, of other "lost-found Negroes," a label covering all those black people who didn't follow or support Muhammad. What better place was there for Malcolm to proselytize than in Harlem, the most widely known black neighborhood in the world? Harlem, with its colorful history and large population, was a wide-open, possibly bountiful fishing ground for a man with skills and commitment and an organization with a credible program. It's important to note that Harlem's wide-openness and its large population didn't, by any stretch of the imagination, mean that fishing in it would be an easy task. Harlem's residents had just about seen it all and heard it all. They had experienced the Harlem Renaissance, the Garvey movement, the Adam Clayton Powell Jr., campaigns, and many smaller versions of these. Just about any black person with an idea or program had, at one time or another, passed through Harlem, so its residents were not easy to impress or persuade.

Malcolm, Ma said, hit the ground running. First he spent hours each day driving and walking through Harlem to see what it was all about. He had been in the neighborhood previously during his street-hanging days, but since he went only to places where one could party or hustle, he didn't see much else that Harlem had to offer. Its theaters, museums, libraries, bookstores, and historical landmarks were of no interest to him in those days.

It's also important to note that, contrary to popular belief, Malcolm never actually lived in Harlem during his hanging-out days. He only partied and ran its streets when he was there for a few days during a train layover on the Boston-New York City schedule. Boston was where he actually lived. That's why he had to thoroughly acquaint himself with Harlem once he became minister of Temple Seven.

Once Uncle Malcolm was situated in New York City, Ma and I would make Harlem a stop on our annual summer trip during which we visited Little, Mason, and Collins relatives in Trenton, New Jersey, Lansing and Detroit, Michigan, and Queens, New York City. We visited Malcolm for a few days every summer between 1954 and 1960. On our first visit in the summer of 1954, he was always on the go. On occasion, time permitting, he would take Ma and me on his rounds, during which he pointed out street scenes to Ma that absolutely shocked me as a child and later as an adolescent. On some of the streets Malcolm drove us through, drug addicts, dealers, and female prostitutes were operating openly, where anyone, even children, could see the action. I had never, in my wildest imagination, envisioned black folks living like that. We saw police officers all over the place, but they seemed totally indifferent to the lawbreaking going on right in front of their eyes.

The police's apparent indifference to the lawbreaking we saw on some Harlem streets reminded Ma and Malcolm of personal incidents with Boston police officers. "Sometimes members of the Boston police force acted like harassing black people was part of their official duty," said Malcolm. He recalled an incident when he was falsely accused of theft by a family member whose fur coat was missing. He was taken to the police station and charged. When the coat was soon found in the very house from which it was reportedly stolen, the police were immediately told that a mistake had been made and that Malcolm was completely innocent. Instead of releasing him, the police, seemingly motivated by the attitude of "We got the nigger; let's charge him," refused to drop the charges. Instead, Uncle Malcolm was given a few months' suspended sentence.

Ma's experience was a more explicit example of why the police are more often the problem when it comes to matters of race than a part of the solution. With me in the passenger seat, Ma was driving on a main highway when a car driven by a young white woman came out of a side street and crashed into Ma's car. Ma was thrown out of the car; I was thrown into the front windshield, resulting in a piece of my nose being cut off. An older woman in the other car was killed. The driver had violated a Massachusetts law by entering the highway without first coming to a complete stop. Despite testimony from two eyewitnesses, one black, one white, that the young white woman had not stopped, as required by law, she wasn't charged with anything. The police tried to say that Ma was the one who was on the side road. They forgot who they were dealing with. Ma, a master at selecting excellent lawyers, soundly beat them in court and used the settlement money from her suit to buy another brownstone building in Boston's South End. Uncle Malcolm, by now in the N.O.I., was very upset with the police's treatment of Ma and wanted to pack the Plymouth Court House with Muslim brothers as a show of support. Ma, knowing that he was still solidifying his position in the Nation, told him that she could take care of things. She was an expert in using one of the white man's own weapons, his so-called law, as a means of fighting white supremacy. She assured Malcolm that she could beat them at their own game. He backed off but kept a close watch on the trial.

The two incidents involving Malcolm and Ma, the latter of which I saw and experienced, and the inaction I saw toward flagrant lawbreaking on those Harlem streets taught me at an early age the very selective way the law is enforced when black people are involved.

One of those drives through Harlem with Malcolm still elicits a smile and a "Thank you, Uncle Malcolm" when I think about it. It was no smiling matter at the time, however. As he was driving us around Harlem, he pointed out people and scenes on the streets to Ma while noting what could be done to change such conditions. I was sitting in the rear seat of the car, leaning forward to hear what they were saying. All the windows were open. Though Malcolm didn't point her out, I remember seeing a very good looking black woman wearing a black dress whose back was open from top to bottom and held together by strings. Other than the dress, she seemed to be completely nude. I was mesmerized, having never before seen any sight even remotely like that. I slowly and discreetly leaned back into the rear seat so I could get a better look at the woman as she walked down the street. I don't think Ma knew what I was doing, but Malcolm noticed. Driving slowly so he could point things out to Ma, he turned and looked around to see what I was doing. I caught his eye. He didn't say anything, but his stern look said, Boy, I know what you are looking at. You know better than to be looking at that woman like that. I quickly looked away from him and the woman, petrified that he was going to tell Ma. It was the only time I ever feared my uncle. But he never told her, as far as I know, and never said anything to me.

During the drive, Malcolm told Ma about the importance of his work in Harlem. I remembered his saying that there were too many "lost-found Negroes" on the streets of Harlem in mindless conditions. "This is my calling," he told Ma. "I want to do Allah's bidding and deliver Mr. Muhammad's message to our people."

Ma, who usually had a lot to say about everything when talking with Malcolm, was more of a listener on those drives. Malcolm was excited and wanted to fill us in on a whole year's activities. "I was happy to see him so involved with our people," she said. "That's what our father and his mother had been doing. He was moving to be the leader that we all knew he could be. I personally wasn't so interested in hearing about Elijah Muhammad's message; I wanted him to get his message, his parents' message, Marcus Garvey's message, the Little brothers' message, to our people."

Sometimes we spent an entire afternoon, four or five hours, riding around New York City with Malcolm. I always remember clearly the stop we made at Harlem's famous National Memorial African Bookstore on 125th Street and Seventh Avenue. With a huge sign above the entrance, the store accurately and boldly described itself as the House of Common Sense and Home of the Proper Propaganda. The bookstore, which was owned and operated by Mr. and Mrs. Lewis Micheaux, provided an important part of Malcolm's social, philosophical, and psychological diet. It was not an ordinary bookstore, but part library and part school, where Professor Micheaux was able and available to teach history better than any professor at any university in the country. Brother Micheaux, a short, brown-skinned man with seemingly endless energy, was an expert on the Harlem

Renaissance. He was one of the two true experts on Malcolm; the other, Dr. John Henrik Clarke, a prominent historian and a confidant of my uncle's, died in July 1998.

The close, nurturing relationship between Micheaux and Malcolm is probably best described by Dr. James E. Turner, founding director of the African Studies Department at Cornell University. Turner said, "I first saw Malcolm at Micheaux's. He would come in there, and he and Micheaux would talk. Micheaux was, of course, well known throughout Harlem as a major nationalist spokesman himself, and he would speak out on the street corner. Sometimes he would have Malcolm speak right in front of the store. He would introduce Malcolm at rallies. The more I listened, the more their broad analysis in terms of our lack of power, our people having no sense of their history, all those basic nationalist tenets—internal self-contempt, lack of ability to cooperate—began to resonate."

When visiting Uncle Malcolm, Ma and I would meet him at Brother Micheaux's bookstore, where he was welcomed any time of the day or night. He spent more time there than anywhere else in New York City. I believed that at times Malcolm may have actually lived in the bookstore. Sometimes he would fall asleep while reading in one of its back rooms. Brother Micheaux would usually have a pile of phone messages or mail for Malcolm when he stopped by, since people who wanted to contact him would often phone or write the store.

There were occasions when Ma, Malcolm, and Brother Micheaux would talk all night about local, national, and international events and people while I slept peacefully among a cavern of books. It was at Brother Micheaux's bookstore in the 1950s that Ma and I first really saw and felt for ourselves how Uncle's words, feelings, and convictions resonated through a crowd in an outdoor space. We had always seen him speak in a temple, inside public arenas, and in television or radio studios. When we saw him speak outdoors in front of the bookstore for the first time, I was tremendously impressed. In the open air, with or without a microphone, he never missed a beat, speaking clearly, bluntly, passionately, and accurately about the racial reality in this country. His words of wisdom would resonate through the crowds of hundreds, sometimes thousands, of people. I had no idea he could touch people like that. I used to think, Boy! That's my Uncle up there speaking to black people about the problems this white man has put on us. Even a person who disliked or hated what he said would be impressed by his oratorical skills.

Though she never admitted it to me, I believed Ma was equally surprised by her brother's commanding presence in an outdoor space. Whenever Malcolm spoke inside with Ma present, he would ask her upon concluding, "How did I do, Ella?" Ma always answered with a smile. "You did good, Malcolm. I'm proud of you." When he spoke outdoors, she beamed even more. Sometimes she was so moved and happy, she would put her arms around his neck or shoulders and pull his head down to her cheek or shoulder. Uncle would smile like a Cheshire cat; he liked that kind of attention from his big sister. Ma was Mrs. Action, a trait she shared with her Little siblings. I got the impression that neither of them cared too much for a lot of lovey-dovey words. I once heard Malcolm tell his wife, Betty, that she liked too much dime-novel romantic talk. He enjoyed poems that expressed strong points and feelings in few words. Ma's biggest compliment to her siblings was to say, "Remember, you are all Pa John's and Daddy's children." She was tremendously proud of her tall, strong brothers and always encouraged me to be like them. In fact, it's more accurate to say that she *demanded* that I be like them. Others put before me as proper role models were Paul Robeson, Nat Turner, and Harriet Tubman. Since she had always dreamed of my being a scientist who would discover something that would help our people overcome oppression and exploitation, she told me about the scientific exploits of George Washington Carver, not because he was a political role model but because of his brilliant creativity and discoveries in a science laboratory.

At a very young age she gave me books to read written by J. A. Rogers and Frederick Douglass. When I was all of seven years old, she gave me a 2,350-page book called *The Volume Library—An Encyclopedia of Practical and Cultural Information Topically Arranged for Ready Home Study.* She signed it "From Mrs. Ella L. Collins to Rodnell Perkins Collins I, Dec. 8, 1952." She told me she wanted me to study all 2,350 pages, just as Malcolm had studied a whole dictionary while in prison. I still have the book. Ma felt so strongly about

Malcolm as a role model that when he was assassinated in 1965, she asked me to promise I would never sell our house at 72 Dale Street, where Uncle had lived with us. "You must always keep it in the family in his memory," she insisted. I intend to keep that promise.

Ma's major concern about Malcolm during his early, premarriage years in New York City was his not taking the time to eat and sleep properly. It's not known by many people, but in the late 1950s his poor eating and sleeping habits landed him in the hospital. Being in Boston, Ma couldn't keep close check on his health. He never had a room of his own during that time, always sharing space with brothers in the N.O.I.. She also knew that he would give his last dollar, if necessary, to anyone who was down on his luck. Of course, he would also use this as a fishing opportunity, telling the person that if he would use some of that dollar to come to the temple, he would learn how not to be down on his luck. Sometimes Ma would offer Uncle Malcolm money, but he wouldn't take it, so she would quietly slip a few dollars into his jacket pocket. Sometimes when we visited him in New York City, Ma would bring him home-cooked food she knew he liked. When he did visit us in Boston, he would sit in his favorite chair reading until he fell asleep. Then Ma had to almost make him go to bed.

One of the things that Ma liked most about Betty, Malcolm's wife, was that after they were married, she did her best to see that Uncle ate right and got sufficient rest. Ma knew from experience that this was not an easy task. Before Malcolm married Betty, whom he first met in Temple Seven, where she was also a member, he was under heavy pressure from all sides about marriage plans. Mr. Muhammad wanted him to get married. Sisters in the Nation considered him prime husband material, as did many women outside the Nation. Ma and her good friend, Sister Saoud Muhammad, concerned about his eating and sleeping habits, strongly believed that he needed a wife. In fact, Ma said that she and Sister Saoud, knowing that he planned to travel to Africa and the Middle East in 1959, were already preparing the way for him to find an African wife on his trip. Malcolm, they knew, had no interest in an arranged marriage, but if he suspected they were involved in such plans, he might make a move on his own. That's exactly what he did. Before leaving for Africa, he married Sister Betty X, a nursing student who lectured on hygiene and medical facts to the Muslim girls' and women's classes. Malcolm wrote in his autobiography: "She's the only woman I ever even thought about loving. And she's one of the very few—four women—whom I have ever trusted." Ma, who was one of the four women Malcolm trusted, was just happy he had a woman to help take care of him. "I was deeply concerned about his health," she said, "and was glad that he now had someone nearby who would see that he ate and slept properly."

Malcolm accomplished with Temple Seven just what he had done with the temples in Boston and Philadelphia. It grew rapidly as hundreds of Harlemites responded to his message about the need for education, economic development, purpose, discipline, self-defense, self-respect, morality, and cooperation. They wholeheartedly agreed with his scathing denunciation of white supremacy in all its insidious forms. It wasn't long before people throughout the country and the world became aware of Malcolm X.

During the years he headed Temple Seven, Malcolm was in and out of Boston, so Ma and I had opportunities to see him other than on our summer visits. When he was in Boston, I often turned to him for advice. In my early teens, after joining the Nation, I asked him, "What should I do now?" He suggested that I sell copies of the *Pittsburgh Courier,* a black-owned, nationally distributed newspaper which often published articles about Mr. Muhammad, Malcolm, and the N.O.I. I remember seeing him selling it on street corners in Harlem when we visited him. That was before he launched *Muhammad Speaks*. While selling the paper, he also fished for new members among his customers and street people. Many of the latter were involved in illegal activities, such as drug selling and using, prostitution, pimping, and shooting craps. Ma and I watched closely and listened carefully as Malcolm fished. He was good at it.

I tried to imitate his style when selling papers in Boston. Though still an adolescent, I sold papers in Boston's Mafia-controlled bawdy district. Looking squeaky clean, I sold papers to patrons of the bars and to the performers. Two of my best customers were women, one black, one white, who danced nude in one of the liveliest bars. Ironically, I sold more papers in the red-light district than to the stuck-up, bourgeois, status-quo Negroes living in Sugar Hill. I mistakenly thought they would be impressed by the sight of a young brother trying to make a few dollars legitimately. They were not. Most wouldn't even look at the paper; others would take one from me, glance through it quickly, and give it back to me. The only Sugar Hill residents who regularly bought papers from me were Mason and Little family members and a few of Ma's friends. Other "friends" of hers would freak out on Ma when they came across articles in the *Pittsburgh Courier* written by or about Elijah Muhammad or Malcolm. With raised eyebrows and clucking tongues, they'd ask: "Ella, are you into those people? Is that what you and Malcolm are into now? We thought you were one of us."

"I really wasn't one of them," Ma noted, "but believed, perhaps naively, that at least some of them could be converted away from their obsession with assimilation. After all, many of them were people with skills that we as a people needed."

In a sense Ma was fishing in another kind of setting than Malcolm was. She even went to social events like the First Diamond Ball, where she was seated at the same table as then Massachusetts governor Christian Herter. Most blacks in attendance were Sugar Hill residents, such as former Massachusetts attorney general and former U.S. senator Edward W. Brooke and Otto and Muriel Snowden, founders of Freedom House, then probably the main meeting hall for blacks in Boston. The Snowdens, pillars of Boston's black elite, made Freedom House a place where proper black folk and proper white folk could meet and mingle. One of its favorite whites was John F. Kennedy, who used it as a platform from which to address the black community.

The Freedom House of that time, the late 1950s and early 1960s, would never have invited Malcolm to speak. After all, he was a militant Black Muslim from Boston. "Those house Negroes," he told Ma, "would flock to hear some white man speak, yet refused to even listen to a black man who was a Muslim. Fortunately, many of the field Negroes did come out to hear what I had to say." It's important to understand that when using "house Negroes" and "field Negroes," Uncle Malcolm was talking about an attitude, a frame of mind. All educated, financially well off black people are not automatically the former, and all low-income, or street-life people, are not automatically the latter. Malcolm had spoken many times on street corners of Boston's Irish, Black, and Jewish areas.

It's entirely possible that Uncle Malcolm, John Kennedy, and Rev. Martin L. King Jr. may have nearly crossed physical paths in Roxbury and Boston's South End during those years. When Kennedy spoke at Freedom House, he was only three blocks from what was to become Temple Eleven, located at 35 Intervale Street. Also, Kennedy often campaigned in Blue Hill, which was off Intervale and was a shopping center for members of the Jewish-American community who still lived in Dorchester and Roxbury. In fact, the building in which Temple Eleven was located had once been a synagogue. Members of the N.O.I. and of the Jewish community basically stayed out of each other's way. Many believed that the latter may have been happy about the Nation's presence in the neighborhoods, since street criminals were wary about hanging around areas where its members had settled. Despite this uneasy coexistence, Jews continued to flee Dorchester and Roxbury as their black populations grew. Many blacks in the Blue Hill neighborhood inaccurately blamed Ma and Uncle Malcolm for the white flight.

As a fascinating historical aside, when Wilfred and Malcolm opened the first Boston temple in 1952/1953 at 405 Massachusetts Avenue, they had no idea that three doors away, at 397 Massachusetts Avenue, was the house in which Martin Luther King Jr. was living while a graduate student at Boston University. It was the first of several times over the next twelve years that the two of them would be in close proximity to each other without meeting. It's amazing to realize that they met only once in their lives.

John F. Kennedy was also often in Boston during that year. When he ran for the U.S. Senate in 1952, he often campaigned extensively in the area because it had a considerable Irish Catholic population. It's almost certain that he was back in the area on occasion in 1953, which means that the three men, all of whom would later be assassinated, were operating in that area at the same time.

When I told Uncle Malcolm about selling papers in the red-light district, he was amused but warned me to be careful. Then, when he heard about the negative reaction of most of Ma's "friends" to my selling the *Courier* because of its regular articles on him, Mr. Muhammad, and the N.O.I., Malcolm told Ma once again that she was wasting her time trying to make righteous black folk out of Sugar Hill snobs. He told Ma she would be more productive as a member of the Nation in Boston. He especially wanted her to work with the Muslim Girls Training Group. Despite her continued misgivings, Ma finally came aboard in 1957. It was a very pragmatic decision. "I had a tremendous amount of respect for my brother," she says. "Eventually I decided that anything he believed in so strongly must have some good points in its favor. Like many, many others, I was attracted to the Nation of Islam by Malcolm, not by Mr. Muhammad. It was he who represented what the N.O.I. claimed to be but what it in too many instances wasn't."

Uncle described his reaction to her decision in his autobiography: "Guest-teaching at the Temple in Boston, I ended, as always, 'who among you wish to follow *The Honorable Elijah Muhammad?'* and then I saw in utter astonishment, that among those who were standing was my sister—Ella! We have a saying that those who are the hardest to convince make the best Muslims. And for Ella, it had taken five years." Malcolm proved to be right about Ma's being a good Muslim, but it was not for long as a member of the Nation.

We were never able to get Dad into the N.O.I. He was a strong sympathizer but wasn't moved to officially sign up. Sometimes Ma and I would both fish him when we were visiting him on his second job with Tracer Lab Inc. Ma would bring his evening dinner. Both of us would sometimes help him clean offices. Eventually, Dad learned to do night office work using IBM's electric accounting machine, the E.A.M., which was part of the first generation of computers. He showed me how it operated, thus introducing me to computers. This interest increased when I began selling newspapers in the neighborhoods around Harvard University and the Massachusetts Institute of Technology (MIT) and had an opportunity to hang out on MIT's campus. While selling papers, I met several student engineers who let me work at the computers in their labs.

All the students I hung around with at MIT weren't computer nuts. Some were African, Asian, and Arab students who attended universities in the Boston area and were tenants in buildings owned by Ma. Most were Muslim. Some have remained friends through the years, most notably Sister Saoud Muhammad, an Egyptian, and her husband, Mahmoud Muhammad, a Jordanian. Sister Saoud later taught Arabic and French at Ma's Sarah A. Little School for the Preparatory Arts. Mahmoud Muhammad was a revolutionary-minded brother who ardently opposed European colonialism in Arab lands.

One year I attended a film festival at MIT hosted by Algerian students. I vividly remember movies they showed about their country's struggle for independence against France. I was shocked by scenes in which French soldiers massacred Algerian women and children. I thought only African Americans suffered such racial brutality from white supremacists and was surprised to see that other people were treated just as badly by Europeans and people of European descent. It was about this time that the case of Emmett Till hit the news. He was a black teenager who had been lynched in Mississippi for allegedly whistling at a white woman. That was the first time I remembered seeing photographs depicting such murderous brutality. When I heard Ma and Malcolm discussing the Till lynching, their condemnation of white supremacists was as harsh as I had ever heard from them. It was the first time that I remember actually disliking, maybe even hating, whites. I was ten years old; Emmett Till was fifteen. That made his death even more personal to me. Malcolm made sure I was aware of that and other atrocities committed against black people by white supremacists.

I wasn't the only one learning from, and being inspired by, Uncle Malcolm. He, along with his brothers, especially Wilfred and Philbert, had provided many thousands of other black folks with the same information and inspiration. Spurred by memories of the Garveyism of their parents, the Little brothers had taken Mr. Muhammad's message to places that even he probably didn't envision.

When Mr. Muhammad launched the first Allah Temple of Islam in Detroit in 1935, he did what so many black Christian preachers had done and still do with that religion—which was to adapt the religious message to the people he was trying to reach. Wilfred and Philbert added their Garveyite beliefs to what Mr. Muhammad was preaching and played pivotal roles in setting up several of the original temples. They, along with Wesley, Reginald, and Hilda, recruited Malcolm. This led to a literal explosion of new temples. "Without the oratorical and organization and the resourcefulness and determination of the Little brothers," Ma said unequivocally, "the Nation of Islam would have remained a nearly comatose, cultlike group that barely made a blip on the world scene. And don't forget Hilda. In those early years, she worked equally hard teaching and inspiring Muslim women." Theirs was a success that would produce both triumph and tragedy.

EIGHT Nation of Islam

From Uncle Malcolm's rapidly growing base at Temple Seven in Harlem, he soon became the N.O.I.'s most persuasive and most productive evangelist. He traveled throughout the country by train and car searching for and converting "lost-found Negroes" to the Nation. Once he began flying, after the launching of the Boeing 707, he was able to do even more fishing. His stops included Los Angeles, Dallas, Phoenix, Chicago, St. Louis, Miami, Salt Lake City, Little Rock, Oklahoma City, Portland, Oregon, Biloxi, Mississippi, Columbia, South Carolina, and Providence, Rhode Island. During Uncle Malcolm's travels, he set up some fifty temples throughout the country, reeling in "lost-found Negroes" like a fervent fisherman going after trout.

"Malcolm knew what it took to build a community, a nation; he knew what 'it's nation time' really meant, in terms of hard work, perseverance, and commitment, before that slogan became popular in the late 1960s," Ma noted. "That's why he so strongly opposed those N.O.I. officials who wanted to keep the organization insular and limited."

When in the Boston area, Uncle Malcolm enlisted Ma's aid in his fishing efforts. He was convinced that the best candidates for conversion to the Nation were people who already believed in some form of Islam, so he asked Ma to host a meeting with Ahmadiyya Muslims whom she knew. One Muslim Ma knew was Sister Zainab, whose building at 216 West Springfield Street was right around the corner from Temple Eleven, at 9 Wellington Street. "Malcolm asked me to invite Sister Zainab, Brother David Ahmad, and other Muslims to meet at my home, still located at 486 Massachusetts. The meeting was not a great success. Though the people present greatly respected Malcolm, they simply were not going to accept Elijah Muhammad as a divine being."

A second group whom Malcolm considered prime fishing prospects were black Baptists. "He used to tell me," said Ma, "that when in a Baptist church, he felt like a kid in a candy shop unsupervised by his parents. The church members were the candy." Surprisingly, Washington, D.C., proved to be a fertile fishing ground. It was there, Ma said, that Uncle Malcolm once enlisted most members of a Baptist church, including its pastor, into the N.O.I. In his autobiography, he noted that there was a similar wholesale conversion in Richmond, Virginia. Another favorite spot for fishing, according to Ma, was Cong. Adam Clayton Powell Jr.'s huge and historic Abyssinian Baptist Church on West 138th Street in Harlem. "He spoke there so often," Ma recalled, "that some people used to wonder jokingly whose flock it was, Reverend Powell's or Malcolm's."

However, it wasn't the prominent churches, such as the Abyssinian, where Uncle Malcolm did his most productive recruiting. It was at those small, evangelical storefront churches whose congregations, as Uncle Malcolm noted in his autobiography, "would go anywhere to hear what they called 'good preaching.' . . . The black Christians we 'fished' to our Temple were conditioned, I found, by the very shock I could give them about what had been happening to them while they worshiped a blond, blue-eyed God. I knew the temple that I could build if I could really get to those Christians. I tailored the teachings for them."

Before fishing among those groups, however, Uncle Malcolm wanted to explain his new beliefs and direction in life to his Little, Mason, and Gray family members in the Boston metropolitan area. "He really didn't expect to get any converts to Islam among our staunchly Christian family members," Ma said. "He just wanted to show them how turning to Islam had changed his life." As he requested, Ma invited all of our family to the gatherings, including Uncle Leonard and his wife, Lowla. Remember, they were the interracial couple who had fled Georgia in the 1930s. Uncle Leonard, said Aunt Sas, was the type of black person who basically accepted whatever whites dished out; he was definitely not a boat rocker.

One gathering took place at our summer home in Duxbury, Massachusetts, about forty-five miles from Boston. At that time, the early 1950s, there were about fifty black people in the town, with most of those being either members of the Mason family, including Leonard, or a group of people who called themselves Cape Verdians. The Cape Verdians were descendants of black Portuguese who really didn't consider themselves black. Leonard was very aware of Malcolm's being a member of the Nation and of the organization's hostile position on interracial relationships. He was not expected to attend the meetings. "If he had," Ma stated, "he and his wife would have been treated cordially. There's no way Malcolm would have been discourteous to them."

As family members gathered at our house, we suddenly heard a loud knock on the door. When Ma opened it, there stood the sheriff of Duxbury in all his official regalia. "I got a report about trouble up here," he said. Ma, knowing that many whites in Duxbury considered her an "uppity" black person who didn't know her place, wasn't overly surprised at the sheriff's appearance. "If too many of us gathered at one place, they always felt the need to check us out," she said, laughing. "Malcolm and I assured him that the report was wrong, and he somewhat reluctantly left."

A few family members who were present when the sheriff showed up were so fearful that they left as soon as he drove off. One of those who departed was Aunt Mary. After that, she never again went to hear Uncle Malcolm speak anywhere. Many family members strongly believed that Leonard was the culprit who phoned the sheriff with a false report of trouble.

Malcolm believed that one of the important factors in his often successful fishing was that many people read the fiery articles he wrote for the *Pittsburgh Courier.* They were widely read and made Uncle Malcolm acutely aware of the importance of a communications instrument. He decided that as supportive as the *Courier* was, the N.O.I. needed its own publication. His first venture in this area was the *Messenger Magazine News,* which he published almost sin-

glehandedly. When it proved to be too costly, he closed it down. He
sent two hundred copies of the magazine to Ma and me for us to sell.
I still have some of them.

Enter Journalist Louis Lomax, whom Malcolm first met in 1957,
when both of them were contributing articles to the *Los Angeles
Herald Dispatch.* Uncle had honed his writing skills in prison, contributing stories and articles to a prison newspaper and writing letters
for other inmates, black and white, to mothers, wives, and girlfriends. His skills were further developed due to a close relationship
with Mr. and Mrs. E. P. Alexander, founders and publishers of the
Los Angeles Herald Dispatch. Mrs. Alexander, especially, coached
him on writing editorials and columns. Though never on the paper's
staff, the time he spent around the office served as a kind of intern-
ship. Malcolm used the time not only to write articles and columns
for the *Herald Dispatch* but also for the *Pittsburgh Courier,* which
was mainly circulated on the East Coast.

Uncle had a professional relationship with Lomax, Ma said, not
a close personal one, as Lomax liked to claim. It led to the now-
infamous and controversial television documentary *The Hate That
Hate Produced,* which introduced the Nation of Islam to host Mike
Wallace and Lomax to national audiences. Lomax was the connecting link in the process. From the time he first met Malcolm and
heard him speak about Mr. Muhammad and the N.O.I., Lomax pressured him to write some kind of story about them. Though personally not interested in such a project at the time, Malcolm told Lomax
that he would pass on and discuss his proposal with Mr. Muhammad.
This was basically a way of putting Lomax on hold, since N.O.I. officials in Chicago didn't have a clue about such matters and usually
accepted Uncle Malcolm's advice.

Lomax, a keen observer who had heard him speak at different
temples and rallies, knew that Malcolm was the brains behind the
Nation. In places such as New York City, Chicago, Los Angeles, and
Washington, D.C., Lomax watched Malcolm instruct and move large
audiences. On several of those occasions, he also heard that while
Elijah Muhammad was a great inspiration to all the N.O.I. members
present, he just didn't communicate well with large audiences. Being
barely literate, Muhammad had difficulty reading notes. Often, Ma

told me, one could see Malcolm coaching him as he spoke. At the 1960 N.O.I. national convention, held at Harlem's 369th Armory, I actually saw Malcolm coaching and orchestrating Muhammad from behind the podium. Lomax had made a similar observation, so he tried to pressure Malcolm into doing a program on the Nation. Being a tenacious newshound, Lomax was not put off by Malcolm's negative response to his first request. Ma said, "Lomax knew that if he got the N.O.I.'s story on film, it would be a major career-enhancing plus with his white bosses."

Malcolm, on the other hand, told Ma he wasn't sure that the organization was ready for such intense and sure-to-be-hostile public scrutiny. He knew enough about the white press of that time to realize that it usually pursued stories on black folks not to educate and enlighten its viewers, readers, and listeners about race relations but to alarm them and reinforce their stereotypes. He was certain that the proposed CBS documentary would depict the N.O.I. as an organization whose members were militant bogeymen who needed to be dealt with. This would accomplish two things—alarm white folks and turn away black folks who might consider joining or at least listening to what the Nation was all about. Despite Malcolm's apprehensions, Lomax's persistence paid off. N.O.I. officials in Chicago overruled Uncle Malcolm and gave permission to go ahead with the project. *The Hate That Hate Produced* was presented to the world in July 1959 and proved to be a shining example of what the white press does best when dealing with racial matters, which is to often miseducate and distort. "Malcolm, ever the good, loyal minister, went along with their decision," Ma said, "because he still believed in Mr. Muhammad."

The Hate That Hate Produced lived down to Uncle Malcolm's expectations. First of all, its very title was deceptive. Though seemingly saying that white hate produced black hate, very little in the documentary depicts white hatred. Between 1955, when Emmett Till was lynched in Mississippi, and 1959, black people in many parts of the South were under siege from white supremacists angered by the growing civil-rights movement. Homes and churches had been firebombed; people had been killed or otherwise brutalized; and jobs had been taken away because of white hostility toward efforts to dismantle legal white supremacy in this country. Then there was the history of hundreds of lynchings in the late 1800s and early 1900s. Jim Crow laws that were mostly passed in the early 1900s were still in effect throughout the South in 1959. There was also the more covert white supremacy in effect in the North, usually centered around housing and employment opportunities. Very little of this racial context was depicted in the Mike Wallace, Louis Lomax documentary. Instead, the focus was on expressions of hatred by members of the N.O.I. "What Mike Wallace called hate," Ma noted, "came across to me as some black people making a commonsense response to all the mostly unpunished brutalities committed on them by white supremacists."

In fact, at the time the show was presented in 1959, no one, including Mike Wallace, could name a single white person whose life had been taken, whose property destroyed, or whose job lost because of any action taken by the Nation or any of its members. In reality, they had as little contact as possible with whites on any level. The program played on the fear that many whites experience when large numbers of black folks get together for any purpose. Many of the black codes of the antebellum South banned five or more Africans being together at one time unless they were under the direct supervision of a white person. That attitude, in a somewhat milder form, has continued to this day and was definitely prevalent in 1959.

So when they watched *The Hate That Hate Produced* and saw several thousand disciplined, committed black people working together in a joint cause, it must have been extremely disconcerting. Knowing the brutal history of white supremacy, most whites just couldn't believe that most black people, no matter how strongly or often they deny it, weren't secretly yearning for or plotting some kind of revenge.

Finally, there was the question of Islam. In 1959 very few people in this mostly Christian country had even the slightest passing knowledge about Islam other than what they had been taught in school. Which was that Islam was out to destroy Christianity. Now they were watching a television show in which scary black folks were proclaiming to be equally scary Muslims. It was too much. "Do whatever is necessary to put a stop to such madness" was probably

the attitude of the typical white Christian after seeing the documentary.

Lomax was aware of all these white feelings. In fact, for marketing
reasons, he counted on them. He wanted a basic theme of the show
to be "There are some angry niggers out there and they are coming
to get you." He knew it would increase ratings, please his bosses,
and give him a jump start into the big time. Mike Wallace, in a more
discreet fashion, was equally eager to do the show as an attention
getter and career enhancer. In his book *To Kill a Black Man,* which
focuses on the assassination of Malcolm and Martin Luther King Jr.,
Lomax wrote that "Mike Wallace was visibly moved—almost to
tears, actually—as he concluded the documentary with the words 'It
is a terrible indictment of America that even a small part of our
Negro population is willing to pay heed to the racist declarations that
we have learned tonight. For them, and for all Negroes, we must
make America live up to the fine language of our creed. We make
ourselves in reality a nation of one people, indivisible, with freedom
and justice for all. In such a nation there would be no place for white
supremacists who disgrace and embitter our society today. And in
such a nation there would have been no occasion to report the mel-
ancholy story of *The Hate That Hate Produced.*" Wallace's pontifi-
cating brings to mind today's talk shows. After presenting guests
who often say and do vile things for an hour of television time, the
hosts trot out psychiatrists or someone similar who piously talk
about the profound meaning of it all. Wallace probably cried all the
way to the bank. As for Lomax, he was unable to build a national lu-
crative career from the show. By focusing almost solely on the
N.O.I. and by not providing an in-depth historical context on race relations in the United States, Mike Wallace, aided by Louis Lomax,
presented a cynically distorted look at race relations in this country.

The documentary was at best a mixed blessing for the Nation.
Malcolm did receive many offers to speak at predominantly white
universities as a result of it and thus moved Mr. Muhammad's message into another area. In the book, *Malcolm X: Make It Plain,* Malcolm was quoted as saying that following the show, "the telephone
in our small Temple Seven restaurant nearly jumped off the wall. . . .
Calls came long distance from San Francisco to Maine. . . . From

even London, Stockholm, and Paris. . . . It seemed that everywhere I went telephones were ringing." The impression given by the quote is that Malcolm was pleased with the documentary. That is not the case. Most of the calls, he told Ma and me, were not from people clamoring to join or support the N.O.I. A sizable number were from members of the international press seeking interviews. Many more came from Muslims and Africans who, while students in the United States, had visited temples or attended an N.O.I. national convention. They were concerned about the one-sided perspective presented by Wallace and Lomax. That wasn't the whole story of the Nation of Islam that they had visited.

Malcolm, said Ma, "was more concerned about the program turning away black folks than he was about it alarming white folks." One such result happened in his own family. "Malcolm knew there was never any possibility of his fishing Aunt Sas and Aunt Gracie into Islam," Ma explained. "They were too devoutly Christian for that, but he hoped that they would at least try to understand what it was trying to do and why he was a member. The Wallace-Lomax documentary ended even that possibility. Though they loved Malcolm, the son of their favorite brother, they were so disturbed by what they considered the anti-Christian position of the N.O.I., that they weren't interested in any good it was doing for black people. Their reaction was probably multiplied throughout the country." Malcolm couldn't even speak about the N.O.I. in their presence.

Malcolm never told the press, the general public, or even most members of the N.O.I. about the letter the documentary elicited from J. B. Stoner, the head of the Ku Klux Klan. "He got a copy of the letter from a black New York City police officer who silently supported him," said Ma. Later, in the summer of 1965, Ma and I had a secret meeting with that same policeman. Dated August 6, 1959, and stamped "Confidential and Top Secret," the four-page letter was addressed to Stephen B. Kennedy, police commissioner of the city of New York. "Dear Fellow Whiteman;" it began. "I have received a report from one of our Klansmen on the New York police force informing me that the nigger Muslims are in rebellion against White law and order. He reports that those blacks have no respect for you honest White Christian policemen. Therefore, in the interests of law and justice, I am offering you the support of the CHRISTIAN KNIGHTS OF THE KU KLUX KLAN."

Stoner then noted that he was "an expert on the black Muslims and have kept up with their infidelic activities for many years. From my knowledge of them, I assure you that they are much more dangerous to White Christian rule in New York than you realize. You and I must join forces to stop the black Muslims now or they will soon drive every White person out of New York City. The largest city in the world will then be an all nigger city of black supremacy where White people will not be allowed to live. The only thing that can stop Elijah Muhammad and his black Muslims from conquering New York is for my Christian Knights and your New York police to join hands and work together to uphold White Christian Supremacy. . . ."

Non-Christian whites should note that Stoner said: "White *Christian* [italics mine] supremacy." He then went on to explain what he meant by a joint effort with the New York City police department.

We need to put the black hoodlums out of business, but we must do it in a legal way with the police and the courts. As a Georgia lawyer, I insist on doing everything according to law. You know what I mean. It is urgent that you persuade the officials of the City and State of New York to immediately repeal all ordinances and laws that prevent Whites from discriminating against niggers because those evil laws constitute an open invitation to all niggers in the South to move to New York City where they will strengthen the Muslims and subject that giant metropolis to black supremacy. . . . Those laws need to be replaced with laws that will help white Christians in New York to imitate us Southerners by keeping the darkies in their place. . . .

The legalities now taken care of, Stoner presented the rest of his plan.

Police Commissioner Kennedy, my dear friend, I now offer you the service of the Christian Knights of the Ku Klux Klan for the purpose of maintaining White Supremacy in New York City

and for keeping New York niggers in their place. I think 5,000
Klansmen could clean up Harlem for you if you would give
them police badges and N.Y. police uniforms to wear instead of
their Klan uniforms. They will leave their robes at home so
New York niggers won't know that your police reinforcements
are White Christian Klansmen. You can use our Christian
Knights as guards to protect every White business in Harlem
and also in other New York areas where nigger customers are
giving trouble to White businessmen. After all, how do the
black jig-a-boos expect to live without White businessmen to
sell them what they need. You can also use our Klansmen to escort White salesmen into Harlem and other parts of New York
City that are suffering from black plague.

Uncle Malcolm took Stoner's letter seriously. Reading it in the
1990s, many may be tempted to laugh at the preposterousness of it
all. However, in 1959, when the civil-rights movement was still basically in its beginning and when white supremacists, including
many in elective office, were snarling against any effort to dismantle
legal white supremacy, when the federal government was still hesitant about passing new civil-rights legislation, when black people
were being threatened and brutalized in many areas for insisting on
equal opportunity and equal protection from the law, Stoner's letter
was no joking matter. "Malcolm was well aware that the Nation of
Islam's bark at that time was much greater than its bite," Ma said.
"He knew that it was not prepared in 1959 to effectively physically
confront Stoner-like white supremacists who would almost certainly
have the active backing, or at least the hear-no-evil, see-no-evil,
speak-no-evil acquiescence, of most white people in the country.
Look at the record. When brutalities occurred, the response of the
federal government was usually that it was a problem the state had to
deal with. It had no jurisdiction. Most whites in the North went along
with that position. That's why Malcolm spoke about Stoner's letter
to a very few people."

As Uncle Malcolm had feared, the Wallace-Lomax documentary
had a negative effect on the N.O.I.'s fishing efforts among black
people and therefore on its continued growth. Many blacks wanted

no part of an organization that might "bring the white folks down on us." Their fears were not unfounded. In his letter, Stoner wrote: "I have had White Christian friends write to many magazines inciting them to denounce Muhammad and his Muslims so as to scare many cowardly niggers away from him. So far I have managed to 'sic' both *Time* magazine and *U.S. News and World Report* on them." Stoner may have been exaggerating his influence on the magazines, but there is no doubt that there was an effort by the press, some politicians, and even some black leaders to scare black people away from joining or supporting the Nation. That doesn't mean that Malcolm ceased fishing for new members and new support. On Harlem street corners, on university campuses, in N.O.I. temples across the country, he continued delivering its message on politics, economics, culture, and religion. He continued his hard-hitting, blistering verbal attacks on those who believed in white supremacy and on a government that hesitated to act when those who not only believed in white supremacy but practiced it in physical attacks on black people broke the laws.

One person fished by Malcolm during that period was Muhammad Ali, then known as Cassius Clay. They first met in 1962, when the boxer and his brother had come to Detroit to hear Elijah Muhammad speak. "Cassius came up and pumped my hand, introducing himself as he later presented himself to the world, 'I'm Cassius Clay.' He acted as if I was supposed to knew who he was. So I acted as though I did." As they got to know each other over the next few weeks, Malcolm wrote in his autobiography: "I liked him. Some contagious quality about him made him one of the very few people I ever invited to my home." Ali's joining the N.O.I. gave it the biggest publicity boost it had had since *The Hate That Hate Produced* was presented to the world.

Probably the most important lesson learned by Uncle Malcolm as a result of the documentary was that the N.O.I. needed its own communications instrument. It simply couldn't depend on other sources to reach its members and the general public. He had proved his effectiveness in verbally communicating with single individuals and large groups of people. Dr. Strickland said that Malcolm's "métier was the spoken word. . . . He was intellectually flexible because his first priority was to communicate in order to instruct. He spoke to people in language that they could understand because he was a people's intellectual, not an intellectual's intellectual."

Malcolm knew, however, that the spoken word was not enough, so he set out to create a publication. The person he asked to help him was Louis Lomax. Malcolm, aware that the N.O.I. didn't have at the time sufficient members with the skills needed to put together a quality publication, very pragmatically turned to Lomax because he possessed such skills. "Theirs was a professional relationship," Ma said, "in which both wanted something—in Malcolm's case, a quality publication, in Lomax's case, another opportunity to boost his career by being where the action was." In his book *To Kill a Black Man,* Lomax wrote that "Malcolm and several other members of the Movement wrote for the paper and I did the editing. I wrote some of the ideas myself after Malcolm had given me ideas he wished conveyed."

The front page of an early edition of the tabloid-sized *Mr. Muhammad Speaks* (the Mr. was later dropped), vol 1, no. 4, dated December 1960, shows graphically what Malcolm was aiming for. Its slogan was "A Monthly Dedicated to Justice for the Black Man," and the lead story, with its large, red-lettered headline, was "Elijah Muhammad Invades Atlanta." Under the headline was a large photograph of members of a crowd with the caption "Part of the thousands who stood in the rain to hear the teachings of Elijah Muhammad at a recent Harlem rally."

Other smaller, red-lettered headlines also appeared on the front page. One said that "Thurgood Marshall Sics Cops on Muslims;" the second that "Muslims Sue Hearst Papers for Cool $3 Million." It consisted of thirty-two pages and cost twenty cents. The Marshall story becomes more fascinating after recent revelations that the former Supreme Court justice once was an FBI informant when working with the NAACP. The most revealing quote came from Jessie James, police chief of Charlotte, North Carolina. According to James, "In the fall of 1959 Thurgood Marshall, chief attorney for the NAACP, invited police chiefs to attend a meeting at his room during the International Police Chiefs Association convention in New York City. At the time, the problems surrounding the activities of the

Black Muslim group were discussed by some of the most important figures in law enforcement today. I was impressed with Marshall's attack on the group. I received the interpretation from Marshall that in his opinion this group was strictly un-American in its objectives. . . . I have talked to chiefs of police about these organized groups in their localized [*sic*] and they feel the groups are un-American in every way. . . ."

The paper soon became an integral part of the N.O.I.'s outreach efforts. Probably the most visible symbol of the Nation for most people in the early 1960s was hundreds of young Muslim men relentlessly selling *Muhammad Speaks* on the streets of every city that had a temple. For many people, that was their real introduction to the N.O.I. Mostly because of Malcolm's oratorical and fishing skills, that meant that the brothers were selling papers in our fifty major cities throughout the country. "One temple opening that was particularly gratifying to him," said Ma, "was the one in Lansing, Michigan, the city in which his father had been murdered and which had treated his mother and her children so badly after Earl Senior was slain. Malcolm greatly enjoyed building and speaking in that temple as a way of showing the blacks and whites who had rejected his family that the Littles were not to be denied." The temple was in a building once owned by orthodox Sunni Muslims who had fled to the suburbs. It was the temple that Ma, Dad, and I attended when visiting relatives in Lansing.

As Malcolm moved around the country fishing for new members and spreading Mr. Muhammad's messages in dozens of different venues, he sent Ma letters and postcards. When he didn't write, he called. At all times he was well aware that the FBI had begun watching his every move. He took for granted that they were monitoring his mail and tapping his phone conversations. He told young brothers in the fruit of Islam that they had done the same to Mr. Muhammad in the 1930s and were certainly still doing so. The FBI was concerned about Muhammad's involvement with Sata Hota Takahashi, a prominent member of Japan's Black Dragon Society. Takahashi was the founder of the American arm of the society, which regarded Europeans and European Americans as "white devils" because of their treatment of people of color in Asia, Africa, and South America. According to FBI files, Muhammad met Takahashi in 1932, a year before he met W. D. Fard. By 1933, Mr. Muhammad was telling black people that "the Japanese will slaughter the white man. It is Japan's duty to save you. Our brothers in the East didn't know we were here sixty years ago. After finding out we were using the name of the devils [whites], they at once went back and told the Asiatic nations that they now know where lost brother was. Now they are only waiting on the word of the prophet. The Japanese army and navy are really strong enough to destroy this devil."

Muhammad also told his followers that Japan had a long history of commercial and diplomatic relations with Ethiopia, a relationship made even stronger when a Japanese princess became engaged to an Ethiopian prince. Because of intense pressure from Italy, which at that time had imperialistic designs on Ethiopia, the wedding was postponed. The Japanese, according to Mr. Muhammad, looked upon Africans as potential trading partners, not as people to be colonized. Its strong commercial ties with Ethiopia reflected that.

Those who deride Elijah Muhammad's interpretation of history as fanciful should remember the fanciful interpretation of the history of Native Americans and the equally fanciful interpretation of the history of Africa and African Americans taught in elementary school, high school, and college.

Besides Muhammad, Malcolm told us, the FBI also kept close tabs on W. D. Fard, with whom Muhammad was aligned in the 1930s. According to FBI files, W. D. Fard came to the United States from India sometime between 1910 and 1915. Eventually he founded the first Ahmadiyya sect in this country. Even before going to prison Malcolm had heard about the Ahmadiyyas from members of the Perry family, neighbors in Boston, who were members of the sect. Brother Abdul, one of the Perrys, told Malcolm that Fard had founded Ahmadiyya Islam in the United States and that whites were not allowed to join the sect.

In 1933, Elijah Muhammad and Fard joined forces. They were both dissatisfied with the Ahmadiyyas for what they considered the sect's reluctance to seriously proselytize among black people. They knew that in order to be successful they had to adapt Islam to the real conditions of black people in the United States. Borrowing some ideas and concepts from orthodox Islam, some from the Ahmadiyyas, some from Takahashi's Black Dragon Society, some from Marcus Garvey, and some from Elijah Muhammad's black Baptist background, they created the Nation of Islam in 1935. There was much hostility toward that orthodox approach not only from the FBI, for political reasons, but from orthodox Muslims and the Ahmadiyyas, for religious reasons. Muhammad actually had to employ bodyguards because of that hostility; some in the Islamic community at large believe the same hostility was behind Fard's mysterious disappearance.

All this history was given to Malcolm by Mr. Muhammad and other N.O.I. ministers when he first joined the organization. He then passed it on to all those people he reached out to. His sole motivation during that time, noted Ma, was his absolute belief in Muhammad and his message.

One way Malcolm showed his commitment was to look out for Muhammad's family. He was the one who, upon discovering that most of Muhammad's children worked for whites, did something about what he considered an intolerable situation. "When Mr. Muhammad had sent me out in his service as a minister," he wrote in his autobiography, "I began to feel it was a shame that his children worked as some of them then did, for the white man, in factories, construction work, driving taxis, things like that. I felt I should work for Mr. Muhammad's family as sincerely as I worked for him. I urged Mr. Muhammad to let me put on a special drive within our few small mosques, to raise funds which would enable those of his children working for the white man to be instead employed within our Nation. Mr. Muhammad agreed, the special fund drive did prove successful, and his children gradually did begin working for the Nation."

The depth of Malcolm's commitment to Elijah Muhammad was revealed in an essay he wrote for the August–September 1956 issue of a publication called *Moslem World and the U.S.A.*

MESSENGER MUHAMMAD is without question the most fearless, uncompromising representative of Allah and Islam. He does not apologize for what His Message of Islam teaches. He says to take it or leave it. . . . Indeed this Christian government is very upset. Its government agents visited me and questioned me so thoroughly concerning this man, I spent sleepless nights wondering what it is about his teachings that has the agents of such a powerful country so concerned and upset. The more they visited and questioned me, the more I came to believe in this man and to know that he is a DIVINE GOD—SENT—MAN. He had never been to college, and his formal education in their school system is very limited, wherein these government agents themselves seemed highly trained and well-schooled in all the higher sciences of life. They are well-learned, yet the teachings of this unlearned man has them upset and stymied. If what he teaches is not true, why then are they so upset? The average unlettered person cannot upset a learned person . . . unless he really has been given something by THE LEARNED ONE (The Best Knower . . .)."

When Malcolm wrote those words, in 1956, Ma noted: "He was probably at the height of his commitment to Mr. Muhammad."

NINE The Split, Part 1: Judas Eye

Malcolm ended the chapter, "Black Muslims," in his autobiography with the following conversation between himself and Elijah Muhammad. " 'Brother Malcolm, I want you to become well known,' Mr. Muhammad told me one day. 'Because if you are well known, it will make *me* better known,' he went on. 'But, Brother Malcolm, there is something you need to know. You will grow to be hated when you become well known. Because usually people get jealous of public figures.' Nothing that Mr. Muhammad ever said to me was more prophetic."

"Malcolm was well aware of one source of hostility, which was government agencies, such as the police and the FBI," Ma said. The police had been on Elijah Muhammad's case at least since 1935, when the first of a series of confrontations between followers of Muhammad and the police took place. Muhammad told Malcolm that Detroit police officers provoked the confrontation by arresting a Muslim associated with Muhammad and accusing him of being a terrorist. When some black people vigorously responded to what they considered a case of harassment, the police and press labeled their response a riot. "This was a time when white supremacists, such as the Ku Klux Klan, were frequently brutalizing our people," Malcolm told us at Fruit of Islam classes. "But as far as I know neither the FBI nor the press ever called Klansmen terrorists, which is exactly what they were." Malcolm told us that the lesson he learned from hearing about that 1935 incident and others was that police departments throughout the country and J. Edgar Hoover's FBI could never be trusted to protect the lives and interests of black people.

Through the years, as he learned more about Hoover, he became convinced that the FBI director was an unreconstructed white supremacist.

Ma noted: "At one time Malcolm proposed to Mr. Muhammad that he and the N.O.I. take Hoover and the FBI to court and charge them with violating his and their constitutional rights. Top officials in Chicago, led by national secretary John Ali, rejected Malcolm's proposal."

Why they did so may be explained by an incident that took place in 1958 and was told to Ma by Malcolm. "Malcolm told me that one day when he, his wife, Betty, and John Ali and his wife, Minnie, were all home in a house they shared in New York City, members of the city's special police unit, called the Bureau of Special Services (BOSS), raided their home. They claimed to be looking for a woman named Margaret Dorsey. When Malcolm told them that they didn't know anyone by that name and requested to see a search warrant, the police ignored his request and insisted on questioning him and John Ali. Their questions, he said, seemed more designed to recruit him as a police informer than to elicit information about the mysterious Margaret Dorsey. He didn't take the bait. Malcolm said Ali was questioned at the same time. He told me that though he didn't suspect it at the time, he believed that it was then that John Ali was successfully recruited as an informant. After that he was never the same, Malcolm noted. I must say that in 1960, when Malcolm told me about this and other problems he was having with N.O.I. officials in Chicago, it was the first time he spoke to me about the Nation's official business. We often talked about many things, but until then he never discussed their official business with me because he felt it wasn't proper to do so. Also, because he knew how I personally felt about the N.O.I."

Malcolm was well aware that harassing incidents such as the one in 1935 and the one he personally experienced in 1958 were almost routine for the police and FBI when dealing with what they considered dangerous black militants. The same kind of harassment had been inflicted on Marcus Garvey, his father, and many other black individuals and organizations that stressed the need for a powerful, unified, self-determining black community in this country, one that

controlled its own internal politics and economic and cultural resources. The name Nation of Islam was reflective of the attitude of
Malcolm and many others in the organization, for they saw themselves as part of a nation within a nation. On at least one occasion in
his autobiography, Malcolm referred to "Our Nation." It was probably that concept, more than any other, that distinguished Malcolm
and those who thought like him from members of more traditional
black civil-rights organizations. It was also a position considered
very dangerous and divisive by people like Hoover and their government agencies. So they made their move on the N.O.I.

One of the first things government agencies try to do in such
situations is develop an informant or informants within the targeted
organization. Malcolm knew how they moved, as shown in the following statement from his autobiography: "Black agents were sent
to infiltrate us. But the white man's 'secret' spy often proved, first of
all, a black man. I can't say *all* of them, of course, there's no way to
know—but some of them, after joining us, and hearing, seeing and
feeling the truth for every black man, revealed their roles to us.
Some resigned from the white man's agencies and came to work in
the Nation of Islam. A few kept their jobs to counterspy, telling us
the white man's statements and plans about our Nation."

"What Malcolm didn't take seriously enough in those early years,"
Ma said, "was the possibility that government agencies would be
able to infiltrate into the highest level of the N.O.I. He truly wanted
to believe that all of its officials were as deeply committed to its declared agenda as were himself, his brothers, and his sister Hilda. By
1960, Malcolm was not only hearing rumors about corruption among
N.O.I. officials in Chicago, he was beginning to believe them. But
he wasn't sure just what to do. By that time, John Ali was national
secretary and controlled practically everyone in the Chicago headquarters. His chief allies were Elijah Muhammad's daughter, Ethel
Sharrieff, the supreme instructor for Muslim sisters, and her husband, Raymond Sharrieff, supreme captain of the Fruit of Islam, the
Nation's military wing.

"Since Mr. Muhammad had moved from Chicago to Phoenix, Ari-
zona, because of his severe asthma, John Ali's power had increased
to the extent that rumors were floating around that Mr. Muhammad

himself was afraid of him. There were now three power centers for the N.O.I.—headquarters in Chicago, where John Ali, Raymond Sharrieff, and Herbert Muhammad reigned supreme; Phoenix, where Mr. Muhammad and his entourage lived; and Harlem, where Malcolm was based at Temple Seven. Though concerned about Elijah Muhammad's illness, Malcolm was pleased that Muhammad was out of Chicago, where the influence of his enemies was more direct. In Phoenix, Malcolm at least had opportunities to speak with Muhammad away from the glaring Judas eyes and large ears of Ali, Sharrieff, and Herbert Muhammad." There were still problems, however. I once heard Malcolm tell Ma that the minute he left a Phoenix meeting with Mr. Muhammad, John Ali, Raymond Sharrieff, or Herbert Muhammad were flying in to oppose any suggestions he had made.

Ma continued: "Malcolm told me that one of his biggest regrets was having fished John Ali into the Nation. For a while they were so close that John Ali knew Malcolm's moves better than anyone else in the N.O.I., including his own brothers. He used his increasing influence over Elijah Muhammad to become the chief shaper of the organization's present and future. He had a very limited vision of the N.O.I. and strongly opposed Malcolm's efforts to broaden its agenda."

What John Ali and his allies were concerned about was acquiring as much money as possible, Ma said. "It was their obsession with acquiring money that led to rumors that some N.O.I. officials were meeting secretly with white supremacists in the White Citizens Council, the Ku Klux Klan, and the American Nazi Party in the early 1960s. Rumors surfaced of a million-dollar offer to be supplied by a Texas oil millionaire, with which they were supposed to buy land and relocate as many black people as possible out of the inner cities. They were also to stress even more emphatically separatism as a solution to the race problem in this country. In return, the white supremacists would persuade government agencies to adopt a hands off policy regarding *internal* N.O.I. confrontations. When Rockwell attended the N.O.I.'s annual convention in Chicago on February 25, 1962, his presence solidified the agreement with John Ali and his minions in Chicago, which explained why they weren't interested in taking the FBI to court for violating the N.O.I.'s constitutional rights, as Malcolm consistently proposed."

I left the N.O.I. in 1961 mainly because of the now strong rumors of the N.O.I.-Nazi alliance. At the time I was sixteen years old. Ma had already left in 1959 because of those rumors and a general dissatisfaction with what she considered the heartless way members were treated by the officials in Chicago. Later that year, though no longer a member, I attended an N.O.I. rally in Washington, D.C., with friends who were still in the Fruit of Islam. It was at that rally that I actually saw George Lincoln Rockwell, head of the Nazis, and his partner, John Patten, sitting in the front row. My friends Brother Willis James, a former nationally ranked professional boxer, Brother Bussbee, and Brother Kenny 2X were as disgusted as I was, but they remained in the Nation because they, along with three other brothers, were Malcolm's bodyguards when he came to Boston. Except for Brother Kenny, who was the smallest of the six, they averaged six feet three inches in height. All six had been fished into the N.O.I. by Malcolm and remained loyal to him before and after his split from the group. They also still had a strong loyalty to Ma, though she was no longer a member. Their children and babies were enrolled in the school and day-care center she had established.

Some people have criticized Uncle Malcolm for not leaving the N.O.I. as soon as he learned about the million-dollar alliance with the American Nazi Party. "That's easy for someone to say who hasn't believed in someone and something as deeply as Malcolm believed in Mr. Muhammad," Ma declared. "I didn't have a strong belief in Mr. Muhammad, so I could leave without any problem. Malcolm was a true believer in Mr. Muhammad. He didn't want to believe anything wrong about the organization to which he had committed his life, and when he did start believing something was wrong, he wanted to put it all on John Ali in Chicago and not Elijah Muhammad himself. We Littles are not prone to show emotion, under any circumstances, but when Malcolm first told me of his suspicions about the N.O.I.-Nazi alliance, I could see how agitated and hurt he was. 'They're messing up everything we've tried to do,' he said over and over. I don't know if anyone outside of that tight circle in Chicago and Rockwell know the whole story about that alliance and who ended up with the million dollars."

That million dollars wasn't the only money being pumped into Chicago. By 1962, because of Uncle Malcolm and some of the productive people he had fished into the N.O.I., money was steadily pouring into Chicago from throughout the country. Besides direct donations from other temples, they received funds from Muhammad Ali's boxing earnings, from weekly sales of over 100,000 copies of *Muhammad Speaks,* and from large donations made by the faithful on the annual Savior's Day, a tribute to Elijah Muhammad. "Malcolm wanted to use some of that money to make the N.O.I. more economically independent," Ma said. "He had a plan to connect it up with black farmers in the South and to buy farms up for sale and form farm cooperatives with the others. He first proposed this to Mr. Muhammad in 1958. He knew the money was there because Aubrey Barnette, the N.O.I.'s national treasurer, whom he had persuaded Mr. Muhammad to hire, kept him abreast of the amount of money pouring into Chicago."

After leaving the Nation because of the corruption he witnessed in the Chicago office, Brother Aubrey provided details of the financial corruption in articles published in the *Chicago Defender, New York Times, Saturday Evening Post,* and *Chicago Daily News.* Documents from the First Pacific Bank of Chicago, according to Brother Aubrey, showed that some $19 million passed through account number 20–198–7. "That's a whole lot of money," Ma noted. "It could keep those sybarites in Chicago and Phoenix living very well."

So the money was there for the farm project proposed by Uncle Malcolm. The person he wanted to work with him on the project was Brother Frederick Entzminger, a longtime friend from Temple Eleven. "Brother Frederick had helped Malcolm so often," Ma said, "that he was shy about asking him to do something else. He asked me to speak to him, since Brother Frederick was also my friend. I told him I would do so with one condition—that Minister Louis X, head of Temple Eleven, not be involved. I just didn't trust him. Malcolm reluctantly agreed to my condition and spoke with Brother Frederick. He was excited about the project."

Ma, Malcolm, and Brother Frederick met at our home on Massachusetts Avenue to discuss the project. After several meetings they agreed to begin purchasing farmland in late 1960 or early 1961. Brother Frederick was to set up a Massachusetts corporation that would focus on transportation and marketing. The hard part was to get Chicago's approval of the project. Years later, Brother Frederick told me that Malcolm, in strict confidence, related to him that Mr. Muhammad was too sick to run the N.O.I. and that John Ali, in effect, was now running things. Brother Frederick found out personally about the corruption in Chicago when he refused to go along with John Ali's plan to put all purchased farmland under the names of members of Mr. Muhammad's family. When he refused, he was expelled from the N.O.I., which devastated him. Despite what Brother Frederick had found out about corruption, he still loved being part of the Nation. Even today, he faults Malcolm for not somehow arranging his reinstatement. He just doesn't understand that by that time Malcolm had little influence with the crew in Chicago.

When Malcolm informed Brother Frederick about Elijah Muhammad's being too sick to run the N.O.I., he didn't mention to him the rumors about Muhammad having fathered children out of wedlock. My uncle was not one to spread unconfirmed rumors. However, there is some evidence that by 1960 he was beginning to have some doubts about Muhammad's living up to the moral code that he had established for members of the Nation and which was sternly enforced by temple ministers. It was a code that harshly condemned fornication outside of marriage, a code which had been used to expel Reginald from the N.O.I., isolating him so that his own brothers and sisters, still in the organization, were forbidden any contact with him. Now Elijah Muhammad was supposedly involved in that very behavior himself.

Malcolm could no longer ignore Muhammad's transgressions personally, though he could do so publicly. Two letters—one written on September 4, 1955, the other on July 19, 1960—show his personal change. Both letters are reports to Muhammad on activities at Temple Seven. Both address him as "My Dear Holy Apostle" and are signed: *"As-Salaam-Alaikum,* your brother and servant, Malcolm X." The revealing difference is in a statement at the top of the letters: In the first, Uncle Malcolm wrote: *"As-Salaam-Alaikum:* In the Holy name of the Almighty ALLAH, our great and merciful and most Beneficent Savior, who came in the person of Master W. F. Muhammad, the Mighty Deliverer, to whom all praise is due, and the Holy Name of His Last and Greatest Servant, the *Little Lamb Without Spots or Blemishes,* [italics mine] the Honorable ELIJAH MUHAMMAD." The second, much less effusive, statement reads: "As-Salaam-Alaikum. In the Holy Name of ALLAH, the Beneficent, the Merciful, To Whom all praise is due, whom we forever thank for giving us the most Honorable ELIJAH MUHAMMAD."

"Between 1955 and 1960 Mr. Muhammad had ceased being 'the Little Lamb without spots or blemishes' to Malcolm," Ma noted.

TEN The Split, Part 2: Recommitment of Faith

When reading the letter Malcolm wrote to Elijah Muhammad on July 19, 1960, his attempt to smooth over the rumors he had been hearing became obvious. Malcolm wrote:

> I have been following you for 12 years (since 1948) now, an active helper for about six years (here at #7). From the start I have studied those in the Bible who did most to help spread the "Gospel of Jesus" and tried my best to copy them or to walk in their footsteps without anyone knowing it . . . because since they were the most successful followers of that Jesus, I figured that the best way to be a successful follower (and helper) to you is to imitate their tactics and efforts. I've kept my eye closely on the prophecy to avoid being a doubting Thomas, betraying Judas or denying Peter. Instead, I've secretly tried to be a Fisherman, a Gospel Spreading Paul, a letter-writing (Journalist) Paul, a Traveling Paul, a diplomat to all classes of people . . . and ALLAH has blessed me. I would never tell this to anyone but you because no one else would understand me.

All those Christian references are deliberate, since both Uncle Malcolm and Muhammad were sons of itinerant Baptist preachers. Uncle Malcolm continued:

> Also, in picturing you as Moses, I've studied his work to see the tactics of those who helped him, and how they did it, and the area in which he was most in need of help. I studied the role of

Aaron. It is for this reason that I've never feared to go anywhere, anytime, and represent you. And I have found, that whenever you send me, and tell me what to say yourself, it has produced such shocking results that most people look upon me as *extremely gifted* . . . but what they really fail to see is that all my success or fame had come from actually saying that "Mr. Muhammad says . . ." ALLAH has also blessed me to be able easily to learn how people really think and especially what they think of me. You told me about five years ago (upon returning from my first trip to Atlanta) that you wanted me to become known, because the more known I became the more I could make you known . . . but that with publicity and popularity comes jealously, envy and many enemies. I've lived to see the fulfillment of all these things.

After reading that heartfelt, skillfully written letter, Ma said, "Mr. Elijah Muhammad could have no doubts that Malcolm was aware that something was rotten in the state of the Nation of Islam." He also had to be aware that Malcolm, despite what he was hearing from the crew in Chicago, was still a loyal follower and supporter. When he wrote about "jealousy, envy and many enemies," he was not referring to Mr. Muhammad but to N.O.I. officials in Chicago who either outright rejected or considerably modified any proposal he made to broaden the Nation's outreach and impact. Potentially the most devastating problem confronting Malcolm was persistent rumors that some key N.O.I. officials were wheeling and dealing with white supremacists. "When the rumors became more persistent," Ma said, "Malcolm knew he had to do something. He went to his friends, the Alexanders, and asked them to publish an editorial attacking white supremacy. That might at least give pause to any N.O.I. officials seeking to deal with white supremacists. The paper responded with an editorial 'Concept at Liberty' in its April 30, 1959, issue. It had little effect. The rumors got louder and louder."

Later, said Ma, Uncle Malcolm got hold of a letter written by J. B. Stoner, imperial wizard of the Ku Klux Klan, in which he discussed dealing with N.O.I. officials. Malcolm wanted this letter published as part of an effort to possibly shame them from dealing with white supremacists. Once again, Ma came to his aid. "I was friendly with Alfred Q. Jarrette, a former associate editor of the *Los Angeles Dispatch*. He was also a Muslim, not of the N.O.I. variety, who had once lived in Iran. Dr. Jarrette, in 1956, had gone to Atlanta to cover a speech delivered by Malcolm during the first Southern Goodwill Tour of the Brotherhood of Islam, which was a gathering of orthodox and unorthodox Muslims in America. Chicago was not enthused about Malcolm's participation in the Muslim fellowship, but he was determined to develop and maintain contact with other Muslims. He was careful to never mix these activities with N.O.I. business, thus depriving his opponents of ammunition to use against him. It was then that Dr. Jarrette, who covered the gathering for his paper, heard and met Malcolm for the first time. A year later, he interviewed him for his paper. By 1961, Dr. Jarrette had left the paper and founded the Great Western Book Publishing Company." Investors in the new publishing project included Jarrette, Ma, and Mrs. Violet Long of Los Angeles. Her daughter, Janette Long, and I later became friends when she moved to the East Coast. It was Janette who took the photo of me and Malcolm's children at the 1964 World's Fair in New York City.

Dr. Jarrette, said Ma, was the first writer in America to approach Uncle Malcolm about doing a book on himself and the Nation. "Malcolm refused the suggestions because he didn't completely trust Dr. Jarrette. However, in 1961, he offered the publisher a deal. He still refused to cooperate with doing a book but was prepared to support a magazine article if Dr. Jarrette agreed to print the Stoner letter. The deal was cut in 1962, and the premier issue of *Muslims: Black Metropolis* was published. It included the Stoner letter. N.O.I. officials in Chicago, especially John Ali, went ballistic, suspecting that Malcolm had been responsible for the letter reaching the public. They became more determined than ever to put him in his place. All of Malcolm's efforts to block the deal were to no avail; John Ali and that bunch in Chicago were too obsessed with money. They were way beyond shaming out of their corruption."

The anguish caused Malcolm by N.O.I. officials in Chicago scheming with white supremacists paled beside that caused by Elijah Muhammad's out-of-wedlock babies. For years, at least since

1955, rumors had been circulating through Muslim temples about the babies, whose mothers were formerly Muhammad's secretaries. It seems that no one, not his wife, not his religiously devout children, not even the devastating effects that public knowledge of this would have on his organizations, could stop Mr. Muhammad from indulging in extramarital relations.

Initially, Uncle Malcolm admittedly refused to believe the rumors. "There was never any specific moment when I admitted the situation to myself," he writes in his autobiography. "In the way that the human mind can do, somehow I slid over admitting to myself the ugly fact, even as I began dealing with it."

More than anything else, Muhammad's involvement with those women set in motion the series of events that led to the final split between Malcolm and the Nation of Islam. It's important to remember that before the white supremacists began sniffing around and before the scheming by John Ali and some members of Muhammad's family in Chicago, his extramarital relationships with several of his secretaries provided N.O.I.'s enemies with salacious material to use against it.

Ma had an intriguing anecdote about the out-of-wedlock-babies saga. "Malcolm got word," she said, "that when the FBI first found out about the babies, it considered leaking a story that Malcolm was the father of the children, another indication that by then they considered him a far greater threat than Elijah Muhammad. They knew that he had once been engaged to Evelyn and thought that would make the rumors more believable. It's indicative of Malcolm's commitment to Elijah Muhammad's agenda that for a brief time he thought that it might be a good move for the N.O.I. 'It would be less destructive to us if the rumors were about me than Mr. Muhammad,' he told me, 'since I'm not married and have no wife to be hurt.' I was totally opposed to him doing that and told him that if such rumors began surfacing, I would come forward and tell the truth. He knew I was serious and never brought it up to me again."

According to Ma, "We now know from the FBI files that they were aware of the babies and made sure that he and other important N.O.I. officials knew that they knew about them. It was a powerful sword of Damocles to hold over Elijah Muhammad and the Nation. I believe the FBI used their knowledge of the babies to shut Elijah Muhammad's mouth. The knowledge was also used by John Ali and his crew as a trump card to force Mr. Muhammad to support their position in the ongoing struggle with Malcolm about the policies and direction of the organization. Whatever his faults, I am convinced that Elijah Muhammad loved Malcolm like a son. He shared personal experiences with him that he shared with no one else except his mother, Sister Marie. He was impressed with Malcolm's knowledge of history and his remarkable ability to communicate with all kinds of people. But Elijah was in no position to defend Malcolm because of the Chicago faction's knowledge about his out-of-wedlock babies."

Seriously complicating the situation for Malcolm, Ma noted, "was the fact that one of the women Elijah Muhammad had impregnated was Sister Evelyn, the same Sister Evelyn to whom Malcolm had once been engaged and whom he had sent to Chicago to be a secretary to Elijah Muhammad. He regarded her as an innocent victim about whom he felt pangs of guilt.

Ma had a different perspective about Sister Evelyn and the other women. "I deeply cared for Evelyn, having once pressured Malcolm to marry her, but when news of her involvement with Elijah Muhammad reached me, I told Malcolm he shouldn't feel any guilt about the situation. He had done all he could do to help Evelyn. She and the others were grown women who did have some choice about involving themselves in sexual relationships with Elijah Muhammad."

Maybe Sister Evelyn and the other women had done the same thing Uncle Malcolm did when he wrote in his autobiography, "I don't think that I could say anything which better testified to the depth of my faith in Mr. Muhammad than that I totally and absolutely rejected my own intelligence. I simply refused to believe. I didn't want Allah to "burn my brain," as I felt the brain of my brother Reginald had been burned for harboring evil thoughts about Mr. Muhammad. . . ." Malcolm was convinced, Ma said, that "whereas the N.O.I. could survive hostility from government agencies, from the white press, from some Christian preachers and some civil rights leaders, even from overt white supremacists, survival itself would be at stake if word of Elijah Muhammad's out-of-wedlock babies reached the public without careful preparation for the storm that was sure to follow."

First he had to prepare members of the Nation of Islam by changing the focus of his teachings. He began asking them to consider whether a person's good deeds outweighed his bad ones and whether the accomplishments and contributions of a person outweighed his personal weaknesses. "But around 1963," Malcolm wrote in his autobiography, "if anyone noticed, I spoke less and less of religion. I taught social doctrine to Muslims, and current events, and politics. I stayed wholly off the subject of morality." He knew that there were hostile members of the press who were lying in wait for him with questions about rumors they had heard about the babies. He admitted to sometimes feeling like a fool and noted that during his street running days one of the worst insults one could hurl at a street hustler was that he had been duped.

As those feelings buffeted him, Uncle Malcolm confided in very few people other than his wife, Betty, and Ma. One of those few was Minister Louis X, head of Temple Eleven in Boston. In more than a few paragraphs and film clips taken of Uncle Malcolm in the late 1950s and very early 1960s, somewhere in the background can usually be seen a boyish-looking minister, then known as Louis X, now known as Louis Farrakhan. Those visuals, along with the ongoing controversy about Malcolm's assassination and Farrakhan's emergence as leader of a revamped Nation of Islam, prompt many people to speculate on, and inquire about, the relationship between him and Malcolm.

The immediate answer is that at one time the relationship was productive and close—that of any ambitious, intelligent, and talented young man to a mentor under whom he had studied and from whom he had learned. Minister Louis confirmed this with comments made in a 1996 interview in the *New Yorker.* He noted that in 1955, while doing a gig in a Chicago nightclub, he went to hear Mr. Elijah Muhammad speak. He liked what he heard, but "I wouldn't call it a conversion experience, because I wasn't thoroughly convinced." The convincing happened when he later heard Uncle Malcolm preach for the first time in Boston. "I'd never heard any man talk like that," he

said. "Then I was convinced that this was where I wanted to be."
Once fished into the N.O.I., Louis provided the entertainment before
Malcolm provided the teaching. In one of two mentions of Farrakhan in his autobiography, Malcolm included him among a group
of young Muslim ministers whom he was praising for their contributions to the Nation of Islam. About the current Minister Farrakhan,
whom he had selected to succeed him as minister of Boston's Temple Eleven, Malcolm wrote: "The Boston Temple's outstanding
young Minister Louis X, previously a well-known and rising popular singer called 'The Charmer,' had written our Nation's popular
first song, titled 'White Man's Heaven Is a Black Man's Hell.' Minister Louis X had also authored our first play 'Orgena' ("A Negro"
spelled backwards); its theme was the all-black trial of a symbolic
white man for his world crimes against non-whites; found guilty,
sentenced to death, he was dragged off shouting about all he had
done for 'the nigra people.'" I still remember a compelling performance in the play by a light-skinned, green-eyed member of the
Fruit of Islam. His performance as a "white devil" was so believable
that he actually frightened many of us, even those who, like myself,
were young teenagers.

   Orgena was first presented in Boston in May 19–21, 1961, at the
Connelly Memorial Theatre, located on the corner of Massachu-
setts Avenue and Norway Street, right around the corner from the
Christian Scientist Mother Church. I sometimes wonder if May 19,
Malcolm's birth date, was deliberately chosen for the play's pre-
miere performance.

   Following the Boston performances, which attracted large audiences, *Orgena* was presented in New York City, Philadelphia, and
Chicago. To Malcolm, the play, whose opening scene dealt with the
exploitation of Native Americans by European settlers, was a good
public-relations vehicle for the N.O.I. as well as a means by which
to educate audiences about the real history of this country, as con-
trasted to that taught in public and private schools. He was anxious
to make it available to the general public, a position that caused further conflict between himself and key officials in the Chicago headquarters.

   Those officials, namely, national secretary John Ali, its supreme captain, Raymond Sharrieff, and two of Mr. Muhammad's children, Herbert and Ethel, formed a formidable anti–Malcolm X faction, which generally opposed anything they thought might enhance Malcolm's influence and power. Because they saw a national tour of *Orgena* as something that would do just that, they used their influence with Muhammad to block a tour by the play. Muhammad agreed with them, but only up to a point. He said that the play could be toured but presented only to members of the Nation of Islam. In Christian terminology that is called "preaching to the choir." Malcolm, though disappointed, accepted Muhammad's compromise. The incident, although not known to the general public, graphically illustrated divisions that had developed within the N.O.I. "Louis X wasn't blind," Ma said. "He carefully noted all the intrigue and was aware that Malcolm's support and the enthusiastic response the play received from N.O.I. audiences opened up all kinds of possibilities. Malcolm spoke highly of him to me, once saying that there was no one in the Nation better to work with than Louis. I don't think he ever told Louis that, but I'm convinced Louis knew how Malcolm felt."

Ma, however, didn't share her brother's feelings about Louis X. "I was always wary of him. He had too much of a lean and hungry look for me. More importantly, he wasn't his own man. His mother made all his important decisions."

Ma was a strong-minded woman herself but, as she said, "I knew that Malcolm would eventually make his own decisions. He would listen to other people, including me, digest and analyze what we said, and then decide what action to take. He wasn't about to let us make his decisions. I didn't get the same impression with Louis Eugene Walcott and Mrs. Walcott. Whatever she said or believed, Louis said or believed. For instance, she was the one who advised him to suspend me from Temple Eleven. She also advised that he not handle the suspension himself but to let Malcolm handle it. Malcolm had to come to Temple Eleven and personally suspend me. I understand why he did what he did, but I always believed he should have forced Louis to handle it himself."

Another problem with Louis X, as far as Ma was concerned, was that "I knew that Malcolm had initially chosen him as his successor at Temple Eleven because of his light skin. Malcolm was very much aware of the light-skin, dark-skin thing in Boston. At that time, it would be hard enough to talk about the Nation of Islam to such people even if a Colin Powell–like person was the spokesperson; with a dark-skinned person, it would have been nearly impossible. Malcolm, still striving to build up the N.O.I., took the position that if anyone could make even a slight dent among people with that attitude, it was Louis X."

Because of the hostility toward Malcolm coming from envious officials in Chicago, he needed all the allies he could get. Among his few close friends in the N.O.I.'s hierarchy were two of Elijah Muhammad's sons, Akbar and Wallace, both of whom eventually left because of disagreements with policies advocated by the Chicago faction. Wallace later returned and took the organization, under a new name, on a new path, toward more orthodox Islam, after Elijah Muhammad's death. Louis Farrakhan kept the old name for the organization he now heads. One person whom Malcolm felt close to and greatly admired, Muhammad's mother, died before the more serious divisions erupted.

When Malcolm told Ma that he had confided in Louis X about the best way to handle the potential babies-born-out-of-wedlock scandal, she warned him about getting caught in the middle of the situation but went along with his plan to deal with the pregnancies, if possible by finding some theory that would work under orthodox Islamic law. "I supported my brother because I knew he still deeply believed in the N.O.I.'s agenda as a means for liberating our people. By then he had lost much faith in Elijah Muhammad but not the organization itself. However, I urged him not to directly attack Mr. Muhammad, to let him sink of his own weight. That way he couldn't be blamed for it."

Ma was among the few people, including Betty, who knew just how deeply Malcolm had been hurt by the situation. She was so concerned about his emotional and mental state that she went to Chicago to see Muhammad. "I told him that as a father of sons, he should understand how Malcolm was being torn apart. I reminded him of Malcolm's immense contributions to the Nation, how he had made it an organization known all over the country and much of the world, how he devoted most of his waking hours pursuing N.O.I. business, how he still preached what 'the Honorable Elijah Muhammad says' when dealing with the press and the public, thus showing his acceptance of his leadership. I also reminded him that both he and his mother, Sister Marie Muhammad, had often expressed affection for Malcolm, how he had sometimes referred to him as 'my son, my seventh son.' Mr. Muhammad was cordial, even friendly, as I spoke, but I left him feeling that he was a sick man who no longer controlled his organization."

In fact, as far back as 1957, there had been rumors about Elijah Muhammad's health problems. "There was so much concern," Ma recalled, "that there was internal speculation about who would take over if Mr. Muhammad was unable to continue, Malcolm or his son, Wallace Muhammad. In 1958, when Wallace was indicted for failing to report to the draft board, the *Pittsburgh Courier* commented that Malcolm might have to run the N.O.I. The commentary quoted Louis X as saying that if Malcolm was unable to take control, he would do so. This was a gambit by Louis X. He knew that Mr. Muhammad, not Malcolm, was the sick person. Louis was moving cautiously because he was well aware of the fate of others who had opposed Mr. Muhammad. He was not going to put himself on the outside, as Kallat Muhammad had done in 1935, when he split from Mr. Muhammad and formed another group. Kallat Muhammad was Mr. Muhammad's younger brother, who, in 1933, claimed that W. D. Fard had designated him as his successor. In 1935, after an internal struggle with his brother, Kallat Muhammad and another brother, Augustus Muhammad, who was Elijah Muhammad's chief assistant in Chicago, left him to form their own group in Detroit. Neither of the brothers had much concern for the black community. They basically looked upon it as something you prey upon. Soon after leaving, they both died. It was said that Mr. Muhammad called their deaths an act of Allah, punishing them for their hypocritical acts. W. D. Fard had disappeared earlier. Reginald had heard rumors about Mr. Muhammad's involvement in the disappearance of W. D. Fard. He also had heard other unconfirmed rumors about Mr. Muhammad and had witnessed some things that disturbed him. I was, and still am, convinced that the federal government knew something about Mr. Muhammad's connection to those two deaths and Fard's disappearance but did nothing to press the matter. They dismissed it as just some darkies killing other darkies. It was also another thing to hold over his head."

Despite all the problems, Malcolm continued devoting his life to the Nation. "The FBI probably assumed that Malcolm would leave the N.O.I. after learning of Mr. Muhammad's liaisons with his secretaries," Ma said, "but they had misjudged the depth of his commitment to the N.O.I.'s message." Though devastated by the information, Malcolm went about his work. "Malcolm didn't just reach out to people with his teaching," Ma said. "He actually did things for people. He didn't just talk Islam; he lived it. He visited the sick in hospitals and at home. He was available to listen and give advice. As a result, Temple Seven was a place that really worked. It was also the highest-grossing temple in the country, an accomplishment it achieved without beating people up who didn't make quotas, as was done in many other temples, including Temple Eleven. There the beatings took place in the basement. Minister Louis X lived right next door."

Among the people helped by Malcolm at Temple Seven was Captain Joseph, whom he had rescued from alcoholism by fishing him into the N.O.I. Joseph was accepted into a substance-abuse program Malcolm had set up at Temple Seven. Its basic tenet was to stress to substance abusers that by abusing themselves and wreaking havoc on their neighborhoods, they had become willing, destructive tools of a system whose goal was to keep them, their families, and their people unfocused and powerless. Because of the program's success with Joseph and others, it was offered to New York City's government. Of course, the offer was rejected. No plan, even a successful one, would be accepted from Malcolm X. Joseph, by the way, later became one of Malcolm's bitterest enemies because of a misguided belief that Malcolm blocked his appointment to the position of national supreme captain in Chicago. He became so bitter that he eagerly became John Ali's man in Temple Seven, never realizing that the Chicago crew regarded him contemptuously as a little minnow who was still considered a wife beater. His only use to them was as a spy to keep them informed about Malcolm. I once heard Malcolm say to Ma, "Everything I do, Ella, Joseph takes to John Ali."

Though Malcolm continued to believe in the N.O.I.'s agenda, if not in Muhammad himself, Ma, after the meeting with Muhammad, was convinced that the organization, under John Ali and his Chicago crew, was too far off track to make continued efforts worthwhile. Many nights during that time between 1960 and 1963, I saw her and Malcolm involved in deep, sometimes painful discussions about what was happening to the N.O.I. Ma later told me that her position was unambivalent. "I told Malcolm that he must either fully control the direction of the N.O.I. or leave it. I was convinced by now that Elijah Muhammad was no longer in control and that the leadership in Chicago had no vision and no intention of creating an organization that could be a mighty force in liberating our people. Some of the temple ministers were serious about liberation, but unfortunately, because of the way the Nation was structured, they had little influence and no power. I again reminded him that the Little brothers and Hilda had given life to a near comatose organization. Even before Malcolm came onboard, Wilfred and Philbert had set up three or four temples. Malcolm greatly accelerated the pace. The Little siblings, I reminded him, hadn't come to the N.O.I. with no idea of what was happening in the world. They had seen and heard their Garveyite parents in action. With their intelligence, talent, commitment, and organizational skills, they could take care of business with or without the N.O.I. If Elijah Muhammad had stuck with them instead of listening to people like John Ali, Raymond and Ethel Sharrieff, Herbert Muhammad, Captain Joseph, Louis X, and a few others, the Nation would have worked wonders among our people. The FBI knew that, which is why they were determined to destroy the N.O.I., as reflected by the Little siblings, and accommodate an N.O.I. under the control of self-indulgent, money-obsessed people like those in Chicago."

In response to Ma's suggestion that he either fully control the N.O.I. or leave it, Malcolm said he "didn't want to be a Brutus to Mr. Muhammad's Caesar." Even after discovering flaws in the Messenger, he wasn't prepared to deny the validity of the message. Unlike the Chicago crew, Malcolm still believed that the message should not be limited solely to those who joined the Nation. It was equally important to reach out to "lost-found Negroes." Malcolm was concerned about what other black people thought about the N.O.I.; John Ali seemingly didn't care. That this was a profound point of dissension between them is evidenced in an observation made by Malcolm in his autobiography:

> If I harbored any personal disappointment whatsoever, it was that privately I was convinced that our Nation of Islam could be an even greater force in the American black man's overall struggle—if we engaged in more *action*. By that, I mean I thought privately that we should have amended, or relaxed, our general non-engagement policy. . . .
>
> It could be heard increasingly in the Negro communities: "Those Muslims *talk* tough, but they never *do* anything, unless somebody bothers Muslims." I moved around among outsiders more than most other Muslim officials. I felt the very real potentiality that, considering the mercurial moods of the black masses, this labeling of Muslims as "talk only" could see us, powerful as we were, one day suddenly separated from the Negroes' front-line struggle.

According to Ma, Uncle shared these very private feelings with only a few people other than Aunt Betty and herself. They included Cong. Adam Clayton Powell Jr., Brother Lewis Micheaux, Harlem historian Dr. John Henrik Clarke, and Louis X. That's why she was so upset when Louis didn't support him in his ongoing struggles with the Chicago crew. "Malcolm's trust in Louis X remained intact," Ma said, "until events around the 1962 killing of N.O.I. member Ronald Stokes by a member of Los Angeles's notoriously racist police department." On April 27, 1962, Los Angeles police officers attacked fourteen unarmed N.O.I. men, one of whom, Ronald Stokes, was killed. Six others were seriously wounded. Ma said that Malcolm was bitterly angry following the unprovoked attack and wanted to go after Stokes's killer legally, if possible, otherwise, if necessary. "I urged him to stick to legal means, since they had a strong case and it was an issue about which the N.O.I. would receive strong support from the larger black community. Police brutality was something most every black adult knew about or often felt threatened by."

Malcolm moved to mobilize black public opinion. He put out a special issue of *Muhammad Speaks* that harshly condemned the killing of Stokes and spoke fervently about it at rallies throughout the country. I remember the Boston rally during which Malcolm showed us a chilling, blown-up photograph of Stokes's body. It stunned, angered, and galvanized us. Louis X was there reacting as emotionally as the rest of us. Ma was also present as a show of support. I don't think I had ever seen my uncle as angry as he was that day. As a seventeen-year-old, I sat mesmerized by the absolute fury in his voice, a fury we all shared by the time he finished speaking. Every now and then I would catch a glimpse of Louis X, who was intensely watching Malcolm. Years later, I realized that on that and other occasions he studied Malcolm the way one would study a textbook. What he learned can be seen in the Minister Louis Farrakhan we see today.

On March 29, 1962, there was another huge rally protesting the killing of Stokes in Detroit's Olympic Stadium. Eight thousand people were in attendance to hear Elijah Muhammad's reaction to the killing. To Malcolm's surprise and joy, Muhammad directly attacked the federal government for its inaction and called for a Justice Department investigation of the Los Angeles police for a possible civil-rights violation. Malcolm was even more pleased when Muhammad, in an unprecedented move, asked for a coalition on the issue between N.O.I. and civil-rights leaders like Harlem congressman Adam Clayton Powell Jr. He had long urged Muhammad to reach out in such a manner.

But Malcolm's joy didn't last long. The Chicago crew was strongly opposed to his angry response to the killing of Stokes, preferring to let it blow over. It was obvious they had won, Ma stated, when, in 1963, "Mr. Muhammad responded favorably to a call from a Los Angeles police official demanding that he order Malcolm to leave Los Angeles. When Elijah Muhammad ordered Malcolm to leave Los Angeles and return to New York City, Malcolm, still loyal, reluctantly went home as ordered."

He further angered the Chicago faction by proposing that the N.O.I. provide badly needed financial support for Stokes's widow and for the families of the six other Muslims severely wounded in the police attack. As usual, John Ali and his cohorts strongly opposed his proposal, insisting it would be too costly. Of course, there was also the dreaded possibility that it would also enhance Malcolm's prestige, and that would never do.

Though Louis X had responded just as emphatically and emotionally as most everyone else to Malcolm's reaction to the killing of Stokes, his support was not forthcoming when help was needed to combat Chicago's opposition to the way Malcolm handled the affair and his proposal to support the victims' families. When Malcolm asked Louis X to join him in delivering eulogies at Stokes's funeral, he was also rebuffed. Louis X, who had been gung ho when Malcolm spoke at the Stokes rally in Boston, cooled off considerably when Chicago showed its opposition. "Louis X's tepid response to events around the killing of Ronald Stokes finally convinced Malcolm that he should not be considered a trusted confidant," Ma said.

Several years later, when hearing or reading some of the vitriolic statements made by Minister Louis X, now Louis Farrakhan, about Malcolm after he left the N.O.I. and before and after his assassination, Ma and I remembered a night back in 1956 when a beaming Louis X, exuding charm and humility, thanked Malcolm for presenting him to N.O.I. members after he received his X. That Louis was a very different person, or so we thought, from the Louis of the harsh words. In reality, events have proved that they are one and the same person. "Louis had already decided whose side he was on," Ma said. "By the time the split became public in 1963, he had very little contact with Malcolm."

What made the split public was Malcolm's statement in response to the assassination of President John F. Kennedy, on November 22, 1963. Muhammad, fearful of possible repercussions from the government or even from the general public, including many black people, had ordered all his ministers to refuse comment on the assassination. Malcolm, in response to a direct question, violated that order with a statement that included the allusion of it being a case of "the chickens coming home to roost."

What he meant by that, Ma explained, was that if a government allows a climate of violence to exist among its people, that violence will eventually reach into the government itself. No one can deny that such a climate of violence existed in the United States in 1963. Earlier that year, civil-rights activist Medgar Evers had been murdered by a white supremacist on his own doorstep. Four adolescent black girls had been murdered by other white supremacists who blew up the Birmingham, Alabama, church which they were attending. Teenager Virgil Lamar Ware was also murdered in that city by white supremacists.

Birmingham was also the place where white-supremacist police chief Eugene "Bull" Connor had his officers sic dogs on civil-rights demonstrators and attacked them with water from fire hoses. In other cities in the South, homes, businesses, and churches were firebombed and demonstrators were brutalized, all without any effective response from the federal government, which basically said it had no jurisdiction. It was a state problem. All this happened in 1963 alone. It was in that violent climate that President Kennedy was assassinated.

No matter the accuracy of Malcolm's statement, the Chicago crew now had the smoking gun it had longed for. Malcolm was suspended. The split was now public. "I don't believe Elijah Muhammad would have suspended Malcolm for the 'chickens coming home to roost' statement if he had been free to act on his own," Ma insisted. "By that time, the Chicago crew had convinced him that Malcolm was a serious threat to the deal they had cut with the white supremacists and to money continuing to pour into headquarters."

ELEVEN An Awakening

Malcolm's split from the Nation of Islam was not only due to his disappointment and disillusionment over Elijah Muhammad's out-of-wedlock children and his disgust and anger over the financial and moral corruption of N.O.I. officials in Chicago; it was also the result of his growing belief that the Islam taught to members of the Nation was not compatible with the Islam of the Holy Qu'ran. "By the early 1960s," Ma said, "Malcolm had become convinced of the need for our Afro-Americans to have a stronger connection with orthodox Islam. He knew that this could never happen as long as the N.O.I. was teaching that Elijah Muhammad was a divine being. As he moved closer to a more Sunni traditional Islam, the crew in Chicago became more and more agitated, considering this a threat to their financial well-being, since the members' belief in the divinity of Elijah Muhammad kept the money pouring in."

This religious side of Malcolm is too often ignored or downplayed by those who write about him. In doing so, they have to dismiss his own words when he declared: "I don't pretend to be a divine man, but I do believe in divine guidance, divine power, and in the fulfillment of divine prophecy."

Uncle Malcolm's religious side was recognized by a young preacher named Rev. Edward Alston, whom Peter Bailey, a journalist and the co-author of this book, heard when attending Queens Chapel A.M.E. Church with his father in Hilton Head, South Carolina. Peter was surprised to hear the pastor of that very small, 133-year-old traditional black Christian church urge the congregation to lead spiritual lives of commitment "like Richard Allen, Daniel Payne, Martin Luther King Jr., and Malcolm X."

That Malcolm had such beliefs really should not be surprising, since he was the son and grandson of Baptist preachers and was greatly influenced by Elijah Muhammad, who was the son of a Baptist preacher as well as the cofounder of the Nation of Islam. Like many others, Uncle Malcolm went through a period of religious observance as a teenager and young adult and a return to it as he matured. Of course, when he returned to religion, it was not to Christianity, the religion of his childhood and young adulthood, but to Islam as taught by Elijah Muhammad. "Malcolm, even as a youngster, never seemed convinced that Christianity had anything to offer him," Ma noted. "His experiences with the white Christians who had murdered his father and institutionalized his mother and the black Christians in Lansing who offered no help to his family had already soured him on that religion. When he first came to live with me in Boston, prodded by Aunt Sas and Aunt Gracie, he dutifully went to church, but his heart was never really in it. I never tried to influence him about Christianity because of my own ambiguous feelings. I had been raised a Christian and remember as a child riding in the wagon with Pa John as he made the round of churches in Reynolds, Butler, and Talbot County to preach. As I got older, I began to see the connection of Christianity with white supremacy. One of the most effective arguments used by the N.O.I. when it fished black Christians was that Christianity was 'the white man's religion,' Malcolm used that argument very effectively when fishing."

Ma mentioned accompanying Pa John when he preached at churches in rural southwestern Georgia. On a visit to southwest Georgia, Peter and I came across one of those churches in Junction City. Bethel Baptist Church was first established in 1869 and, according to their deacons, is the oldest black church in the area. The current church was built in 1918. I vaguely remember Ma mentioning it when she told me about attending various churches with her grandfather. We saw several Little and extended family graves from the late 1800s and early 1900s in the church cemetery.

Malcolm's condemnation of Christianity was not total. He readily acknowledged the courage and contribution of such outstanding black Christians as David Walker and Henry McNeal Turner. Walker, in 1829, wrote his brilliant and fiery *David Walker's Appeal*, which was directed "to the Colored Citizens of the World, But in Particular, and Very Expressly to Those of the United States of America." In it he wrote:

> I believe if any candid person would take the trouble to go through the Southern and Western sections of this country, and could have the heart to see the cruelties inflicted by these *Christians* [italics his] on us, he would say, That the Algerians, Turks and Arabs treat their dogs a thousand times better than we are treated by the Christians. . . . See the hundreds and thousands of us that are thrown into the seas by Christians, and murdered by them in other ways. They cram us into their vessel holds in chains and in hand-cuffs—men, women and children, all together!! O! save us, we pray thee, Thou God of Heaven and of earth, from the devouring hands of the White Christians!!!"

Turner, a bishop in the A.M.E. Church, according to the book *Black Leaders of the Nineteenth Century*, realized that

> blacks must reject all teachings of the white church that confirmed their inferior status. He was particularly sensitive to the symbolic significance of "whiteness" in Christian teachings and discouraged singing of such verses as "Now wash me and I shall be whiter than snow," explaining that the purpose was to make one clean, not white. More dramatic was his assertion, often repeated, that "God is a Negro." When this statement drew criticism from whites—and from a few blacks—Turner patiently pointed out that historically every race of people had portrayed God in its own image; but he also lashed out at those whites and "all of the fool Negroes" who "believed that God is a white skinned, blue-eyed, projecting-nosed, compressed-lipped and finely-robed *white* gentleman, sitting upon a throne somewhere in the heavens." Turner was deeply disturbed by the negative influence of white Christianity upon the black psy-

che: he knew that "Christianity" reflected the values of the greater society, and he despaired of any significant improvement in the self image of Afro-Americans so long as they were subjected to daily indoctrination by the dominant culture. "As long as we remain among the whites," he wrote in 1898, "the Negro will believe that the devil is black and that he (the Negro) was the devil . . . and the effect of such sentiment is contemptuous and degrading." This is one of the reasons, Turner concluded, "why we favor African emigration."

In their condemnation of the connection between Christianity and white supremacy, David Walker, Henry McNeal Turner, and Malcolm were soul brothers. Where they differed is that the first two remained Christians even while attacking its hypocrites and Uncle Malcolm left it for Islam as taught by Elijah Muhammad. Like Muhammad, Malcolm's first contact with Islam was with the Ahmadiyya Muslims in Boston. Both of them found the Ahmadiyyas too insular and not really set up to meet the needs of our people. "Their attitude," Malcolm told Ma, "was that people should seek them out. They had no agenda for really reaching out to our people. That's why I found Mr. Muhammad's teachings more appealing."

Once Malcolm joined the N.O.I. he became a true believer, as most converts tend to do. He listened to and learned from Wilfred, Philbert and Hilda, Muhammad, Mr. Micheaux, and Dr. John Henrik Clarke. What he learned was then passed on to others in classes he held in N.O.I. temples throughout the country. I became aware of the depth of his faith and his knowledge when, as a teenager, I joined the Nation. In male-only classes for the Fruit of Islam, Uncle Malcolm taught us about geography, history, public speaking, etymology, current events, moral conduct, and manners. All classes were taught from a strong black perspective, based on his belief that we should return to our system of thought and not get caught up in the Greco-Roman system of thought that they had stolen from our ancestors and distorted for their own purposes. He reminded us constantly in black history and black-revolution classes "to remember that a knowledge of our history was important no matter what career choice is made. It's critical if you're to be successful. One of the rea-

sons that the so-called Negro in America has not been more successful in achieving political, economic, and cultural power is our lack
of knowledge of history. There are blacks who are masters of
physics, the math sciences, medicine, and the law who can even help
put spacecrafts into the atmosphere. Yet these same people too often
have very little knowledge of our history. We have too few masters
of our history."

He said that this included a lack of knowledge about our religious
history. "The white man has never separated himself from Christianity," Malcolm told us. "When you hear the white man bragging, 'I
am a Christian,' he's bragging that he is a white man. Because of a
lack of historical knowledge about Christianity, a Negro who brags
about being a Christian is saying that he wants to be white. He doesn't
know that the first Christian church outside of the holy city of
Jerusalem was in Africa. They don't know that the African Christians, originally, did not believe in the divinity of Jesus as taught in
theology today. The Romans, as part of a peace treaty in A.D. 300,
which ended many years of struggle, forced the kingdom of Axum in
Ethiopia to accept their European Christianity, which stressed the divinity of Jesus.

Axum, Uncle Malcolm told us, emerged in the pre-Christian mil-
lennium and became the dominant kingdom in northeastern Africa
during the third and fourth centuries A.D. It was an advanced political state with trade relations with other African kingdoms, the Middle East, and the Far East. One of its emperors, Ezana, is credited
with making Christianity an official religion on the African continent. Another had given protection to the Hebrews, and they have
been in Ethiopia since. "You would know these things if you studied
your history," Malcolm would tell us.

As Malcolm told us these things, we sat there in awed silence. All
of us had spent years in public and private schools, but had never
heard such history. Our classroom was set up in such a way as to
provide a proper setting for the lessons we were learning. It always
contained a big blackboard on which was drawn an American flag
with the words "Slavery, Suffering and Death" over it. On the right
of the flag was drawn a tree with a black man hanging on a rope
from one of its branches. On the other side of that was a Muslim flag

with a star and a crescent. In each corner of the Muslim flag was the slogan "I for Islam, F for Freedom, J for Justice and E for Equality." Written in the center of the blackboard was the question "Which one will survive the War of Armageddon?"

Malcolm knew where he stood on that question. To him Christianity had weakened our people. "Think about what you were taught in school, what images you saw in your churches and the songs you were taught to sing," he said. "My mother and father were Christians who were also Garveyites and black nationalists, yet I remember hearing them sing songs in church with lyrics that went 'Wash me white as snow.' That's expressing a desire to be white. Many of our people get resentful when they hear me talk like this. They shouldn't be resentful; they should remember what they were taught in history, Bible studies, and geography and how so much of it was designed to make us look down on black and up on white."

Continuing his lessons on Christianity, Malcolm said, "Jesus himself didn't call his beliefs Christianity. That name didn't appear until two or three hundred years after he was dead. Right or wrong?" (At intervals during his teaching, Malcolm would say, "Right or wrong?" after making a statement. We'd respond with an enthusiastic "Right!") "Any history book can tell you this; any theologian knows this. Most Negroes will contend this, but when you tell it to a white man, he shuts his mouth because he knows it is true." At that point Uncle Malcolm added: "What makes the white man a devil is not the red tail you and I look for but his great deception when he knows the truth."

Many members of the audience, when hearing such religious history for the first time, looked a little nervous at discovering that their teachers and preachers had misled them for years. Malcolm continued: "Those who have studied a little deeper will say to me, 'Before God called it Christianity, it was called Judaism.' Isn't that what they say? Their position doesn't follow logically. If Christianity was named after Christ was born and before Christ was born the religion was called Judaism, this means it got its name from a son of Jacob whose name was Judah. But history tells us that Jacob was bending down before Judah was born, which shows us that Jacob's religion couldn't have been Judaism. Abraham was Judah's great-grandfather, meaning that Abraham was on the scene long before Judah. Thus, you can't call Abraham's religion Judaism, since there was no such thing as Judaism during his day. So what was God's religion before they called it Judaism? This is something that the white man has never taught you and me because he's afraid to let us know what God's religion was called in Abraham's day." Malcolm would then provide us with the teaching of Mr. Muhammad about Abraham. "The Honorable Elijah Muhammad teaches us that Abraham's religion was Islam." Malcolm was giving Elijah Muhammad credit for a knowledge of religious history that he didn't possess, according to Ma. "It was Malcolm's extensive knowledge of history that he gained from much reading and listening to people like Mr. Micheaux, Dr. Clarke, and others that made him so aware of the role played by white supremacy in Christianity," she said.

It's important to remember that Malcolm didn't speak of the end of Christianity itself when he said, "Religiously, I believe that we are living at a time when we are seeing the end of the wicked world of slavery and colonialism that has been inflicted on us by white Christians." He was speaking of the white supremacist version of Christianity practiced by those "who wanted all to know that 'I'm white, therefore I'm right and superior to you dark races.'" Such people, he told us, "do not act like human beings who are white, but act more like devils when it comes to dealing with dark-skinned people."

Malcolm was speaking at a black forum at the Rev. Adam Clayton Powell Jr.'s Abyssinian Baptist Church when making the above statement. I attended that forum. What I remember most about it was not Malcolm's statements about religion but his response when Rev. Powell asked him to "please distinguish between segregation and separation?" Uncle Malcolm responded with an answer that showed why he was such a great teacher. "The Honorable Elijah Muhammad teaches us that segregation is that which is done to inferiors by superiors. Separation is done voluntarily by two groups of people. For example, you will notice that an oriental community like Chinatown is never called a segregated community because the Chinese in Chinatown control all their businesses, all their banks, all their own politics, all their own everything. In the so-called Negro community everything is controlled by outsiders, so we have a regulated, segregated community. We are not for segregation, but we are for separation. When you are segregated, that is done to you by someone else; when you are separated, you do that to yourself."

His explanation made a whole lot of sense to me, as it did to so many others. I used it every time someone tried to brand me a segregationist because I was in the Nation of Islam.

I don't want to give the impression that Malcolm spent all or even most of his time in those classes and lectures attacking white supremacist versions of Christianity and Judaism. He really didn't. Most of it was used to teach us about Islam, as he learned from Mr. Muhammad, and later about Islam in its more traditional form. He was now convinced that Islam should be the religion of choice and salvation for us as black people. Between 1952 and 1959, he traveled extensively, extolling Islam as taught by Elijah Muhammad, with its emphasis on the white man as the devil and the need for total separation from a white supremacist society. It was an Islam whose greatest flaw and even blasphemy, as far as more orthodox Muslims were concerned, was the teaching that Elijah Muhammad was a divine being. "It was that teaching," noted Ma, "that really caused problems between the N.O.I. and other Muslims. The beliefs about whites being devils or at least devil-like in their behavior toward Africans, Asians, and Native Americans and about the need to separate from such people if one is to lead a productive life were at least debatable and worthy of discussion among Muslims. But the concept of Elijah Muhammad as divine was a totally objectionable tenet that no serious Muslim could ever accept. Malcolm was too serious about his religious beliefs and too intelligent to forever stick to such an untenable belief. Even without the out-of-wedlock babies and the corruption of John Ali and his minions, eventually he would have had to challenge the N.O.I.'s position on the divinity of Elijah Muhammad."

In both interpretations of Islam, Uncle Malcolm was a master teacher who made history and religion vibrantly alive. He taught us the five pillars of orthodox Islamic belief from the Holy Qu'ran:

1. To bear witness that there is only one God (Allah) and
   Muhammad is his messenger.
2. To offer prayer five times each day.

3. To pay a portion of your earnings for those less fortunate.
4. To fast during the month of Ramadan.
5. To make the journey to the home of Allah once in a lifetime.

The prophet Muhammad, Uncle Malcolm taught us, said in his last sermon: "I leave you two things; if you cling to them, you will never go astray: the Book (the Holy Qu'ran) and the Sunnah (my example)." The Holy Qu'ran is the last Book of Revelation from Almighty God and is a book of guidance for every aspect of a Muslim's life. The Sunnah, or the practices of the prophet Muhammad, we learned, is documented in compiled books based on statements of those who lived and walked in Muhammad's company. His wife, Aisha, when asked about him, answered, "He is a walking Qu'ran," meaning that every aspect of the prophet Muhammad's life was in harmony with the will of God Almighty (Allah).

When listening to Malcolm's teachings as a teenager, I remember thinking over and over again, We were never taught that in any school I ever attended. Instead, Islam was presented to us as a bloodthirsty religion that enthusiastically advocated "holy wars" as the best means of spreading the faith. A "jihad" is how our teachers described it. That is a distortion of the word *jaahad,* Malcolm said, "which is Arabic for doing your utmost, struggling with all your heart, mind, body, and soul. There can be a *jaahad* of self-improvement, a *jaahad* for self-control, and one for your self-defense. All three require doing your utmost, struggling with all your heart, mind, body, and soul to accomplish your goals."

Malcolm never used the word jihad when speaking about action against white supremacists. When a reporter asked Malcolm, "Mr. X, would your group declare a holy war on white people?" Malcolm answered that "white people went to Africa, Asia, and the Americas claiming to be doing God's holy work. That's what the Crusades were all about. Bringing God into such activity is your game. We let Allah himself take care of you. Mr. Muhammad teaches us that Almighty God will chastise you."

It's obvious that *jaahad* is not the sinister concept falsely attributed to Islam by Crusade-minded Christians. There is no such thing as a "holy war." All wars are ugly and unholy.

One of the most memorable things we learned from Malcolm was that a sizable number of Africans brought to enslavement in this country were Muslims. We had never heard such a thing before. Most of us thought that Islam came to our people with the Nation of Islam. We were overwhelmed to learn that in 1790 the South Carolina legislature granted a special law for a community of enslaved Muslims. We learned about Omar Ibn Said's autobiographical narrative written in 1831. The *American Historical Review*'s July 1925 issue described him as a "Fullah tribesman from Senegal" whose narrative is "the only complete autobiographical narrative written in America by a slave in his own native tongue." He was first brought to Charleston, South Carolina, in 1807 and later fled to Fayetteville, North Carolina. Excerpts from the narrative quoted Said as saying, "There came to our place a large Army, who killed many men, and took me, and brought me to the great sea, and sold me into the hands of the Christians, who bound me and sent me on board a great ship and we sailed upon the great sea a month and a half, when we came to a place called Charleston in the Christian language. . . ."

Said described his first owner as "a small, weak, and wicked man called Johnson. . . . I fled from the hands of Johnson to a place called Fayd-il (Fayetteville). . . . I reside in this our country by reason of great necessity. Wicked men took me by violence and sold me to the Christians . . ."

It excited us to learn about such a long history of African Muslims in this country. It gave us, as Malcolm had intended, a sense of historical connection, the feeling that we were part of something of substance that transcended white supremacy, enslavement, segregation, and European-interpreted Christianity.

Later I learned about other early Muslims, including Yarrow Mamout, who is described in *The Guide to Black Washington* as "a unique citizen of his time (the early 1800s) who lived through the American Revolution, *never gave up his Moslem (sic) religion* [italics mine] and lived to be over one hundred years old. . . ."

Malcolm's teachings were also reinforced by Professor Sulayman S. Nyang of Howard University. In an introduction to the book *Islam, Black Nationalism and Slavery* by Adib Rashad, Professor Nyang noted that many of the Africans brought to these shores to enslave-

ment were Muslims. "The religion of Islam survived on during the
life times of individual believers who tried desperately to maintain
their Islamic way of life. Among the Muslims who came into *antebellum* [italics his] times in America one can include Yorro Muhmud
(erroneously anglicized as Yarrow Mamout), Ayub Ibn Sulayman
Diallo (known to Anglo-Saxons as Job ben Solomon), Abdul Rahman (known as Abdul Rahman in Western sources) and countless
others whose Islamic ritual practices were prevented from surfacing
in public."

Between 1952 and 1959, when teaching in the temples or lectur-
ing to the general public in churches, schools, and public auditori-
ums, Malcolm always prefaced his teachings with the Honorable
Elijah Muhammad says this, the Honorable Elijah Muhammad
teaches that. By 1960, dismayed by Muhammad's out-of-wedlock
babies and disgusted with the money-grubbing corruption among
N.O.I. officials in Chicago, Uncle Malcolm was saying, "Though
we follow the Honorable Elijah Muhammad, we don't believe in
Mr. Muhammad; we believe in Islam."

His change in emphasis began in 1959, after a trip to the Middle
East. He returned with the orthodox English translation of the Holy
Qu'ran written by Yusuf Ali and authorized by Al-Azhar University
of Cairo, Egypt. Malcolm, prodded by people like Ma, Sister Saoud,
Brother Mahmoud, and others, began to believe that ties to a more
orthodox Islam were best for our people. He began teaching from
the English translation of orthodox Islam of the Holy Qu'ran privately to carefully chosen N.O.I. members in New York City, Los
Angeles, and Washington, D.C. Ma, for one, was pleased with his
new religious direction. "Malcolm had outgrown the very limited vision of the Nation of Islam," she noted. "It was too burdened down
with visionless, corrupt leadership that was more concerned with
filling their pockets with money than empowering our people." Ma
had turned to orthodox Islam in the late 1950s and had established a
school and day-care center for Muslim children. The children in
both mostly had parents who were still members of the Nation but
wanted their children to learn to read the Holy Qu'ran from people
who knew what they were doing.

Minister Louis X of Boston's Temple Eleven and the Chicago

crew were very distrustful of Ma's school, considering it a possible hotbed of insubordination. Malcolm, aware of their hostile attitude, made sure to stay away from the school when he visited us in Boston. He knew that Louis X and a few other N.O.I. members were watching him and would report to John Ali in Chicago if they saw him at the school. He still believed in most of Elijah Muhammad's message, if not in Muhammad himself, so he shared his developing feelings about orthodox Islam with only a few people, most notably Dr. M. T. Mehdi, Sister Saoud, Brother Mahmoud, Ma, and me. He knew that Ma was now attending the new orthodox Muslim mosque in Quincy, Massachusetts, where she took her Shahada (to bear witness that there is no God but Allah and that the prophet Muhammad of A.D. 600 was the last of the great prophets of Allah). In 1991 the Society of Islamic Brotherhood presented an award to Ma for her work in the cause of Islam. "I was glad that there was an Islamic alternative to the Nation of Islam," Ma stated. "I knew about the hostility of Louis X and the others toward my move to orthodox Islam even while I was still in the Nation. That was one of the few issues which led Louis X to consider me as insubordinate and later to my suspension. I also knew that it was only a matter of time before Malcolm made a similar move."

Ma said that Louis X usually personally handed out suspensions in Temple Eleven but in her case called Malcolm in to handle it. "I believe he did it for two reasons. The first was to put Malcolm on the spot by having him suspend his own sister; the second was to provide a cover for Louis X. He had washed his hands of the whole situation, or so he thought. Actually, he had shot himself in the foot. His move against me sent shock waves through Temple Eleven. Many members, especially women, wanted to leave the temple but stayed on to see what I would do. Eventually, because of my suspension and other petty moves by Louis X, several important people did leave the temple."

Despite the suspicion and hostility of key N.O.I. officials, Malcolm continued his move toward orthodox Islam. Once he made an intellectual decision, based on his common sense and personal analysis, he wouldn't turn back. He had decided that orthodox Islam was the "religion of action" needed to combat the white supremacy of too many Christians. A gift he brought for Ma on the 1959 trip to the Middle East illustrates that belief. It was the root of a small Resurrection tree. I remember the root looking very dry and very dead. However, Malcolm explained, that tree was like no other. It could have died many, many years ago, but one day, if it was put into solid ground and watered, it would rise up again, blossoming with green leaves. "Our people are like this tree plant, Ella," Malcolm said. "We have been thought dead, but plant us in solid ground and we will raise up again."

For Uncle Malcolm, Islam, initially as interpreted by Elijah Muhammad and later in its more orthodox form, provided that solid ground.

TWELVE The OAAU:
The Preassassination

There were at least three organizations and one individual who, for very different reasons, were very pleased, if not ecstatic, when Malcolm, during a press conference held at Harlem's Hotel Theresa, finalized his split from the Nation of Islam. It was March 8, 1964. In a firm voice that belied the inner turmoil he had gone through since his suspension from the N.O.I. in late November 1963, Malcolm broke with the group that had been the all-consuming force in his life for nearly a dozen years.

His defection greatly pleased Ma, who had long advocated that her brother leave "an organization that had been taken over by a corrupt, visionless leadership solely out to fill their pockets with as much money as they could swindle from its members. There were many good, committed people in the Nation of Islam, but they had no power over its policies and actions. Malcolm was just one of those serious people who finally saw that John Ali and his sybaritic crew had become Muslim versions of jackleg Christian ministers who so often preyed on our people. Malcolm was too knowledgeable and progressive for such narrow-minded, limited individuals."

The Nation of Islam, the FBI, and the CIA, all of which considered Malcolm a formidable threat to their schemes and goals, were similarly pleased. Probably the most relieved by his departure at that time was John Ali and his crew. Malcolm, with his honesty, integrity, and commitment to black people, was, to them, a problem they were happy to be relieved of. Unofficially, he had been gone from the N.O.I. since November 1963, when he was allegedly suspended for ninety days for making "the chickens coming home to roost" observation in response to a question about the November 22, 1963, assassination of President John F. Kennedy. "What he was really suspended for," said Ma, "was his refusal to participate in or condone the rampant corruption prevalent in the N.O.I.'s Chicago headquarters." After that statement John Ali, who now reigned supreme in the organization, beefed up his efforts to divide Elijah Muhammad and Malcolm. Once that was successfully accomplished, he had to make sure that Muhammad Ali, whom Malcolm had personally fished into the Nation, didn't leave with him. John Ali was well aware that N.O.I. would face disastrous consequences if both Malcolm and Muhammad Ali left and worked together to launch a new religious and political movement. Their combined charismatic drawing power would have been irresistible to thousands of black people not only in the United States but throughout the world.

"Probably the most effective action taken by John Ali to gain control over Muhammad Ali," Ma insisted, "was to marry him off to a woman whom they knew was not a proper wife for a young Muslim. Malcolm told me that John Ali and Herbert Muhammad set up the marriage so they would have something to hold over Muhammad Ali's head. The woman was older, much more worldly, and known to be a party girl. Ali, still a babe in the woods when dealing with such matters, never knew what hit him. He told Malcolm that dealing with her was harder than fighting Sonny Liston."

Speaking of Liston, Malcolm told Ma and me that he had suggested that Muhammad Ali taunt Liston before and during their fight. "Ali liked to talk, so I suggested he use his mouth in a more constructive manner. I recognized Liston as one of those weak minded Negroes who believed whatever the white man said. I suspected he could be psychologically broken down by the right kind of taunts."

With a combination of flattery and intimidation, John Ali and Herbert Muhammad persuaded Ali to stay with the N.O.I. The rest is history. Ma noted, "I believe with all my heart that if Muhammad Ali had stuck with Malcolm, he wouldn't be in the condition he's in today."

The CIA and the FBI, having thoroughly infiltrated the Nation using ultrasophisticated surveillance equipment, were aware of all the dissension. They were also well aware of Malcolm's willingness to speak with clarity and righteous anger about the true nature of race relations in America. They were even more aware of, and concerned about, his ability to make a direct connection between the struggle against white supremacy in the United States and the struggle against colonialism then being waged in both Africa and Asia. The agencies considered his truth telling about the connection between white supremacy and colonialism, especially to foreigners at the height of the cold war, as a threat to the security of the United States. For instance, Malcolm was co-chairman of a Harlem, New York, welcoming committee, including Rev. Adam Clayton Powell Jr., which had invited President Kwame Nkrumah of Ghana to Harlem in 1958. President Nkrumah, an ardent Pan-Africanist, was not one of the State Department's favorite African leaders because of his vigorous opposition to the continued economic exploitation of Africa by America's allies in Europe. President Nkrumah once stated: "Neocolonialism is based upon the principle of breaking up former large united colonial territories into a number of small nonviable states which are incapable of independent development and must rely upon the former imperial powers for defense and even internal security. Their economic and financial systems are linked, as in colonial days, with those of the former colonial rulers." He further noted that "colonialism and its attitudes die hard, like the attitudes of slavery, whose hangover still dominates behavior in certain parts of the Western Hemisphere." They knew exactly what President Nkrumah meant by "certain parts of the Western Hemisphere."

Equally upsetting to the FBI, the CIA, and military intelligence was Malcolm's connection to King Ibn Abdullah Saud Al Saud of Saudi Arabia, whom they basically considered an ally. FBI files claim that Malcolm first met King Saud in 1957; Malcolm said that their first contact was made in 1962. Ma set up the contact through her friendship with Kahalil Muhammad, head of the Boston/Quincy Islamic Center and also an Arabic instructor at a school founded by Ma. Malcolm and King Saud didn't meet as planned, but the king requested information on the N.O.I. Unfortunately, before they met formally, King Saud was removed from office because of a report to

Saudi Arabia that some members of his entourage were behaving in an immoral manner in Boston. As a guardian of the holy city of Mecca and of the Islamic faith, it was his duty to keep his people in check. His failure to do so led to his removal by the Islamic Council, to be replaced by one of his brothers, Prince Faisal. "If that meeting with King Saud had taken place," Ma said, "Malcolm might have left the Nation of Islam in 1962. King Saud was to be the key figure in Malcolm's move to orthodox Islam. There was also the added factor that he was not only the protector of Islam (the holy city of Mecca); he was also an important leader in the effort of oil-producing nations to organize the oil cartel. That later became known as OPEC [Organization of Petroleum Exporting Countries]. The FBI and the CIA probably knew that Malcolm was privy to a discussion about the possibility of an oil embargo with King Faisal and President Gamal Abdel Nasser of Egypt in 1964."

The government agencies were agitated by Malcolm's involvement with such world figures. This agitation increased significantly when he later announced the formation of two new organizations, the Muslim Mosque Inc. (MMI) and the Organization of Afro-American Unity (OAAU). The former was for those who shared his religious beliefs; the latter for those who shared his political, economic, and cultural vision. The OAAU was both named and patterned after the Organization of African Unity.

As Malcolm envisioned, both organizations would have strong international connections; MMI with orthodox Islam, the OAAU with the struggle of Africa and Asian people against European colonialism. The MMI was inspired by Malcolm's trip to Mecca, where, he wrote to Betty and Ma, "in the land of Muhammad and the land of Abraham, I had been blessed by Allah with a new insight into the true religion of Islam and a better understanding of America's entire racial dilemma." He saw that whites "who accepted Islam" were capable of transcending white supremacy. Those three words "who accepted Islam" are very important to note because they are so ignored or downplayed by those eager to shout that Malcolm became a born again integrationist after his pilgrimage to Mecca. White Americans who accept Islam probably couldn't fill up a medium-sized auditorium. "That leaves a whole lot of white people still infected with white supremacy," Ma said when reading or hearing such distortions of Malcolm's position.

After writing the first two letters to Betty and Ma, the two people to whom he was the closest at the time, Malcolm wrote to several others about his new Islamic vision, including Wallace D. Muhammad. He wrote to Wallace, Ma explained, because Wallace had once expressed to him his conviction "that the only possible salvation for the Nation of Islam would be its accepting and projecting of a better understanding of orthodox Islam." Malcolm believed that with the help of Betty, Ma, Wallace, and others, the MMI would provide the kind of Islam he had seen during his hajj for black people in America.

What MMI would be for those who shared Uncle Malcolm's religious beliefs, the OAAU would be for those who shared his belief in the need for an organization whose goal was not a nebulous integration but group and individual self-respect, self-determination, self- defense, educational achievement, and political, economic, and cultural empowerment. Ma and I had heard Uncle Malcolm often speak privately about his plans for the OAAU, but it was during a speech in Boston in June 1964 that we first heard him speak publicly about the new organization. The OAAU and MMI chapters in Boston were the first organized outside New York City. Several hundred people, including family members J.C. (Ella and Malcolm's first cousin), John Little, and Aunt Grace, were in attendance. They had many questions for him to address in this his first meeting with them since publicly announcing his plans. What kind of relationship would the OAAU have with Africa? How could they help the Africans while at the same time helping themselves? Could he explain the difference between human rights and civil rights? Most were ready to follow Malcolm but wanted to know where he was going to lead them. "Even though we have every right to be angry at the white man for the injustices he has inflicted on us," Malcolm said in his stentorian voice, "for us to receive freedom, justice, and equality, we should never act out of hate, greed, anger, or revenge. That is how the white man does things. We must act in defense of our human rights by any means necessary. We must take our case to the World Court and accuse the United States government of violating and not protecting our human rights."

His statement about going to the World Court electrified the audience, eliciting enthusiastic applause and shouts of approval. Ma was pleased both with his statement and the audience's reaction. She said, "He was finally speaking for himself, for his own beliefs. There was no more the Honorable Elijah Muhammad says this; the Honorable Elijah Muhammad says that. I was certain that Malcolm would do an even better job in building the OAAU than he had done with the Nation of Islam."

In parts of his speech Malcolm reiterated to us what he had told students at Ghana's Kwame Nkrumah Ideological Institute and members of its parliament during a May 1964 visit to that country. "America has never accepted us as human beings," he told them, and later us. "Thus, it is not interested in human rights for you and me. Yet she claims to be for human rights in Africa, Asia, and South America. She sends Peace Corps workers all over the world. Why? Why doesn't she send them to places like Harlem, Boston, Los Angeles, Little Rock, Mississippi, Alabama? I'll tell you why. America is hypocritical in her racism. Look at South Africa. The only difference between the white racist government of South Africa and that of America is that they preach and practice segregation while America preaches integration and practices segregation. America supports South Africa's denial of human rights for black Africans." By that time, Ma said with a smile, "the government informants in the audience, and you can bet they were there, were probably squirming and anxious to report to their handlers."

"As an orthodox Muslim believing in Allah, the Holy Qu'ran, and Prophet Muhammad," Malcolm continued, "I am compelled to fight for human rights. The Holy Qu'ran compels me to do so. For those of you who want to follow true Islam, you can join the OAAU's fight for human rights. However, if you wish to just be a practicing Muslim, you can join Muslim Mosque Inc. and help us teach true Islam here in North America."

In further describing the OAAU's connection to Africa, Malcolm declared that "we can learn much from the strategy used by American Jews. They have never migrated physically to Israel, yet their cultural, philosophical, and psychological ties to Israel have enhanced their political, economic, and social position right here in America. Pan-Africanism will do for people of African descent all over the world the same that Zionism has done for Jews all over the world."

At the conclusion of Malcolm's speech, the audience erupted with applause. Even Ma, who seldom allowed herself to get publicly excited about anything, smiled broadly and applauded enthusiastically. "The Nation of Islam, the CIA, and the FBI all thought he would be demoralized and broken by the split," she said later. "Now their spies in the audience saw that he had been freed and energized instead." Still a teenager, I was even more enthusiastic than Ma and the others. I was elated and inspired by my uncle's speech. Man, I remember thinking, he's going to hook us up with world Islam and Pan-Africanism. He's really on the case.

Malcolm's international plans weren't entirely new. Marcus Garvey and W. E. B. Du Bois had both been committed Pan-Africanists who had developed contacts with African leaders, but when Garvey set up his organization in the early 1920s, most of Africa was under near-total domination by European colonialists who were supported by the United States. Thus, he was unable to establish the kind of contact with African leaders that Malcolm later had. By the time sufficient African countries were independent enough to be even a minor factor on the world scene, Du Bois was too advanced in age to take advantage of the new situation. Malcolm, however, was in his robust thirties, and due to the emergence of semi-independent African countries and advancements in communications and transportation, he was able to communicate with and directly meet many African politicians, diplomats, scholars, businessmen, and students both in the United States and on the African continent.

There was nobody more cognizant of Malcolm's potential with the OAAU than the CIA, the FBI, and military intelligence. Even before the June 1964 Boston speech, they had been busily doing everything they could to isolate and undermine him. In February 1964 both the *Amsterdam News* (a black newspaper based in Harlem) and the *New York Times* reported that Malcolm might split permanently from the N.O.I. "They probably got that from the FBI,"

Ma said. FBI files revealed that in March 1964 both it and the CIA had their informants spread rumors that Malcolm intended to form an organization that would rival the Nation. Rumors, spread by the informants, were rampant in the streets of Harlem that Malcolm was nothing without Elijah Muhammad, that he was desperate to get back in his good graces, that he could only lead with his help. Another rumor was that Malcolm had told Muhammad that he would return to the N.O.I. only if he (Malcolm) and Wallace D. Muhammad shared control, which meant that the Chicago-based sybarites John Ali, Raymond Sharrieff, and Herbert Muhammad would be replaced. According to this rumor, Malcolm insisted on receiving an answer by March 4, 1964. The objective of all the rumors, Ma said, was to keep things at a boiling point between Malcolm and Elijah Muhammad. "By that time Elijah Muhammad was only concerned about two things—staying alive and continuing to enjoy the pleasures of his personal harem. He was afraid that the Chicago crew might deny him both if he didn't go along with their attacks on Malcolm."

It must be said that there was a period in early 1964 when Malcolm seemed to agonize over the possibility of splitting from the N.O.I. He was sending out ambiguous messages to those who supported him, including loyal supporters such as Aubrey Barnette and his wife, the Wiley James family, Brother Busbee, James 6X, the Thompson family, and Brother Charles 37X and his family. The latter was Sister Evelyn's brother, the same Sister Evelyn to whom Uncle Malcolm had once been engaged and who was one of the young women impregnated by Elijah Muhammad. "I believed that Malcolm owed something to those who were supporting him," Ma stated. "He needed to state his position forcefully and clearly so there would be no ambiguity about where he stood. I told him as bluntly as possible that I had absolutely no interest in supporting him in the N.O.I. or in an N.O.I.-type organization." Ma was unyielding. I once heard her tell Malcolm that she would not allow family members and friends to be led astray by another of the likes of Muhammad. "I once left you in jail because you were acting foolishly," she said. "You need to remember that."

I didn't hear the rest of that conversation, one of several they had, sometimes lasting all night, but I do know that by the time Uncle Malcolm spoke to us in Boston, in June 1964, his position was unambiguous. The firm conviction in his voice established that he had finally freed himself emotionally from Elijah Muhammad.

Besides the speech, there was another factor about Uncle Malcolm's visit to Boston during that time that sticks in my mind. It was the importance of the concern for his safety. He had received a barrage of hostile commentary, including physical threats, from several key N.O.I. officials. By that time, Ma said, "the sinister, luxury-loving John Ali, the obsequious, luxury-loving Louis X, the conniving, equally luxury-loving Herbert Muhammad, the equally obsequious, shallow Raymond Sharrieff in Chicago, and the bellicose, easily led Captain Joseph in New York City were all well aware that Malcolm was not going to quietly fade away. They also knew that no matter what Malcolm said, any orthodox religious organization he set up was going to harm the cash cow they were operating in Chicago. Without Malcolm there was a real chance that the Nation of Islam would return to the comatose state it was in before the Little brothers energized it. Their belligerent statements were designed mainly to intimidate possible supporters of Malcolm, both within and outside the Nation. Louis X knew he was coming to Boston to speak, and I was afraid he might attempt to provoke a confrontation that would discredit what Malcolm was trying to do."

As a result of the threats, tension was very high when Malcolm arrived in Boston. He stayed with us. Ma, in her usual fashion, made him as comfortable as possible. She cooked his favorite foods, washed and ironed his clothes, listened to him, speaking only when answering questions, and insisted that he take the opportunity to rest instead of visiting the dozens of family members and friends who had extended invitations. When she thought he was sufficiently relaxed, she raised the question of security. Her concern about this was magnified because of a call earlier that week from Brother Leon Ameer, one of Malcolm's most trusted supporters. Brother Leon, who had once been a bodyguard for Muhammad Ali, had been approached by an N.O.I. official about killing Malcolm. He immediately informed Malcolm about the request. That's why Ma took his call very seriously. When Uncle's response was too lackluster, she told me that if Malcolm didn't become more diligent about security, "I will develop a plan to have him kidnapped and taken somewhere where he will be safer." This may sound outlandish and extreme to some, but I had been around Ma long enough to know that she meant every word she said. And I knew I would be involved in some kind of way. The thought of helping to kidnap my uncle, even for his own safety, really shook me up. Fortunately, it didn't come to that point. Malcolm finally acknowledged Ma's concerns; he knew her well enough to know that she wouldn't let up.

After discussing several plans, Ma settled on one that shocked both me and Malcolm. "Rodnell, you are to go inconspicuously to that public telephone booth in front of the storefront church in Roxbury. You will call the FBI, with a disguised voice, and tell them that 'Malcolm X is going to be bumped off. I'm going to do it today.'" Malcolm vigorously protested when he heard the plan. "Ella, what will I look like asking the FBI for help?" Ma was respectful but adamant. "You are not asking them for help. Anyway, I don't give a damn what it looks like. People, including your family, need you here and now, not when you are dead." Malcolm continued protesting, but less vigorously. He had enough faith in Ma's commonsense approach to problems to reluctantly go along with her audacious plan.

I was extremely angry about the threats made against Malcolm; that anger gave me the motivation to carry out Ma's plan. Malcolm watched as Ma and I rehearsed what I was supposed to say and how I was supposed to say it. While walking the several blocks to the phone booth, I silently repeated my lines. The call itself was almost anticlimactic. I spoke my lines like a pro, hung up the phone, and quickly left the booth. I forced myself to walk casually home—I really wanted to run—where Ma and Uncle Malcolm were waiting. Things were somewhat relaxed by then. Both of them smiled as I calmly told them about my successful mission.

Ma's plan worked to perfection. Shortly after I returned home, we saw several agents sitting in a car across the street. Ma graciously offered them refreshments, which they graciously refused.

According to Clayborne Carson in his book *Malcolm X: The F.B.I. Files,* the FBI recorded the reception of a call from "an unknown source" at about 1:40 P.M. the afternoon of June 12, 1964. The source is no longer unknown.

Some ten years later I asked Ma how she felt about the incident. "Some people will say it was hypocritical considering how we all feel about the FBI," I reminded her. Ma was unrepentant. "Listen, my brother was being threatened by a bunch of corrupt men who had no compunction about harming him. I had also heard that white supremacists had put up an offer of ten thousand dollars to anyone who killed him. The FBI was not only aware of those threats, but considering what we know now about their activities during the 1960s, they probably encouraged them. That call threw them off temporarily. Out of sheer curiosity, if nothing else, they had to check things out."

Malcolm covered much territory in that Boston speech, but there was one plan he had for the OAAU which he didn't deal with that day. I don't know how many other people knew about it, but he told Ma and me that the OAAU would recruit technologically skilled black Vietnam veterans to fight with liberation forces on the African continent. They would first study at the Kwame Nkrumah Ideological Institute, then be sent to freedom-fighters camps throughout Africa. Their payment would include land and an opportunity to further their education at the University of Ghana.

The concept behind this first arose when he spoke privately to African freedom fighters in London. When he sought their support for the human-rights struggle in the United States, they asked what he was prepared to do for them in return. That was when he first mentioned the black Vietnam vets who knew how to use some of the most advanced military equipment then available. Because of Malcolm's assassination in 1965, and the U.S.-backed overthrow of President's Nkrumah's government a year later, the plan never got off the ground.

Of all the issues Uncle Malcolm dealt with in his speech, none stirred the audience as much as the OAAU's plan to charge the U.S. government, before the World Court, both with violating and failing to protect the human rights of its black citizens. The concept was not entirely unprecedented. On December 18, 1951, an integrated organization, the Civil Rights Congress, filed a petition to the UN General Assembly charging the U.S. government with a failure to protect its black citizens from genocide. The petition was written by Paul Robeson and William L. Patterson and signed by, among others, W. E. B. Du Bois and civil-rights leader Mary Church Terrell. Its opening statement set its tone:

> The responsibility of being the first in history to charge the government of the United States of America with the crime of genocide is not one your petitioners take lightly. The responsibility is particularly grave when citizens must charge their own government with mass murders of its own nationals, with institutionalized oppression and persistent slaughter of the Negro people in the United States on the basis of "race," a crime abhorred by mankind and prohibited by the conscience of the world as expressed in the Convention on the Prevention and Punishment of the Crime of Genocide adopted by the General Assembly of the United Nations on December 9, 1948.

The statement reads like a horror story. It lists overwhelming, documented evidence of hundreds of mostly unpunished lynchings, beatings, and other brutalities and blatant denial of voting rights and access to public accommodations between 1944 and 1951.

The Civil Rights Congress's petition was faced with at least two formidable obstacles. The first was the near glaring absence of independent African and Asian countries in the United Nations at that time. Only Ethiopia and Liberia were ostensibly independent. The rest of sub-Saharan Africa was controlled by European colonialists. The second obstacle was that the U.S. government was able to successfully red-bait it because of the communist affiliation of many of the signees. This offset, in the minds of most white people and too many black people, the accuracy of the evidence presented in the petition.

In the early 1960s, when Uncle Malcolm was developing his plan, there were over twenty African countries in the United Nations. According to historian Dr. John Henrik Clarke, at least six of those were definitely prepared to support Uncle Malcolm's efforts, and several others were considering it.

As for red-baiting, try as they might, government agencies and the press couldn't successfully hang that tag on Malcolm. As a black nationalist, he considered the Russians as basically just another group of white supremacists trying to economically exploit African and Asian people. On several occasions, Malcolm told us that when it came to dealing with people of color, the white communist Russians weren't that much different from the white capitalist Americans and Europeans.

The foundation for Malcolm's foreign policy, as expressed by the OMU, was laid in the late 1950s and early 1960s, when he established contact with, and developed relationships with, a number of world leaders, including President Kwame Nkrumah of Ghana, President Gamal Abdel Nasser of Egypt, Prime Minister Jomo Kenyatta of Kenya, and Prime Minister Milton Obote of Uganda. From the mid-1950s on, he also developed relations with African diplomats at the United Nations and African and Muslim students who were attending colleges and universities in the United States and Europe. Without the approval of the small-minded N.O.I. leadership in Chicago, Uncle Malcolm joined the 28th Precinct Community Council in Harlem. Another member was Cong. Adam Clayton Powell Jr., with whom he had developed an amenable working relationship. One of the council's functions was to invite African diplomats and leaders to Harlem, thus challenging the lie told to them by State Department officials that blacks in this country weren't interested in them or even were hostile toward them.

Malcolm, on his own, went further than just handling official welcomes; he often helped African diplomats find housing and schools for their children. Finding decent housing was especially difficult for them, since housing discrimination was rampant in the New York City metropolitan area. It was so bad in New York City and the Washington, D.C., area, in fact, that the ardent accommodationist Carl Rowan, then with the State Department, was forced to warn President Kennedy about the trouble it could cause for American foreign policy in Africa. "Americans who humiliate African diplomats by subjecting them to racial discrimination betray their country," Rowan reportedly told Kennedy. Rowan, who was no fan of Malcolm's, may have been aware of his outreach efforts.

Malcolm also took African, Asian, and Caribbean diplomats and students on personal tours of New York City. He used the time to educate them about the real state of race relations in the United States. He especially enjoyed directing them to Mr. Micheaux's bookstore and the Schomburg Center for Research in Black Culture, where they could find books about their own history not yet available in their countries.

Malcolm's most effective effort to reach out was the annual Afro-American Bazaar, which was launched on November 5, 1960. Dozens of African, Asian, and Caribbean diplomats and students were invited to the Rockland Palace in Harlem to enjoy food, nonalcoholic beverages, and conversations with several thousand grassroots Harlemites. They could also attend and participate in workshops designed to educate them about the connection between white supremacy and colonialism. As far as I know, no one else at that time was making such an ongoing effort to reach out to representatives of the emerging independent countries. Later, on the world professional tennis circuit, I occasionally met people who had attended one of the bazaars. Their remembrances were best reflected by an Asian Muslim who told me that Malcolm "was the first person in America who made me feel at home: I'll always remember Brother Malcolm and his smile."

Malcolm had a particularly close relationship with Ambassador Alex Quaison-Sackey of Ghana, the first African to be elected president of the UN General Assembly. Other important foreign leaders with whom he had ongoing relationships were Abdul Rahman Babu of Tanzania, Premier Patrice Lamumba of the Congo, King Faisal of Saudi Arabia, and Che Guevara of Cuba, second-in-command to Fidel Castro. Babu, Tanzania's minister of commerce and cooperatives, once spoke to OAAU members at Malcolm's invitation. When introducing him, Malcolm said, "I was honored to be on the platform with Africa's leading revolutionary. Our people need an education on what a revolution really is. We need to know what it costs. Here is a brother who can tell us."

Following an enthusiastic ovation, Babu praised Malcolm for his efforts to connect the struggle against white supremacy with that against colonialism on the African continent. Malcolm was pleased, just as he had been earlier when, in a UN debate over the Congo, several African diplomats had publicly made the same connection. "That was unprecedented," Ma said. "It resulted from the hard work Malcolm had been doing for five years."

Adlai Stevenson, U.S. ambassador to the United Nations, was livid with the Africans' statement, describing their language as "irrelevant, irresponsible, insulting, and repugnant." Stevenson's fervid response confirmed that the connection hit home. "Malcolm knew he was on the right track," Ma said.

Presidents Nkrumah and Nasser were two of Malcolm's most supportive contacts. "Malcolm told me that he felt like they were his brothers in the struggle against white supremacy and Western political and economic imperialism," Ma said. "He described them as serious about what they were doing, not babblers of rhetoric, as were too many of their colleagues." In fact, it was President Nasser who alerted Uncle Malcolm about an anti-Nasser African American Muslim who worked for the U.S. government and who might try to get next to him. It's not surprising that Presidents Nkrumah and Nasser, considering their adamant positions as foes of economic exploitation and imperialism, were on the State Department's "A" list of world leaders it could do without.

Ma was especially fond of Nasser. "If we had ten more black men like him," she insisted, "we could take back what is ours." Malcolm beamed when she talked like that. It showed how in sync they were in the struggle for human rights.

Malcolm first met most of his African peers on two visits to the continent in 1964. On the first, of five weeks' duration, between April 13, 1964, and May 21, 1964, he also took time to meet with King Faisal of Saudi Arabia. The king declared him a state guest, thereby awarding him the treatment usually reserved for visiting heads of state. He was provided with a car, a guide, a translator, a hotel suite, and a chauffeur. Their meeting, the main focus of which was Uncle Malcolm's move to orthodox Islam, was set up by Dr. Mahmoud Youssef Shawarbi, director of the Federation of Islamic Associations in the United States and Canada. The king, by the way, was considered a U.S. ally in the Middle East.

Malcolm cultivated those and other relationships at a time when

most other black leaders in this country barely paid lip service to foreign affairs. He criticized U.S. policy on white supremacist control
of South Africa and the Vietnam War, while others discreetly limited
their comments to civil rights. More so than any other prominent
black leader, he spoke out publicly in 1960 about U.S. efforts against
African nationalist Patrice Lumumba of the Congo. (Joseph Mobutu,
longtime president of Zaire, as the Congo was known during the
cold war, was one of the U.S. lackeys hostile to Lumumba. The
United States lavished millions of dollars on him as their pet leader
in Central Africa.) Malcolm first met Lumumba in 1960, when the
latter spoke at Howard University in Washington, D.C. He was so
impressed with the Congolese leader that during their private talk he
invited Lumumba to come to Harlem and present his message about
exploitative colonialism. They became such good friends that Malcolm named one of his daughters after him. Lumumba was determined to wrestle control of his country's mineral wealth from the
greedy and bloody hands of Belgium and its allies. For his efforts,
Lumumba was assassinated by forces supported by the United
States. Malcolm strongly condemned the U.S. role in Lumumba's
demise.

Malcolm also supported the Cuban revolution, not because of an
unquestioning commitment to Fidel Castro but because he knew that
under most previous Cuban leaders, black Cubans, the majority population on the island, were denied access to public accommodations
in restaurants, hotels, beaches, and other public facilities owned by
white Americans, including gangsters.

Malcolm was led to his position by his vast knowledge of black
history in the United States. He constantly reminded us that the
highly praised U.S. Constitution not only did not recognize human
rights of black people; it did not even acknowledge our ancestors as
full human beings. To placate southern enslavers concerned about
their representation in the House of Representatives, the "freedom-
loving," Christian founding fathers decided that each African would
be counted as three-fifths of a person. Is there any other written constitution in world history that described some of its residents as
three-fifths of a person? "With that as a beginning," said Ma, "it's no
wonder that the federal government for over two hundred years had

no qualms about failing to protect the human rights of our people. To make a strong case at the United Nations, all Malcolm had to do was cite the three-fifths clause in the Constitution and list all the documented occasions, from enslavement to lynchings to Jim Crow laws, that the federal government failed to protect our human rights. There was no need to distort or magnify that history."

Traditional civil-rights leaders knew that history as well as Malcolm did. "However, they also knew the history of what happened to black leaders who spoke forcefully on foreign affairs," said Ma. "Marcus Garvey, whose slogan, 'Africa for Africans,' deeply disturbed the colonialists, was jailed, then deported; Paul Robeson was flagrantly harassed and denied a passport for travel; W. E. B. Du Bois, who attended most of the early Pan-African conferences, was flagrantly harassed and also denied traveling rights. He eventually decided to live permanently in Ghana. Later, three years after Malcolm was assassinated, Martin Luther King Jr. was assassinated when he spoke the truth about the Vietnam War."

Malcolm refused to bow down before that history. He persisted in his advocacy for human rights and for connecting that struggle to the larger one going on in Asia and Africa. His efforts paid off big time in July 1964 when the Organization of African Unity (OAU), in an unprecedented move, invited him to its annual conference in Cairo as an unofficial observer-representative. He had attended the 1963 OAU Conference in Addis Ababa, Ethiopia, as an unofficial observer-representative of African Americans, his official status at the OAU. Delegates at the 1963 conference were impressed with his extensive knowledge of African affairs and his obvious deep commitment to the continent. Now that he was back by invitation, he was well prepared to take advantage of that unprecedented opportunity.

When Uncle Malcolm arrived in Cairo, he was warmly greeted by many of the delegates and other Africans. Though not allowed to speak, he was able to distribute a statement to the delegates, the press, and the general public that included the following:

The Organization of Afro-American Unity, in cooperation with a coalition of other Negro leaders and organizations, has decided to elevate our freedom struggle above the domestic level of civil rights. We intend to internationalize it by placing it at the level of human rights. Our freedom struggle for human dignity is no longer confined to the domestic jurisdiction of the United States government. We beseech the independent African States to help us bring our problem before the United Nations on the grounds that the U.S. government is morally incapable of protecting the lives and property of twenty-two million African Americans. . . . We assert the right of self-defense by whatever means necessary and reserve the right of maximum retaliation against our racist oppressors no matter what the odds are against us. . . . We are well aware that our future efforts to defend ourselves by retaliating—by meeting violence with violence, eye for eye and tooth for tooth—could create the type of racial conflict in America that could easily escalate into a violent, worldwide, bloody race war. In the interest of world peace and security, we beseech the heads of independent African states to recommend an immediate investigation into our problem by the U.N. Commission on Human Rights. If this humble plea that I am voicing at this conference is not properly worded, then let our elder brothers, who know the legal language, come to our aid and word our plea in the proper language necessary for it to be heard. . . .

That statement also reminded the Africans that as Malcolm explained, "recently three students from Kenya were mistaken for American Negroes and were brutally beaten by the New York City police. Shortly after that, two diplomats from Uganda were also beaten by New York City police, who mistook them for American Negroes. . . . Our problem is your problem. No matter how much independence Africans get here on the mother continent, unless you wear your native dress at all times when you visit America, you may be mistaken for one of us and suffer the same psychological humiliation and physical mutilation that is an everyday occurrence in our lives."

When put into the context of the time, Malcolm's statement was almost restrained. The years 1955–65 were a period when white supremacist terrorists embarked on a murderous and brutalizing rampage. Between 1955 and July 1964 alone, terrorists lynched fifteen-year-old Emmett Till in Mississippi, supposedly for whistling at a white woman; lynched Rev. George Lee in Mississippi for leading a voter-registration drive; lynched Lamar Wade in Mississippi for organizing black voters; assassinated local Jackson, Mississippi, NAACP head Medgar Evers for his civil-rights activities; and bombed a black Baptist church in Birmingham, Alabama, thus killing four adolescent girls—Addie Mae Collins, Denise McNair, Carole Robertson, and Cynthia Wesley. There had been thirty Birmingham bombings before the one that killed the girls, a factor that led some people to refer to the city as Bombingham.

Shortly before Malcolm left for the OAU conference, the terrorists struck again. On June 21, 1964, three civil rights workers, James Chaney, Andrew Goodman, and Michael Schwerner, were abducted and murdered in Philadelphia, Mississippi. On July 11, 1964, Lemuel Penn, a lieutenant colonel in the U.S. Army Reserves, was slain while driving north through Colbert, Georgia.

At the time Malcolm distributed the statement, not one person had been punished for those and dozens of other such atrocities. Presidents Dwight Eisenhower, John Kennedy, and Lyndon Johnson insisted that the federal government had no jurisdiction, that punishing such criminals was the responsibility of individual states. It was a responsibility that the states barely went through the motions of meeting. As a result, many known terrorist killers freely walked the streets of southern cities and towns in a position to either persist in their murderous assaults or at least urge others to continue the bombings, threats, harassments, and killings. The posture of Presidents Eisenhower, Kennedy, and Johnson underscored Malcolm's basic premise that the federal government was either unable or unwilling to protect the lives and property of black people. It was a powerful and persuasive argument.

While Malcolm was in Africa solidifying the OAAU's foreign-policy goals, racial tensions remained high and racial incidents continued to make headlines. Probably the most compelling event was the Harlem uprising in the summer of 1964. It was ignited on July 15, two days before the conference opened, when a white police officer, claiming to have acted in self-defense, shot and killed fifteen-year-old James Powell. Young Powell was the latest of a long list of black people killed by a law-enforcement officer claiming self-defense. And it was not the first time that the weapon—in this case a knife supposedly used by the attacker—was not anywhere to be found.

While Malcolm was in Africa, another major event was taking place. The Democratic Party refused to seat the Mississippi Freedom Party's (MFP) delegates at its national convention. The courageous Fannie Lou Hamer and others had formed the MFP to challenge Mississippi's white supremacist–dominated, regular Democratic Party delegates. Malcolm made sure that Africans with whom he spoke were aware of those and other such incidents. By the time he left Africa, in November 1964, he had carried the OAAU's message to many thousands of Africans, especially students.

In a statement summing up his views on the OAAU conference's response to his first statement, Malcolm said: "Upon my arrival in Cairo, I was met with open arms by the African leaders and their various delegations. They asked me to prepare a memorandum on the real status of our people in America. . . . My memorandum charged that this same racist element in the State Department knew that our newly formed Organization of Afro-American Unity was planning to internationalize America's race problem by lifting it from the level of *civil* rights to a struggle for the universally recognized *human* rights, and on these grounds we could then bring America before the United Nations and charge her with violating the UN Declaration of Human Rights and thereby of also violating the UN charter itself." To combat the OAAU's plan, Malcolm continued, "the racist element in the State Department very shrewdly gave maximum worldwide publicity to the recent passage of the Civil Rights bill which was only a desperate attempt to make the African States think the United States was sincerely trying to correct the continued injustices done to us and thereby maneuver the African governments into permitting America to keep her racism 'domestic' and still within her sole jurisdiction."

Later, when others joined the State Department in challenging his position on racial conditions because of the passage of the 1964 civil rights legislation, Malcolm retorted: "When someone sticks a knife into my back nine inches and then pulls it out six inches, they haven't done me any favor. And if they pull that knife which they stuck in my back all the way out, they still haven't done me any favor. They shouldn't have stabbed me in the back in the first place." The enslavement of African people was that initial stab in the back.

Helping the State Department with its spin control were members of the Peace Corps, who supposedly were in Africa for humanitarian reasons. Malcolm, who described some Peace Corps members as "missionaries for neocolonialism," was somewhat amused at their antics, especially those of the black volunteers. "Ella, you should have seen them," he told Ma. "Everywhere I went there they were, always trying to get me off to some dance, some dinner party, all designed to keep me from meeting with African leaders, students, businessman, and educators. They appeared completely oblivious to the fact that most of the African leaders and I knew they were Uncle Toms sent there to look out for the interests of the white man. Their main function was to help drive a wedge between us and the Africans."

Malcolm praised African leaders for passing a resolution supporting the OAAU's request, adding: "This resolution has so many frightening implications for America's future image and position in the world, especially for her foreign policy in this crucial election year. It is not surprising that the American press completely smothered the fact that the Second Summit Conference passed such a resolution despite the fact that it was sent over UPI wire services to all the American news outlets."

"After Malcolm distributed those two statements at the OAU conference," Ma said later, "there was no turning back. The FBI and CIA now knew that he was serious about exposing their lies and distortions about race relations in this country to the world. And more and more people were listening to him, here and abroad. I must admit to having had mixed feelings about his great success. On the one hand, I was as proud of my brother as I had ever been. I had envisioned him as a national leader of our people; he had become an international one. On the other hand, I've already noted the evils that confronted black leaders who spoke truthfully and forcefully to foreign countries about race relations in this country or who made the connection between white colonialism in Africa and Asia and white supremacy in the United States. When I shared my concerns with Malcolm, he said passionately, 'Ella, if they want you, they get you. They got Kennedy. So what can I do?' I couldn't answer that question."

Ma, mixed feelings and all, was among a host of OAAU and MMI members who enthusiastically greeted Malcolm when he returned in November after eighteen weeks of promoting his foreign policy in Africa. They had read the full text of both of his statements in issues of the *Blacklash,* the OAAU newsletter edited by A. Peter Bailey, so they were aware of his huge accomplishment. That Malcolm by then had spent some twenty-three weeks, nearly half a year, establishing and solidifying contact abroad demonstrated to them the crucial importance he gave to the necessity of moving our struggle against white supremacy into the international arena.

As Malcolm arrived through customs at Kennedy Airport, he looked up and saw a couple of dozen supporters standing behind the glass wall, waving, smiling, and holding signs of welcome; he smiled broadly and waved back. He later told us that it was a moving sight which he hadn't expected.

Ma was not with us at the airport. "Betty and I decided to greet him at home. We shared a concern about his safety and would have preferred that he return quietly and get out of that airport terminal as quickly as possible. We knew that people representing the corrupt N.O.I. leadership in Chicago, the FBI, and the CIA were most certainly lurking in Kennedy Airport that day. After Malcolm's statements were distributed in Africa and his first public statement in October 1964 about Elijah Muhammad's out-of-wedlock babies, his enemies knew that he couldn't be silenced by threats. That left them one option—to kill him."

All the while Malcolm was gone, the N.O.I.'s leadership subjected him to a constant barrage of vitriolic verbal and written personal attacks. In some cases, actual physical attacks were made on some of his supporters. I knew personally just how far some of them would go based on an incident that occurred in early July 1964, shortly before Malcolm left for the OAU conference. Because of the great hostility toward him emanating from Louis X's Temple Eleven we took special security precautions when Malcolm came to Boston.

We would spread the word that he would be speaking at four or five places at the same time. We also would use someone, equally tall and physically shaped like Malcolm, as a decoy. For that appearance the decoy was Brother Benjamin X (Goodman), formerly of Temple Seven in Harlem, who left the N.O.I. with Malcolm. After he spoke, we all gathered at one of Ma's properties on Massachusetts Avenue. We knew that members of Temple Eleven in parked cars were watching our house. To throw them off Malcolm's trail, Brother Benjamin was dressed in such a way that caused the N.O.I. crew to believe it was Malcolm we were taking to Logan Airport. As we drove off in Ma's four-door 1959 Cadillac, three cars filled with N.O.I. operatives followed us. I was driving. Brother Benjamin sat in the backseat with a brother on each side of him. When we entered Callahan Tunnel on the way to the airport, traffic was very slow. One of the N.O.I. cars began bumping our car from behind, which caused me to bump the car in front of me. Suddenly, when traffic briefly stopped, occupants from one of the N.O.I. cars jumped out of their car, ran back to ours, and tried to open the two back doors, where they thought Malcolm was sitting. What no one else knew was that I had put an unloaded shotgun in the car, keeping the bullets in the glove compartment. When I told the others about the gun, Brother Benjamin told one of the brothers to get the gun, open the window, and point it at the person pulling the door. When he did that, the at-tacker jumped back, screaming, "He has a gun! He has a gun!" That, plus the fact that traffic was now moving again, enabled me to pull away from them. When we got to the airport, state police, called by someone who had witnessed the confrontation in the tunnel, drove up in a few minutes. The N.O.I. attackers, who were still following us, saw this and quickly sped away. We were all arrested, including Brother Benjamin, but we were bailed out that afternoon. It was a heady experience for a nineteen-year-old, one that graphically illus-trated to me the very real danger faced by Malcolm. The one positive point was that our plan worked. While the action was taking place in Boston, Malcolm, without distractions from N.O.I. zealots, was lis-tening to a debate at the United Nations.

While the N.O.I. was making threats, the FBI was active on an-other level. In September 1964, during the period Malcolm was visit-

ing Africa, Hoover received two pieces of correspondence from the
Department of Justice's Internal Security Division requesting his
help and direction on using the Logan Act against Malcolm. This is
an act which allows the prosecution of "any citizen of the United
States . . . who, without the authority of the United States, directly or
indirectly commences or carries on any correspondence or inter-
course with any foreign government or any officer or agent thereof."
Malcolm, devoid of any quixotic illusions about his government enemies, was well aware of the Logan Act, Ma said. "We had several
lengthy discussions about it. He actually considered registering as a
spokesman for the OAU in this country. This was no big secret,
since he had already inquired about the possibility. The CIA asked
the State Department to refuse him that status. His assassination
ended all those moves on their part and his. Obviously they had decided that he had to be eliminated, not just harassed."

Ma and others kept Malcolm abreast of those activities, so he knew
what to expect when he returned. Despite that knowledge, from November 24, 1964, when he returned, until February 21, 1965, when
he was assassinated, he steadily pressed forward with his agenda on
both the domestic and international fronts. Domestically, among
other activities, he spoke at four OAAU rallies (he was assassinated
at the fifth), at the Harvard Law School Forum, at a rally in Detroit, in
Selma, Alabama, where he supported the Martin Luther King Jr.–led
campaign for voting rights, and at a Harlem Youth Opportunities
Unlimited Forum in Harlem. He also announced his support for Fannie Lou Hamer and the Mississippi Freedom Democratic Party and
was a guest on several television and radio programs in different
cities. A personal highlight was the December birth of his fourth
daughter, Amiliah.

Internationally, Malcolm was equally busy. He participated in a
debate at Oxford University in England, addressed the First of the
Council of African Organizations in London, delivered another
speech at the London School of Economics, and was interviewed on
a television program in Toronto, Canada.

Besides dealing with several particular issues, in all his speeches
Malcolm reiterated his position that the U.S. government was either
unable or unwilling to protect the lives and property of black people,

thus compelling us to take our case to the UN Commission on Human Rights. Malcolm was never naive enough to believe that the United States, with all its military and economic power, would have to obey a UN resolution, but the propaganda implications were enormous. That's what the State Department and the CIA wanted to avoid at all costs.

What the Nation leadership wanted to avoid at all costs was any discussion about Elijah Muhammad's out-of-wedlock babies. They went into an apoplectic rage every time Malcolm responded to questions on the subject. He rarely initiated the discussion but responded when asked direct questions. Ma wanted him to shut up about the subject no matter how many questions were asked. "I urged him to say absolutely nothing to anyone at any time about those babies," Ma said. "The women involved were all adults, not children. They made a choice, a bad one as it turned out, but it was their choice. The problem was that Malcolm believed he had to get involved because one of those women was Evelyn, to whom he had once been engaged and whom he recommended for employment with Elijah Muhammad. That, along with the added factors that he had helped spread Elijah Muhammad's strict guidelines on sexual morality to many thousands of people, had even punished fellow members of the N.O.I., including one of his own brothers, who violated the guidelines, compelled him to speak out when asked."

Ma continued: "I was among those close to Malcolm, including Betty, who wanted him to take a breather from the struggle and focus for a while on himself and his family. I urged him to take a little time and build up his financial situation so he could better take care of his family and his agenda for the OAAU. After totally devoting over ten years of his life to the struggle for human rights, there were times he was so broke he couldn't even afford to buy a suit. I once teased him that Captain Joseph, a Temple Seven functionary, dressed better than he did."

Shirley Graham Du Bois, widow of the late great educator activist and Pan-Africanist W. E. B. Du Bois, was another person who suggested a new direction for Malcolm. When he visited her home in Cairo in July 1964, Mrs. Du Bois proposed that he accept a teaching position at a university in Ghana and that he take over the project of compiling the Encyclopedia Africana, begun by her husband, Dr. Du Bois, who died before it was completed. Malcolm, who greatly admired Du Bois for his Pan-Africanism, was honored by Mrs. Du Bois's proposal. According to Ma, he was considering it when he was assassinated.

We believe that Mrs. Du Bois knew about the severe pressures on Malcolm, since she had seen her husband experience somewhat similar ones from government agencies. The pressures culminated in two ominous incidents occurring less than two weeks before Malcolm was assassinated. The first was his being banned from France on February 9, 1965. He was scheduled to speak at a rally sponsored by the OAAU affiliate in Paris and to meet privately with several African and Asian freedom fighters. When he disembarked from the plane at Paris's Orly Field after a flight from London, French officials were waiting. Without even letting him go to the terminal to make a phone call, they put him on another plane that took him back to London. Many people, including Ma and me, believed that the French government acted upon a request from the U.S. State Department, which was aware of the purpose of Uncle Malcolm's visit. Later, Ma was told that that was not the case. In fact, the French government, knowing of the CIA's plans to eliminate Malcolm, had double-crossed the United States. "They didn't want any action taken against Malcolm on French soil," Ma explained. "They knew about the failed attempt to kill him by poisoning when he was in Africa and were concerned that another attempt would be made on his life in Paris, an attempt that would be blamed on French colonialists angry about Malcolm's close relationship with Ahmed Ben Bella." Ben Bella was an Algerian nationalist detested by those who wanted to maintain French control of his country. For that reason and because of France's concern about his scheduled private meetings with the freedom fighters, de Gaulle declared Malcolm persona non grata.

The second ominous incident, the firebombing of Malcolm's home in the East Elmhust, Queens, section of New York City, occurred five days later, on February 14, 1965. It was particularly ominous because for the first time the lives of Malcolm's pregnant wife and four young daughters were directly endangered. Ma and I sped to New York City from Boston the minute we heard about the cowardly attack. Ma barely spoke as we made our way to the city. I was seething with anger, as any nineteen-year-old would be, vowing to exact revenge on those who had attacked my uncle, aunt, and cousins. We knew that some in the Nation were enraged about Malcolm's responses to questions about Mr. Muhammad's out-of-wedlock babies, but we really didn't believe they would attack a pregnant woman and small children.

Those two incidents, happening so close together, confirmed that the threat to Malcolm had increased dramatically. It was both infuriating and frustrating for those of us close to Malcolm to be so aware of the threat but so helpless to do something about it. Ma actually began reconsidering plans to kidnap him and move him to a place where he would be safer. That she would even contemplate such an utterly impractical plan illustrates the depth of her concern. "I was absolutely convinced that a live, less visible Malcolm was more important to us in the long run than a martyred Malcolm," Ma told me later.

As family members, we seethed when we listened to or read about threats directed toward Malcolm by John Ali, Raymond Sharrieff, Captain Joseph, and Louis X. The latter still adamantly denies any involvement in the assassination but has admitted to helping create an atmosphere bloated with the kind of tension, confusion, and intrigue that allowed skilled killers, used to carrying out political assassinations, to operate with deadly effectiveness.

Government agencies, as we later learned from FBI files, gleefully wanted and in some cases orchestrated the move on Malcolm. They were the puppeteers, with N.O.I. operatives acting as willing puppets. For more comprehensive details on how the sinister campaign was carried out, three books—Karl Evanzz's *Judas Factor;* Zak A. Kondo's *Conspiracys: Unraveling the Assassination of Malcolm X;* and Clayborne Carson's *Malcolm X: The F.B.I. File*—are highly recommended.

It was the atmosphere that Louis X admits to helping create that we had to live with during the last year of Uncle Malcolm's life. If it was hard for us, surely it was unimaginably stressful for Uncle Malcolm. It was that same atmosphere that set up the events of February 21, 1965.

THIRTEEN The Assassination

February 21, 1965, was a cold, sunny, clear day in Boston. Ma and I had returned earlier that morning after a hectic week with Malcolm in New York City. We had gone to the city the previous Sunday following the firebombing of his home. Though nearly bone-tired I was still too hyper to sleep, so shortly after arriving back in Boston, I went to visit a friend. It was there that I first saw the television newsflash about Uncle Malcolm's assassination. I didn't even wait to watch the entire report. My first reaction was to race home to be with Ma. I made the normally ten-minute drive in record time. When I raced into the house, our eyes met; Ma saw immediately that I had heard about the assassination, and I was sure that she knew. Her bearer of bad news was Sheik Ahmed Hassoun, a short, slender, ebony-hued Sudanese Muslim elder who for the past several months had been Malcolm's spiritual adviser and grandfather-like friend. As Betty stood by, he had told Ma the devastating but not totally unexpected news. Ma, still as calm and controlled as ever, told me that we would be leaving for New York City in the next few minutes. I knew Ma was emotionally wrought over the news, but like her Little brothers and sisters, she wasn't about to show it, especially when there were important things to do.

I wasn't so calm. I was consumed with a rage I had never experienced before, my mind flooded with a million ways to seek revenge on those murderers responsible for my uncle's assassination. I was especially livid with the N.O.I. leadership and members who had directed continuous venomous threats against a person I loved and re-

spected above all others. Being with and around him had been a
never-ending learning process.

In my early teens, I had joined the Nation because of Uncle Malcolm. I had heard him speak, on his trips to Boston or on ours to
New York City, and the learning process continued. I soaked up
every thing he said. He usually stayed with us in Boston, and I will-
ingly gave up my bedroom and my favorite rocking chair to him. I
traveled around Boston with him—as much as he or Ma would
allow—and was never happier than when I could drive him to his
meetings and other appointments. The learning process continued
during those drives. Sometimes he spoke with me about what he was
currently doing; other times he read or sat silently in deep contem-
plation. I felt very grown-up at those times.

As Ma and I drove to New York City, there was very little conversation, but I could see that she was hurting. All I could think about
was how we could have let this happen. We knew what was coming.
Why hadn't we found some kind of way to stop it? All of us around
Uncle Malcolm were nothing but chumps, I thought to myself; we
talked a big game but really were useless.

I relived in my mind the previous week. The firebombing of Malcolm's home was the last straw for Ma. "More than ever I wanted
Malcolm to take his family and get away for a while," she said. "I
still believed he was more valuable to us and the movement as a live
leader than a dead martyr. 'Just leave, Malcolm,' I urged. 'Go to
Africa for a few years. Take one of those positions you have been offered.' He was concerned that Betty wouldn't want to make such a
major move. 'Yes, she will,' I said. 'If you leave, Betty will follow.'"
Malcolm wasn't so sure. Betty strongly resisted moving away from
the America with which she was very familiar and where she had
friends around to be with her when he was on the road pursuing his
political goals, as he often was. Malcolm also thought a pregnant
Betty might be too frail for such a move. "Betty is much stronger
than she appears," Ma insisted. "You should tell her straight out that
we are going to pack some suitcases, get the children ready, and
move on."

When the move-to-Africa proposal was rejected, Ma made another suggestion—move to our summer home in Duxbury, Massa-

chusetts. Again, Uncle Malcolm hesitated. In addition to Betty's resistance to moving, he strongly believed that it was important for
him to be in New York City, where the international action was.
"That's just why you need to leave New York City for a while," Ma
argued. "You need to get away from the action for a while." Ma was
very upset with Malcolm most of that week because he seemed
oblivious to safety concerns; with Aunt Betty for not insisting on
their moving away from the dangers lurking in New York City; with
those forces threatening her brother's life; with key members of the
OAAU for bedeviling Malcolm with their petty turf disputes; and
with herself for being unable to convince Malcolm to lay low for a
while. Once, she actually blew up, declaring that "everyone is walking around like zombies just waiting for Dr. Death to knock on the
door."

Sheik Hassoun was even angrier than Ma. Some people in the
OAAU, most notably James Shabazz, the organization's chief admin-
istrator, often dismissed Sheik Hassoun as a backward old man totally out of touch with the times. When he walked through Harlem's
streets in his Sudanese dress and with his sturdy walking cane, one
could swear he was from the time of Moses. But Sheik Hassoun was
well aware of what was happening around Malcolm. The two of
them had developed a loving relationship, one that made Hassoun
very concerned about Malcolm's safety. According to Ma, "Sheik
Hassoun told me that no matter what Malcolm said, every person
who came to OAAU meetings or to the office should be searched.
He was also deeply suspicious of the loyalty of some of the people
around Malcolm."

For some reason, we learned later from Sheik Hassoun, Malcolm
ordered him not to come to the Audubon Ballroom for the OAAU
rally on February 21. When Malcolm saw him there, he snapped at
him, for the first time, ordering him to "get away from here." Sheik
Hassoun stayed. Because of Malcolm's stubbornness about security,
Sheik Hassoun maintained later, Malcolm was assassinated; made
the call to Ma, with whom he also had a close relationship, and we
were relieved that he would be there comforting the family when we
got to New York City.

By the time we got to Tom Wallace's home in Queens, where

Betty and the children were staying, I had cooled down considerably, aided by Ma's stern warning that if I didn't get myself together I wouldn't be much help to Betty and my little cousins. I knew that one of my responsibilities would be to help with the children. It was early evening when we arrived. We had covered the normally five-hour drive in four hours. We found all present to be in a calm frame of mind. There were tears but no hysteria. The adults spoke with a kind of deliberate calmness designed to soothe the children who were milling around. "I was really impressed with and proud of the way Betty handled the children that evening," Ma said later, "especially the way she soothed them." The children obviously realized the gravity of it all and seemed determined to be as calm as the adults. I was outwardly calm, but inwardly I was still considering ways to wreak havoc on those who had murdered my uncle. I shared Sheik Hassoun's position that the OAAU security force should have ignored Malcolm's order not to search everyone who came through the door. After all, I reasoned, the president of the United States has little, if any, say in security operations. If he says no, they say, "Too bad. Our job is to look out for the larger issue of your safety and the country." Malcolm was, in essence, our president. We should have had the same attitude. Now it was too late.

Just how late it was became official on February 22, 1965, when I accompanied Ma, Betty, and Percy Sutton, Malcolm's attorney, to the city morgue to identify Malcolm's body. When I saw his bullet-riddled body on that stainless-steel table, I experienced a twinge of anger even at the man whom I deeply loved and respected. You gave up on your safety, Uncle Malcolm, I thought. This wouldn't have happened if you and the rest of us had been more security conscious. All this was done inwardly, since Ma had sternly warned me that there were to be no emotional displays in front of the whites present. I knew she wasn't joking.

After that odious task, we returned to the Wallace home, where Ma, Betty, and Mr. Sutton began discussing funeral arrangements. That task provided the first concrete evidence of how successful the assassination had been in frightening and intimidating people. Several funeral homes and major Harlem churches, fearful, they said, of possible violence, refused to handle Malcolm's funeral. Though I now try to understand their fears, at the time I added them to the ever-growing list of people to be loathed and despised. Cong. Adam Clayton Powell Jr. would have let us use the Abyssinian Baptist Church, but his board of trustees said no. Ma and Betty, still as calm as ever, never showed how the rejection hurt them. Finally, Unity Funeral Home agreed that his body could lie in state there, and Bishop Alvin A. Childs's Faith Temple Church agreed to be the site of his funeral services. To them, especially to Bishop Childs, we are eternally grateful.

Once sites were secured for the services, Ma and I had to hurriedly return to Boston to get more clothes and more money. Malcolm spent most of his time taking care of movement business, not making money. Unlike his former colleagues in the N.O.I., he had not enriched himself at the expense of the people he led and for whom he spoke. The money Betty had, mostly coming from the autobiography advance, was needed to take care of basic expenses for her and the children. There was none for funeral expenses. Ma agreed to take care of those. While in Boston, Ma, in a February 25 press conference, announced that at Malcolm's request she would now head both the MMI and the OAAU and that she would pay off his debts. She followed through on that pronouncement.

When we went back to New York City for the February 27 funeral service and burial, I stopped by Unity Funeral Home and saw some of the thousands who over the past few days had come to pay respects to Malcolm. Still angry, I was not impressed. Where were you thousands when he was alive and needed political, moral, and financial support? I wanted to ask every single one of them. Uncle's body was in a glass-topped, sealed-tight casket selected by Ma and agreed to by Betty. Ma's plan was to eventually bury Malcolm in a tomb or take his body to Mecca.

Imam Sheik Hassoun prepared the body for a Muslim funeral, and Imam Hashaam Jaaber said Islamic prayers at the burial site in Hartsdale, New York's Ferncliff Cemetery. When time came to spread dirt over Malcolm's casket, I felt strange when I saw the cemetery's white employees doing it. "I'll do that," I said firmly. I was assisted by three other brothers, who also joined me in Muslim prayer at Malcolm's burial site after everyone else had gone.

After the funeral and burial, Ma and I returned to Boston, where we really had to begin confronting the fact that Malcolm was dead. He had been a central and connecting presence in our lives for as long as I could remember. However, there was little time to dwell on grief. As head of the MMI and the OAAU, Ma had much to take care of, and I had to help her. One of her first tasks was to arrange for Sheik Hassoun's return home. He was anxious to leave, having become thoroughly disgusted with all the threats and violence and all the petty infighting among members of the MMI and the OAAU. "I have no desire to be part of such discord," he told Ma. With the help of Brother Ahmad Osman, she arranged for him to go home.

Then she had to deal with a human-rights petition several OAU members were planning to present to the General Assembly of the United Nations. "I soon realized," Ma said, "that without Malcolm's drive, commitment, and persuasive skills, the petition had little chance of success. The government agencies who were the puppeteers behind his assassination knew that better than anyone else."

The event that just about guaranteed that the petition plan would fail was the U.S.-backed overthrow of President Kwame Nkrumah's government in Ghana on February 24, 1966, one year and three days after Malcolm was assassinated. President Nkrumah was a deeply committed Pan-Africanist and probably Malcolm's closest contact on the African continent. His overthrow was a devastating blow to Pan-Africanism.

While the petition plan accusing the United States of violating and failing to protect the lives and property of African Americans was sidetracked, another goal of Malcolm's foreign policy was more fruitful, even after his death. That goal had been to convince Africans and Asians, especially the former, that their struggle against white colonialism on their continents was directly tied to our struggle against white supremacy in the United States. There were several indications that at least some African UN diplomats had heard Malcolm. On March 12, 1965, less than a month after he was assassinated, a *New York Times* article, headlined "World Court Opens African Case Monday," noted: "The United Nations World Court of Justice would entertain oral proceedings starting Monday linking the American Negro's struggle against segregation in the United States with the

fate of Africans in South Africa. . . . African complainants, searching
for arguments to defeat the race-separation policy of South Africa,
have hit on the obvious parallels between the two situations. . . . The
World Court proceedings at The Hague could have significant repercussions through much of Africa."

In February 1966, a year after Malcolm's assassination, the same
paper published an article which said that "a London group calling
itself the Council of African Organizations had violently attacked
the United States over the murder of Malcolm X (El-Hajj Malik El-
Shabazz). The group is made up of students and other unofficial
African representatives here. A press release described Malcolm as a
leader in the struggle against American imperialism, oppression, and
radicalism. It said, 'The butchers of Patrice Lumumba are the very
same monsters who murdered Malcolm X in cold blood.'"

Such reactions, along with dozens of editorials and articles printed
about Malcolm in African and Asian newspapers, prompted Carl T.
Rowan, then director of the U.S. Information Agency, to take action.
Rowan, considered by many the quintessential "house Negro," said,
among other things, that when he first heard of Malcolm's assassination, "I knew there was a real danger of it being grossly miscon-
strued in countries where there was a lack of information about what
had actually taken place, what Malcolm X was, what he stood for, or
what was being espoused by those Negroes with whom Malcolm X
was in conflict. I asked my colleagues in the agency to do an extra-
zealous job of getting out the facts, of informing the world in order
that we might minimize damaging reactions based on emotion, prejudice, and misinformation." To Rowan's dismay, many Africans and
Asian leaders, students, and newspaper editorialists, ignored his reaction to Malcolm's assassination, which was based on Rowan's
personal prejudice and misinformation. He simply could never accept Malcolm's political beliefs.

Those reactions didn't just happen out of the blue. Malcolm laid
the foundation for them in the late 1950s when he befriended
African and Asian diplomats and students who were puzzled and angered when encountering white supremacy in this country. It was a
plan designed to take advantage of the opening made by the fero-
cious cold-war propaganda struggle between the United States and

the Soviet Union over which of the two predominantly white powers was going to control the mineral resources of the newly emerging African and Asian countries. The so-called cold-war struggle, he often told us, had very little to do with human rights and justice. The FBI's and CIA's unrelenting hostility toward Malcolm must be put into the context of that struggle, which was probably at its hottest and fiercest in the early 1960s.

I did what I could to help Ma with her MMI and OAAU responsibilities. For some two years after Malcolm's assassination, knowing how it affected me, she was lenient with me. After that, she demanded that I shape up and get a life. Often during those two years of grace, I thought about and relived some of the unforgettable moments I had listening to, working with, and otherwise supporting Malcolm. I remembered when Ma, concerned about Malcolm's security, bought him a very expensive pair of gloves to wear when driving his car. They had heard about a chemical poison developed by the CIA that, when put on the steering wheel, could enter a person's body undetected via the fingertips and cause death. "It made death look like the result of a heart attack," Ma said. "We heard about it from one of Malcolm's Asian contacts."

I remembered Malcolm once jokingly telling Ma that if he had known that Martin Luther King Jr. lived so close to the N.O.I. temple when he was a graduate student at Boston University in 1952, he would have attempted to fish him into the Nation. It's very ironic that their paths crossed only once when they were alive. Those people who always like to insist that Malcolm had made a dramatic change in his outlook should read Dr. King's rarely mentioned last book *Where Do We Go From Here, Community or Chaos?* My co-author, Peter Bailey, says he once read the following Dr. King statement which students thought was made by Uncle Malcolm:

A second important step that the Negro must take is to work passionately for group identity. This does not mean group isolation or group exclusivity. It means the kind of group consciousness that Negroes need in order to participate more meaningfully at all levels of the life of our nation. . . . This form of group identity can do infinitely more to liberate the Negro than any action of *individuals* [italics his]. We have been oppressed as a group, and we must overcome our oppression as a group.

Talk about a dramatic change. Except for the words "our nation," Malcolm would totally agree with that statement.

I remembered the time when Ma and Malcolm worked on disguises, including a false beard that he sometimes used, especially when in Boston, home of the very hostile Louis X and Clarence X (Gill) of Temple Eleven. She was even prepared to disguise him in a dress if necessary.

I remembered Malcolm visiting us sometimes just to relax. He would sit in my Shaker rocking chair, with its big burgundy cushion, and read or silently look out the bay window, in deep thought.

I remembered that one chilling moment when Malcolm, fatigued and temporarily disheartened, said in response to Ma's question about his safety, "I'm already dead, Ella." I can't express in words the look on Ma's face when he said that. I was crushed.

I remembered that Malcolm loved books with a passion. He seemed to be in seventh heaven when in Mr. Micheaux's Harlem bookstore or in the basement of his home, where books abounded on the floor, on shelves on the walls, on tables and desks. On many occasions, he sent me to the Harvard Square newsstand in Cambridge to pick up a variety of magazines and newspapers, whose contents he devoured.

I remembered Ma receiving many phone calls from angry activists throughout the country who supported Malcolm; they were seeking her backing for their plan to take revenge on N.O.I. officials in New York for what they considered their role in Malcolm's assassination. Ma refused their requests. "Malcolm wouldn't want that," she insisted. "If he had been interested in something like that, he could have launched it when he was alive. All he had to do was give the word and much blood would have been shed, to the delight of white supremacists." Some of the activists ignored her plea. It's believed by many that they burned down Temple Seven the evening of the assassination.

I remembered how emotional Malcolm got when he sat in the United Nations and heard Ousmane Ba, Mali's foreign minister, make a blistering attack on U.S. policy in the Congo. Ba bitterly denounced the "imperialistic forces of reaction, obscurantism, and racism" that were responsible for the murders of "Dag Hammarskjöld, Patrice Lumumba, and John F. Kennedy." Malcolm told Ma how moved he was to hear racism included in Mr. Ba's speech, for he had been encouraging African diplomats to do just that.

I remembered being a bit jealous during my teenage years about having to share my uncle with other family members, N.O.I. members, and later, OAAU and MMI members when he was in Boston.

I remembered once asking Uncle Malcolm if Ma had really thrown him and Sophia (the white woman he was involved with in his preprison, street-running days) down the stairs when she caught him sneaking her into the house. "While I was sneaking Sophia in," he told me, "Ella must have heard me opening the door to the downstairs hallway. She waited until I opened the door, then dumped dozens of books from the upstairs bookcase all over us. I never could fool your mother."

I remembered Ma telling me how upset Malcolm was when he came to visit one day in the mid-1950s and found out she had a blond-haired German tenant. She used to cook in our kitchen. I learned my first German words from her. "How could you have that white devil in your house, cooking your food?" Malcolm asked Ma. "She needed a place to stay. I needed the money," Ma responded, looking straight at her brother. He let it go.

Finally, I remembered the evening of February 20, 1965. We were all crowded into Tom Wallace's home, a situation with which Malcolm was very uncomfortable. He feared that his presence was endangering the lives and property of the Wallaces, especially after the firebombing. The Wallaces assured him that they were doing what any good and supportive neighbor would do. "The Wallaces were real heroes," Ma said later. "They came through when many others had been scared off. We owe them eternal gratitude." Tom Wallace, his wife, and his children, Gail and Tom Junior, Betty, the four children, Sheik Hassoun, Ma, Malcolm, and I were in the house. A regular visitor was Malcolm's attorney, Percy Sutton, who was later elected as Manhattan borough president. At about 9:00 P.M. in the evening, Betty and Mrs. Wallace cooked dinner for everyone. Gail and Tom junior were watching the children—Attilah, Qubilah, Ilyasah and Amilah—who were busy running through the house. It was past their bedtime, but no one really tried to put them to bed. Malcolm was scheduled to stay in a hotel that night, but he wouldn't leave until the children were in bed. "I want to say good night to them after they're in bed," he told us.

Ma, Tom Senior, Sheik Hassoun, Malcolm, and I were in the front room. Malcolm often looked nervously out the window, checking out the street and his car. That made Tom Senior and the rest of us very nervous. Finally Tom Senior said, "Please, Brother Malcolm. Stay away from the window. I'll check things out for you." Malcolm, who seemed rather listless, didn't argue with him.

He then decided that he needed a briefcase that was in the car. Ma and Sheik Hassoun told him there was no way he was leaving the house to get that briefcase. "Let Rodnell get it," Ma said. Somewhat reluctantly, Malcolm gave me the keys to his four-door Oldsmobile 98, one of the few things he had accepted from the N.O.I. when he headed Temple Seven. Unlike his former colleagues in Chicago, he didn't believe that the hard-earned money given by dedicated members should be spent on personal items for N.O.I. officials.

When I returned with the briefcase, I gave it to him but held on to the keys, hoping he would forget about leaving for the hotel. I wanted him to stay with us, his family. It still pains me to recall how listless and despondent he looked most of that evening with us. He was moving around almost zombielike. That was the only time I ever saw him look like that; I expected him to be his old self by the next day.

Sometime between 11:00 and 11:30 P.M., hoping it might liven him up, I asked Malcolm to join us for a picture-taking session. While the pictures were being taken, he asked me for his car keys. I pretended I didn't know where they were. "You must have misplaced them," I suggested. He gave me a look similar to the one Ma gave to let me know I had better do what she said or else. "Rodnell, *you* have my keys," he said firmly, looking me straight in the eyes. I gave them to him. The picture-taking session did relax him somewhat, but when looking at the photographs later, I saw the sadness in his eyes.

It was sometime between midnight and 12:30 A.M., February 21, 1965, that the children, now completely worn out, went to bed. Malcolm quietly went into their room and tenderly kissed each of them good night, which means that the last thing his daughters received from their father was a good-night kiss. He also lay down for a while with them and Betty. After that he was ready to leave for the hotel, which, contrary to popular belief, was not in midtown Manhattan but in Queens, near Kennedy Airport. It was to be several hours, though, before he got to the hotel. With mostly everyone settled in, he wanted to speak privately with Ma and me. Since that couldn't be done in the crowded house, we went to his car. He sat in the driver's seat, Ma next to him in the passenger seat, and I sat in the back. He knew that there was the possibility that New York City Bureau of Special Services agents might be able to listen to us with their ultramodern surveillance devices, but we really had no other choice but to use the car.

Malcolm did most of the talking. Ma mostly listened but every now and then would ask a pertinent question. I just listened. I believe that he had asked me to be with them because he knew that whatever he wanted Ma to do, I would have to help her. For the next couple of hours he spoke about a variety of things, most notably his wife and children. He told Ma that she must be prepared to help raise the children if that became necessary. He expressed regret that pursuing his political and economic agenda had deprived him of more time with the girls. "I believe that what I've been trying to do to fight white supremacy will benefit them later in life," he said. "That's my only consolation."

He expressed annoyance at Betty's obstinate position against moving from New York City. "With her being pregnant and her being a nurse, I understand her concern about the quality of medical care available in Ghana or Saudi Arabia [the two places most prominently mentioned as sanctuaries]," he said, "but if necessary she could be flown to Europe for delivery of the baby. She just doesn't seem to fully understand how worried I am about her and the children remaining here if something happens to me. If she doesn't go to Ghana or Saudi Arabia, they have to be with you, Ella." Ma just nodded. "I very seriously doubted that Betty had any intention of moving to

Ghana, Saudi Arabia, or Boston," she later said, "but I kept my doubts to myself. I knew Malcolm wanted to talk, so I had decided to listen very carefully."

Malcolm also told Ma that events of the past month had forced him to reconsider who was the main force behind the attacks he was subjected to. "I know what John Ali and the Nation can and cannot do," he said. "I don't even believe it's the FBI anymore. It's the CIA that's behind all of this. They're extremely afraid of my contacts in Africa and Asia." It was that statement by Malcolm which later led Ma to resist those who wanted her to approve of revenge-driven attacks on members of the Nation of Islam.

Malcolm also spoke about his money problems. "There are several nations from whom I could get money," he said, "but the State Department is just waiting for me to accept so they can accurately accuse me of Logan Act and Smith Act violations."

"Don't worry about money right now," Ma told him, "It's very important but can be dealt with later."

By that time, I realized, to my utter dismay, that my Uncle was talking like someone who wasn't going to be around much longer. I was stunned but still didn't speak. I was hoping that Ma would revise her plan to arrange for the kidnapping of Malcolm to get him off the streets for a while. I was definitely going to encourage her to do so when we were alone.

As they continued talking, my age and my total fatigue after a hectic, stressful week overwhelmed me, and I fell asleep. I will regret falling asleep for the rest of my life. When Ma woke me up, it was a couple of hours later. She never told me all of what they talked about while I slept. Her death in August 1996 means that no one will ever know unless the police's listening devices were operating.

I shook Malcolm's hand when Ma and I got out of the car. They embraced. We waved as he drove off to the hotel. Ma and I left immediately for Boston, going home for the first time in a week. The next time I saw my much-loved, brilliant, and loving uncle, his body was lying on a steel-gray table in a New York City morgue.

FOURTEEN Symbolism Without Substance

The first six to eight years after Uncle Malcolm's assassination were extremely difficult ones for Ma. Among the many challenges she personally dealt with was the devastating loss of a brother whom she deeply loved and respected; she also had to keep the Organization of Afro-America Unity (OMU) afloat. That eventually proved to be almost a lark compared to another responsibility she had assumed, which was to strongly challenge those forces that, for various reasons, wanted to use Malcolm's name and legacy to gain recognition and financial rewards.

Those who approached her for information and material were usually of two types—individuals who planned to treat Malcolm as some kind of dangerous, violence-advocating demagogue who got what he deserved and those who, while mostly agreeing with his political, economic, and cultural beliefs, were concerned about his legacy insofar as it enabled them to achieve their political and financial goals.

Ma, who was deeply skeptical of both types, was inundated with calls and letters from scholars, journalists, prisoners, foreign diplomats, black-power groups, community activists, politicians, radio and television talk-show hosts, book publishers, and film producers. "All wanted me to provide them with insight and information on Malcolm's life," Ma said. "All, especially in the first few months and years after his assassination, seemed to be in a hurry to get something out. That alone turned me off. I knew that my brother's life was too important and too complex to be done hurriedly. After all, I didn't know who most of them were and wasn't about to speak about Malcolm to anyone I hadn't been able to check out. I must make it clear that everyone who contacted me about Malcolm was not out to exploit his name and legacy. Some were sincere and really believed in him. Those I cooperated with to some degree."

Malcolm had fought hard for too long for the liberation of our people, Ma emphasized, "for those of us who were close to him to allow ourselves to be used as tools and fools by those who wanted to use his name and legacy for their own purposes. Malcolm was a freedom fighter, a believer in the proposition that our people everywhere had the right to free themselves from the shackles of colonialism and white supremacy by any means necessary and a learned, well-read leader who had put together a carefully considered, evolving plan to advance their struggle.

"He was also a loving father, husband, brother, nephew, and cousin and a man respected abroad for his intelligence and commitment to expanding the human rights of our people. Anyone who was not willing to comprehend or understand that of Malcolm X wasn't going to get any contribution from me. I didn't have the power to stop them from presenting an image of Malcolm X, symbolism without substance, but along with others, I did have the knowledge and skills needed to challenge their half-truths, distortions, and evasions about my brother's life."

Those who believe that Ma was overly concerned about the symbolism-without-substance issue are advised to delve into general American history, as it was then taught (the late 1950s and 1970s) in most public and private educational institutions, and see how they treat those labeled as "black militants." Nat Turner, the great revolutionary leader who led an armed uprising against enslavement in Virginia that caused tremors throughout the South, was basically ignored. If mentioned, he was usually treated as a "crazy, ungrateful Negro" who repaid a kind enslaver with violence. *David Walker's Appeal,* written by the former slave David Walker, is probably the most revolutionary statement ever made against the enslavement of Africans in this country, yet it was rarely taught in schools on any level. Now it is at least mentioned in more schools but still treated as the ranting of a violence-oriented militant rather than as a righteous declaration of war against those who bought, sold, exploited, and brutalized African men, women, and children.

John Brown, the great white abolitionist who sacrificed his life in the battle against enslavement, is generally taught as being some kind of fierce fanatic rather than as a genuine freedom fighter. For years, in history books and other scholarly compositions, enslaved Africans who used every trick in the book to avoid working for enslavers were depicted as being genetically "lazy" rather than as captives using nonviolent protest against their captors. In the beginning of the twentieth century, right up to the civil-rights movement of the 1960s, black men and women who challenged the legal white supremacy of Jim Crow laws were denounced and sometimes killed for being "uppity" rather than being heralded as courageous for fighting a system that attempted to consign them to permanent second-class citizenship.

These and countless other examples graphically illustrate why Ma's concern about how Malcolm's life and legacy were recorded by writers and filmmakers was very real and not a sign of raging paranoia. Such opinion molders came to Ma because they knew she had been one of Malcolm's closest confidantes, whom he held in great esteem. He made that clear in his autobiography. "What those who approached me didn't know," said Ma, "was my belief that to contribute to any project that would miseducate or mislead people on Malcolm would be a betrayal at the highest level."

Ma, of course, was not the only member of Malcolm's family approached by those seeking to capitalize on his life and legacy. Others, most notably Wilfred and Philbert, his brothers, and Betty, his widow, were also besieged. "Unfortunately," Ma lamented, "we were not a united family due to the trauma caused by the assassination and deep divisions about how to respond to events. Wilfred and Philbert were still in the Nation of Islam and thus caught in the middle of commitment to an organization to which they had dedicated their lives for so many years and a commitment to their younger brother, whom many thought had been assassinated by members of that organization. They had justifiable concerns, considering the times, about the safety of their families. Betty, pregnant with four young daughters to care for"—it was six with the birth of the twins later in 1965—"was in no position to think about what must have seemed like esoteric things like legacies. Her husband, unlike Dr. King later, was not treated after his assassination as a great American hero, so she didn't get the tremendous outpouring of support received by Mrs. King. This made her more susceptible to approaches from predatory writers, book publishers, and filmmakers. If we had had more family unity, we would have been able to exercise more control over the way Malcolm was treated in books and movies and documentaries. We could have insisted on their presenting the Malcolm that we all knew rather than one they envisioned. By not having that unity, we let him down."

I remember vividly at least two occasions when the lack of family unity severely hurt our efforts to make sure that what happened to many other black heroes in books and films didn't happen to Malcolm. The first occurred in 1964, after he left the Nation. At a press conference called by the N.O.I. in Chicago, Philbert bitterly denounced Malcolm as pursuing "a dangerous course which parallels that of the precedents set by Judas, Brutus, Benedict Arnold, and others." Segments from that press conference were later included in the 1972 Marvin Worth documentary on Malcolm. Many family members were livid with Philbert. Aunt Gracie called him "a disgrace," adding, "I never want to see him again." Ma had always taught me to love and respect my uncles, but as a teenager I found it extremely difficult to respect Philbert after what he did. "I am just as angry and hurt as you are," Ma said, "but I try to understand the incredible pressures Philbert must have felt. We don't know what kind of threats John Ali and others made to him. What we do know is what they had done to others they considered threats to their money-making machine called the Nation of Islam. We have to take that into consideration." It was many months before I could accept Ma's position.

The second incident involved Betty. Justifiably traumatized by the assassination, which she, along with her children, had actually witnessed, Betty made a serious mistake. During the evening following Malcolm's burial, she ordered Leon Ameer, one of his most dedicated supporters (initially hired to assassinate my uncle), and another member of the OAAU to dump all of Malcolm's papers, including handwritten notes, into the trash. They had been stored in the basement of Tom Wallace's home since the firebombing of their home shortly before the assassination. I had helped move them there. Brother Ameer and I were anguished by Betty's order but didn't know what to do. I called Ma, hoping she would talk Betty out of throwing the papers away. To my surprise, Ma refused to get involved. As best as I could understand her motivation, she didn't want to make Aunt Betty more upset than she already was. Brother Ameer, despite his misgivings, decided it was a family matter; he had no choice but to follow Aunt Betty's order. The papers were thrown into trash cans near the Wallace home. I'm sure that members of the FBI and of New York City's Bureau of Special Services, who were watching the Wallace home from a car across the street, eagerly rescued the papers from the trash cans and filed them away somewhere. They probably couldn't believe their good luck. If our family had had better communications and more unity, Betty could have given those papers to a Little family member for safekeeping and preservation. The disunity resulted in the deplorable loss of valuable primary information on Malcolm.

Despite that severe loss, Ma still had her memories of, and insights into, her brother—information that a diverse cast of characters sought to get from her. From 1965 up until her death from the effect of diabetes and two leg amputations in 1996, she received innumerable requests for interviews, comments, and observations. Included among the cast of characters were journalist Louis Lomax, who helped Malcolm launch the Nation's newspaper *Muhammad Speaks* and who played a pivotal role in putting together *"The Hate That Hate Produced,"* the infamous CBS documentary about the N.O.I.; author James Baldwin, whose work Malcolm respected; Alex Haley, cowriter of his autobiography; Spike Lee, director of the flawed 1992 film on Malcolm's life; and film producer Marvin Worth, who signed a lifelong agreement with Betty to do a film on Uncle Malcolm.

The first of the above to contact Ma was the overly enthusiastic, exuberant Louis Lomax, a keen observer who knew before any other that Ma was a primary source of information and insight into Malcolm. In the spring of 1965, only a couple of months after Malcolm's assassination, Lomax contacted Ma about collaborating with him in producing a film that would include much of the information he had gathered for his book *When the Word Is Given*. The book, while including extensive information on Malcolm, focused on Elijah Muhammad and the Nation of Islam. That in itself was a problem with Ma, as evidenced in a letter to her lawyer, later sent to Lomax, which stated: "Any motion picture concerning the life of Malcolm X will under no circumstances glorify the Muslim movement, but will, in fact, show the breach or split when he left their movement, and his great continuing influence throughout the world, following his murder." Though this was written in 1968, it expresses exactly what Ma felt in 1965 when first contacted by Lomax. His request came to the OAAU and was passed on to her by James Shabazz, who had been Malcolm's chief secretary. The excuse she gave Lomax at the time for not becoming involved with his project was that she was too busy planning the first annual May nineteenth birthday memorial for Malcolm. She suggested he contact Betty. Again, the response was negative. She was too busy taking care of her fatherless daughters.

Lomax was nothing if not persistent. Fired up about the project, he called Ma two or three times daily in efforts to pump her up about the proposed film. Lomax, despite his being a keen observer, just didn't understand that Ma was not the type of person who got pumped up about things. She was thorough, cautious, and skeptical and not susceptible to Lomax's impassioned blandishments. "Lomax was always too eager for my taste," Ma said. "I didn't believe he would have done anything intentionally harmful to Malcolm's life and legacy, but with his eagerness to rush things out, he came off as ready to present anything his white bosses wanted, anything that would gain him recognition. He didn't have a sufficient commitment to what Malcolm was all about for the kind of film I envisioned. He had talent—of that there's no doubt—but I knew that any kind of collaboration agreement with him had to be airtight."

That's why Ma, after nearly three years of talking and negotiating, had her lawyer draw up a contract clearly stating what she wanted from such a collaboration. That was sent to Lomax's office in Los Angeles. After several weeks of back-and-forth negotiating with Lomax's office, Ma decided that he wasn't in a position to deal with her concerns, so she had her lawyer contact Henry Klinger, head of Twentieth Century-Fox's office in New York City. Those negotiations were temporarily suspended, at Klinger's request, after Martin Luther King Jr.'s assassination on April 4, 1968. Ma agreed to his request because she planned to attend Dr. King's funeral in Atlanta.

"I soon found out, however, that Dr. King's assassination wasn't the only reason for the suspension of negotiations," Ma explained. "Through a valuable contact in the New York City Police Department, I learned that J. Edgar Hoover had contacted a Twentieth Century-Fox executive and demanded they not do any film 'on niggers like Malcolm X and King that depicts them as some kind of heroes and martyrs.'" My mother and I had obtained this information from this high-ranking police official at a secret meeting in Central Park in the fall of 1965. It should be noted however that Hoover didn't object to a film on Malcolm, just to one that would depict him as a hero or martyr. "That leaves me to believe that he would have gladly supported one that focused on Malcolm as a hustler and demagogue, one that dealt with him as symbolism without substance. I wasn't about to support nothing like that," said Ma.

Hoover got his way. By May 1968, widely read syndicated columnist Leonard Lyons wrote in the *Los Angeles Times* that "20th Century Fox probably will cancel *When the Word Is Given,* the Louis Lomax film on the late Malcolm X." Hoover's diatribe wasn't necessary. When I later read a section of the document Twentieth Century-Fox sent to Ma in January 1968 discussing her role in the proposed film, I could only laugh at their monumental arrogance and ignorance about whom they were negotiating with. It read: "Our right to portray factually and/or *fictionally* [italics mine], and to such extent and in such manner as we *in our sole discretion* [italics mine] may elect, your likeness, personality, life, activities and career, under your name or under any other such name selected by us in or in connection with the photoplay and to exhibit, distribute and otherwise exploit the photoplay by and all media, devices and places now known or hereafter devised."

"They must have been joking" was my reaction upon reading their contract. "No, they weren't," Ma said, "and that was for the portrayal of my character. Can you imagine what they would have done to Malcolm's?"

The whole question of the Lomax film became moot in late 1968 when he was reportedly killed in an automobile accident.

The next major effort to do a film on Uncle Malcolm involved Ma, James Baldwin, and Marvin Worth in the late 1960s and early 1970s. Ma was more receptive to a Baldwin-written screenplay because Malcolm had spoken so highly of him as "a firebrand with a pen who brilliantly expressed the feelings of our people." In fact, Ma said, "Malcolm had really wanted Baldwin to work with him on his autobiography, but their schedules were a problem." Because of Malcolm's high regard for him and what she had read by and heard about him, Ma believed Baldwin would be "a strong ally in the battle to present a Malcolm X of substance in a film."

They didn't meet until after the assassination, when Baldwin consulted with her about a short play he planned to write about Malcolm's life. "After we met," Ma said, "I became even more convinced that Baldwin would do justice to a movie on Malcolm and that he was just as concerned about substance over symbolism as I was."

Others involved with the project were Art Aveilhe, of J. B. Lippincott Company, a book publisher; Bruce Perry of the Socialist Press Media; Arnold Perl, Baldwin's business partner; and a relative of a prominent banker. The last became a real problem, often coming to meetings completely intoxicated. "I wonder if he has to drink in order to negotiate with black people," Ma wondered. One day, at a meeting held at the new OAAU offices on West 139th Street in Harlem, the banker's son fell down in a drunken stupor. "I had had it," Ma noted. "I wasn't prepared to waste my time with an alcoholic white man."

It was generally agreed that Aveilhe would work with Ma on her memoirs and Baldwin would write the screenplay. Worth, of course, would produce the film. "Baldwin and I agreed we would stick to our guns on how Malcolm's story should be told," Ma said. "We envisioned a film that would focus on him as a black nationalist, as a man serious about his Islamic religious beliefs, as a man with a prophetic vision about race relations, as a man of international stature who had been received abroad as a representative from his people, and as a committed foe of white supremacy wherever it reared its violent head."

That was not the film envisioned by Marvin Worth and Warner Bros. What they were looking for is best reflected by a 1972 documentary on Malcolm produced by Worth, which mainly focused on Malcolm as a street hustler, a convert to the Nation of Islam, and an adversary of the N.O.I. It was in this documentary that Philbert was shown denouncing Uncle Malcolm. "That documentary was a disaster," Ma declared. "Controversy and conflict was the name of the game. Symbolism without substance was rampant. After seeing it, I knew that Marvin Worth, Warner Brothers and I would never agree on a movie about my brother."

The crucial question was Where did Baldwin stand? "I had enough common sense," Ma said, "to know that it wasn't my objections that thwarted the film they wanted to make. I didn't have enough clout to stop such action, only perhaps to make them a little uncomfortable. Baldwin was the key. I was very grateful when he dropped out of the project when they insisted on changing his script. I have never forgotten that."

However, people like Bruce Perry and Marvin Worth didn't go away. The film Worth wanted to produce in the 1970s, one that focused on Malcolm's days as a street hustler and on his conflicts with the Nation of Islam, was the film directed by Spike Lee in 1992. It was described as an adaptation of the script James Baldwin had dropped in the early 1970s. Spike Lee promoted his film as having the support of Malcolm's family. It's more accurate to say that it was supported by some members of Malcolm's family, most notably Betty. Other members, most notably Ma, didn't support it in any way, shape, form, or fashion. "I wasn't disappointed with Spike Lee's film," explained Ma, "because having gone through those experiences with Lomax, Twentieth Century-Fox, Klinger, Worth, and Warner Brothers in the 1960s and 1970s, I didn't expect anything with real substance in the first place. Spike Lee created a classic example of Malcolm as symbolism without substance. Malcolm's depth as a person, leader, and family member is barely touched upon. There's much more about his street-life days than about his life as a respected national and international spokesman against white supremacy, much more about his conflict with the Nation of Islam than that with the U.S. government. Marvin Worth finally got the film he had wanted twenty years earlier. The most lasting, positive thing about it was actor Denzel Washington's portrayal of Malcolm. I first saw him portray Malcolm in a play in New York City, which I believe was called *When The Chicken Comes Home to Roost*. In both the play and the film he was excellent. I just regret he was denied the opportunity to portray the whole Malcolm X."

There's at least one other thing to clear up about Spike Lee's film. The year 1990 marked the twenty-fifth anniversary of the assassination. This was also about the time that speculation began about Spike Lee's proposed film. The press likes to credit its coverage and the film, from its proposal to its release, for having "revived" interest in Malcolm. That is at best a half-truth. From the year after his assassination right up to the present, thousands of African Americans held memorial tributes on the anniversary of the assassination and celebrations on the anniversary of his birth. Annual pilgrimages are made to his gravesite in Westchester County. During those times, forums are held, plays written, programs presented, and a host of items, such as T-shirts, cassette tapes, and posters, are sold and distributed celebrating his legacy. Streets and schools in black neighborhoods in cities throughout the country were named in his honor.

In 1971, at Ma's request as president of the OAAU, Eugene A. Leahy, mayor of Omaha, Nebraska, issued a proclamation designating May 16–22 as Malcolm X Week. "Now let it be resolved," the proclamation read, "that we acknowledge the contributions of Omaha-born Malcolm X on the occasion of his forty-sixth birthday, May 19, 1971, not as a gesture to a certain segment of the community but rather as a genuine indication that the city of Omaha can be proud that a man of his temperament arose from our midst."

In 1984, Iran issued a stamp commemorating Malcolm on the Universal Day of Struggle Against Race Discrimination. "Neither of these events are mentioned in books or documentaries. Spike Lee does not elucidate them and other issues in his film because they give even more substance to Malcolm's life and legacy," Ma said.

Malcolm was not forgotten by thousands of African Americans

despite his treatment as some kind of a nonperson by the mainstream press. The press ignored all that activity until 1990, when they became aware of dozens of activities planned around a twenty-fifth anniversary of the assassination. They then belatedly jumped on the bandwagon. They may have helped expand interest in Malcolm, but they certainly didn't revive it.

In her battle against symbolism without substance, Ma focused on films and television documentaries because they reached millions of people faster than other forms of opinion-making and opinion-influencing communications. However, she was also concerned about the books being published on Malcolm, especially those being used in schools. As could be expected, most of the writers, like their film and television counterparts, analyzed, commented on, and philosophized about his teenage street life, criminal activity, his conflict with the Nation of Islam, and his reported St. Paul-on-the-road-to-Damascus change in regard to race relations. In the latter, they often claimed that he had moved from being a violence-preaching black separatist to a Johnny-come-lately believer in nonviolent protest and integrated brotherhood forever. They ignored the fact that he was neither of the above.

Most of the books, especially those published by prominent publishers, never mentioned the international Malcolm X who was treated by several important African and Asian countries as a foreign minister representing African Americans. They were impressed with his cohesive philosophical position, based not on street-corner rhetoric but on a comprehensive analysis of the deep ties between white supremacy in the United States in the 1950s and early 1960s and colonialism, as practiced by Great Britain, France, Belgium, and Portugal. One of the reasons Ma liked *Black Power—Potere Negro* by Italian writer Robert Giammanco (written in Italian) and *Malcolm X: The Man and His Times,* edited by Dr. John Henrik Clarke, is that they did place Malcolm in that context.

Just as determined to put Malcolm into a context of their own choice were those who wrote from a European socialist perspective. They wrote about changes in Malcolm, but they focused on his supposed change from a committed black nationalist to an integrationist type Marxist. They pounced on a vulnerable Betty soon after the assassination and secured rights to publish Malcolm's speeches. "To me," Ma said, "they were all exploiters, no different from Spike Lee/Marvin Worth/Warner Brothers film, conniving to make money off Malcolm's name and legacy."

The pivotal book, by any measure, is Malcolm's autobiography written with Alex Haley. Ma had no serious problems with what was in the autobiography, but she often "wondered what was left out and what was put in after Malcolm's death. His not being there for the final editing does raise those kinds of questions."

Something we knew was left out was five chapters that basically outlined Malcolm's political, economic, social, and cultural positions that were expressed in the OAAU's aims and objectives. They were hyped by the press and among some observers as the "mysterious missing five chapters." They really weren't missing. Ma and I knew about this, as did Alex Haley, who seemed to have enjoyed all the intrigue around the mystery that was created. Attorney Gregory Reed, of Detroit, Michigan, who purchased the working manuscript at an Alex Haley estate sale in 1992 and whose legal services I once used, said that inclusion of the chapters in the autobiography would have made it "more scholarly." When I told him that much of the information was available in the OAAU's aims and objectives, he was surprised that the OAAU was still in existence.

Ma wished that the chapters had been included in the autobiography because "they would have provided all those people, probably numbering in the millions, who read the autobiography a more detailed look at what Malcolm was aiming to do politically, economically, and culturally. He had a plan of action. I don't know why Haley or his editors excluded them. Maybe sometime in the future he planned on using them as the foundation for another book on Malcolm."

Among other things, the OAAU's aims and objectives that Malcolm helped develop and approved of stated:

Basically there are two kinds of power that count in America, economic and political, with social power deriving from those two. . . . Organization of Afro-American Unity will organize the Afro-American Community, block by block, to make the

community aware of its power and potential. We will start immediately a voter-registration drive to make every unregistered
voter in the Afro-American community an independent voter;
we propose to support and/or organize political clubs, to run independent candidates for office, and to support any Afro-American
already in office who answers to and is responsible to the Afro-
American community.

The OAAU's aims and objectives stressed responsibility, self-help,
self-defense, discipline, education, and a commitment to unity. There
is no doubt that their inclusion in the autobiography would have enhanced its already strong emphasis on substance.

The struggle that Ma and others launched to keep control of Malcolm's life and legacy is ongoing. Every time we are tempted to believe that the job is done, we must check out historical precedents.
For instance, in the 1950s, when Kenyan freedom fighters launched
an armed uprising against British domination of their country, they
were denounced in books, newspapers, on television, and on radio as
Mau Mau savages and terrorists by the descendants of the same people whose ancestors, in 1776, staged an armed uprising to rid their
country of British control. Apparently, how such people and events
are treated by the image creators and preservers depends on who is
in power. Ma clearly understood that from the beginning and put us
on the right track. It's our responsibility to stay on track by challenging the distortions of the manipulators and exploiters who want to
depict Malcolm as symbolism without substance.

APPENDIX

The information contained in these never-before-published letters, not their grammatical structure, is the historically important element, thus our decision to publish them verbatim.

Ma invited Malcolm to leave Michigan and come to live with her and his two elderly aunts in Boston. The letter, written on August 17, 1940, forever changed their lives.

Friday Afternoon

Dear Malcolm:

I don't know how to write to you. But I will try. Everybody is fine here. Sas lives in the mailbox looking for a letter from you. Gracie thought maybe you would be back by now. *I know better.* I had one of those long nightmares & dreams about you last nite. In fact every nite since you left. We miss you so much. Don't swell up & buss but honest everything seems dead here. Lots of boys called for you. Ken just left. Dorothy hasn't been here since you left. I was in town to a party Sunday nite. Had a swell time. Sas & Gracie are fine & want you to come back. I would like for you to come back but under one condition. *Your mind is made up.* If I would send your fare could you pay all your bills? Let me know real soon.

I'm going to move out of here next week. I'm going to take a small place until I can get the house on the corner street straightened out. Which will take at least 2 months. You should treat Miss McQuire like a sister. I think Wilfred wants her for a wife. Ruth just called & told me Dorothy is going to a hospital tomorrow morning to stay for two or three months. She thinks she might have TB. I hope not. Mary & Shirley was here yesterday. I had a letter from Reginald Tuesday. He wants to come to Boston. Let me know if you can bring Yvonne with you. How is Wilfred, Hilda & Philbert? Write soon.

Ella

⁓

This letter to Ma from her sister, my Aunt Hilda, was written shortly after they first met each other for the first time. The two sisters were getting to know each other.

4111 So. Logan St.
Lansing, Mich
Aug. 21, 1940

Dear Ella,

How are you? I'm sorry I didn't write to you before this. We are all ok here. Reginald had an operation. He's been home from the hospital 2 wks today and he's getting along just fine.

How is everybody there? I didn't know Aunt Gracie was sick and in the hospital. Katy has a baby girl. Wilfred was in Detroit Sunday before last and our cousins told him they would come to see us in a few weeks.

School starts in a couple of weeks. I kinda hate to go back but I guess I will. What are you doing with such a large house? I should think you would be afraid to stay in it.

I had another job working for an old stingy couple. The woman was fussy and the man was off in the head. I thought maybe I could put up with it, but when the man came walking in the kitchen one day with a hammer and a butcher knife, it didn't take me long to quit. I haven't worked since. I would like something to do before school starts though.

I'll tell Yvonne and the rest of the kids to write to you. Reginald's address is 609 Birch St. instead of Birks St. Well I don't know of anything else to say, so I'll close now. Everybody sends their love. Write soon.

Hilda

P.S. I had some pictures of me to send to you, but after I looked at them a couple of times I decided not to. But you can still send me that picture of you that I wanted. I think is was the 1st one. Well, so long again.

Hilda

∽

This letter from Wesley, Ma's brother, illustrates his then deep belief in Islam as taught by Elijah Muhammand, the pivotal role played by the Little brothers in the expansion of the Nation of Islam, and their never-ceasing efforts to "fish" Ma into the N.O.I.

17940 Mackay Street
Detroit 12, Michigan
April 17, 1951

Dear Ella,

I received your letter last Friday and it found all of the family here in good health and doing fine. I hope these few lines find you and your family doing likewise. You also have a new sister-in-law now. She is a very nice lady and is one of the secretaries in the Temple here. I hope you are not too angry with us for waiting so long to write you.

Our Temple here is progressing very rapidly and new converts are coming in, both young and old. Not only our Temple here but all of them are showing unlimited progress. Temple No. Nine has just been opened in Youngstown, Ohio and is well on the road to success.

Our celebration on the 26th of February was a total success and was a big impression on our Lost Brethren. We invited Moorish American, Sufi Bengali, Armadyya, and Marcus Garvey followers, doctors, lawyers, preachers and so-called Christians as well as foreign born Muslims from all over the world and all so-called Negroes in general. There were Muslims from all of our Temples and believers where Temples have not yet been set up. We had a full house.

His subject was "understanding" and you know as we all know that what has been lacking among our people. We went over big-

ger than you can imagine and the city of Chicago is all stirred up
as never before. The preacher of one of the biggest churches in
Chicago stood and confessed before thousands that he had been
teaching the white man's Christian religion only for a living and
he was not a bit more satisfied with anything than we were. He
also said he was at our service and we could use his church anytime we desired.

The foreign born speakers from India, Palestine, Persia,
Morocco, and other places all said we had a superior teaching than
them and the Muslims following our leader, Elijah Mohammad
lived more like Muslims and were in more unity than any group of
people they have ever known. Also they wished they were a so-
called Negro because they know what is prepared for those who
accept Islam in the last days. They too wanted to follow our leader.

We just learned last Sunday the Moorish Americans and Marcus
Garvey followers of Chicago want to unite their strength with ours
by following our leaders too. It is time for all of us to come
together now because the devil is getting harder and harder on us
everyday.

A house divided against itself cannot stand and there is no
government today more divided and confused than this
government. President against the Senators, Senators against Gov-
ernors, etc. helps to bring them to their destruction which is fast
approaching.

Tell Kenny, Rodnell, Dorothy and all of the others hello. I just
wanted to write to you a few words of encouragement. I wrote to
Malcolm last week and I told him I would send him some pictures
by you. I wish you could come out here and some to the others
too. Maybe if you go to New York, you can go to the Temple
there. It is at 36 West 135th Street, New York City 30. It is a new
Temple (1947) and is progressing well. Tell them (if you go) you
are the sister of Brother Wilfred X of Temple No. 1, Detroit,
Michigan or myself.

I heard Mary Ann was on her way there so I guess she is there
by now. I will write you again very soon and send you the
pictures. I would like to have a picture of Earl like your mother
has in the living room. Also of you, Mary, Rodnell and Kenny for

my family album. If you can have one made of Earl let me know
and I will send the money for it. Tell everyone hello and write
soon.

Your brother
Wesley

Please excuse this poor writing.

⤳

*In 1959 Malcolm received a copy of this letter from a friendly source in the
New York City Police Department. It graphically illustrates the depth of the Ku
Klux Klan's white supremacy and how it saw members of the NYPD as possi-
ble "soul brothers."*

1 Thessalonians 2:14-16   St. John 8:44-48

Christian Knights
of the
Ku Klux Klan

Archleader, J. B. Stoner,   Suite B, 702 Barret Avenue
    Imperial Wizard   August 6, 1959   (Corner of Barret & Broadway)
                          Louisville 4, Kentucky

National Headquarters
P.O. Box 48
Atlanta, Georgia

Honorable Stephen P. Kennedy
Police Commissioner of New York City
CONFIDENTIAL AND *TOP SECRET*
New York, N.Y.

Re: the black Muslims

Dear Fellow Whiteman:
    The Christian Knights of the Ku Klux Klan is composed of all
loyal White people, both Catholics and Protestants, native born

and foreign born, young and old. We are working to unite all of the forces of White Christendom in the struggle to Preserve the great White Race. The future of civilization depends upon the survival of the beautiful intelligent White Race-the bearer of Christian truth.

I have received a report from one of our Klansmen on the New York police force informing me that the nigger Muslims are in rebellion against White law and order. He reports that those blacks have no respect for you honest White Christian policemen. Therefore, in the interests of law and justice, I am offering you the support of the CHRISTIAN KNIGHTS OF THE KU KLUX KLAN.

I am an expert on the black Muslims and have kept up with their infidelic activities for many years. From my knowledge of them, I assure you that they are much more dangerous to White Christian rule in New York than you realize. You and I must join forces to stop the black Muslims now or they will soon drive every White person out of New York City. The largest city in the world will then be an all nigger city of black supremacy where White people will not be allowed to live. The only thing that can stop Elijah Muhammad and his black Muslims from conquering New York is for my Christian Knights and your New York police to join hands and work together to uphold White Christian Supremacy. Without the support of my Christian Knights, the Muslims will continue to force you to retreat until you and the great Mayor Wagner and all other White officials and judges will be ousted from office. Elijah Muhammad will then give your job to a nigger and put in a nigger as mayor of New York. Then he will only allow niggers on the N.Y. City Council and all judges and all policemen will be niggers. By then, the Muslims will have driven all White people out of New York, without exception. Don't let the black Muslims fool you when they demand entrance to schools in White neighborhoods or demand houses or apartments in White areas. They only wish to enter White neighborhoods and White schools so they can then proceed to drive all of the Whites out. Take my advice and we will put the niggers in their place instead of letting them take over New York City and all the national power that goes with it.

We need to put the black hoodlums out of business, but we must do it in a legal way with the police and the courts. As a Georgia lawyer, I insist on doing everything according to law. You know what I mean. It is urgent that you persuade the officials of the City and State of New York to immediately repeal all ordinances and laws that prevent Whites from discriminating against niggers because those evil laws constitute an open invitation to all the niggers in the South to move to New York City where they will strengthen the Muslims and subject that giant metropolis to black supremacy. Those laws need to be replaced with laws that will help White Christians in New York to imitate us Southerners by keeping the darkies in their place. You might be interested in knowing that some Southern business men and farmers are complaining because their darkies are leaving the South and moving to New York where they can get higher pay. Wealthy Southern housewives are complaining because it is becoming harder to find colored maids and cooks who will work for a dollar per day; they want you to send them back and cut out those high wages for niggers in New York. They are moving to New York in large numbers to work for higher wages on account of your laws against racial discrimination. Remember, every nigger who moves from the South to N.Y.C. makes the Muslims more powerful.

You need to learn more about that evil genius, Elijah Muhammad, or you will never stop him and his niggers from taking over your city. He claims to be the re-incarnation of that infidelic 7th Century prophet, Mohammad, who almost conquered the known world and he may be him because he is much more clever than the other niggers.

I think we need to put Muhammad out of business in a legal way and not use the criminal methods that the communist F.B.I. is using against him. I hear that the F.B.I. is hiring nigger pimps to join up with the Muslims so they can spy on them. They also start arguments in meetings so as to disrupt them. They also try to turn niggers away from Islam by accusing Muhammad and other Muslim officials of stealing money out of the Muslim treasury because the F.B.I. knows that most niggers will believe those kind of false charges without any proof. Even though I would enjoy seeing Muhammad hanged from a Harlem lamp post, I have to admit that he does not steal from his own followers. We are both familiar enough with red F.B.I. methods to know that the F.B.I. plans to frame the Muslims by having nigger F.B.I. pimps use violence and then blame it on the Muslims. Instead of using illegal F.B.I. police state methods, I suggest that we put the Muslims out of business with the White Christian methods that have worked so well in the South. Besides, any spies you put among the Muslims will probably be killed. Those Muslims are the meanest niggers in the world.

You need to realize that Muhammad has organized several hundred thousand niggers throughout America. His Muslim temples are springing up everywhere; he has several temples in my home city of Atlanta. If you were a student of Race, you would know that Christianity is the Whiteman's religion and has only been successful in White countries; whereas, the Muslim religion of Islam is a nigger religion which appeals to the nigger's black racial instincts. That is why the Muslims grow stronger every day even though every nigger that becomes a Muslim will go to hell when he dies. If we fail to stop the Muslims now, the 16,000,000 niggers of America will all soon be Muslims and you will never be able to stop them. Reports from Christian missionaries say that Islam is sweeping over all of Africa so don't underestimate the Muslims.

Up to and including its edition copyrighted in 1956, the Encyclopedia Britannica admitted under the heading of "Negro" that the nigger is closer to the anthropoid ape than the White man in every respect except one. It also revealed the niggers to be natural born cannibals. For more information about the facts of Race, I suggest you read "Take Your Choice, Separation or Mongrelization" by the late U.S. Senator Bilbo of Mississippi and "White America" by Earnest Sevier Cox. Both are in the Library of Congress. Another valuable Race book is "The Cult of Equality" by Stuart O. Landry, 305 Chartres, New Orleans, La. Therefore, you can easily see that your problem is with black savages. We will help you put the blacks in their place before they turn all of your great city into a barbaric jungle.

The NAACP is a bad gang but I assure you that the Muslims are ten times more dangerous. The NAACP is a cream puff compared to black Islam. The NAACP likes White people so much that its members try to associate with us Whites every day, but the Muslims think they are better than us Whites even though everybody knows that we Whites are superior to the nigger coons. I guess you know that the NAACP is headed by a man who is not a nigger, but there is a bad nigger at the head of the Muslims.

I have had White Christian friends write to many magazines inciting them to denounce Muhammad and his Muslims so as to scare many cowardly niggers away from him. So far I have managed to "sic" both "Time" magazine and "U.S. News & World Report" on them.

Police Commissioner Kennedy, my dear friend, I now offer you the service of the Christian Knights of the Ku Klux Klan for the purpose of maintaining White Supremacy in New York City and for keeping New York niggers in their place. I think 5,000 Klansmen could clean up Harlem for you if you would give them police badges and N.Y. police uniforms to wear instead of their Klan uniforms. They will leave their Klan robes at home so the New York niggers won't know that your police reinforcements are White Christian Klansmen. You can use our Christian Knights as guards to protect every White business in Harlem and also in other New York areas where nigger customers are giving trouble to White business men. After all, how do the black jig-a boos expect to live without White business men to sell them what they need. You can also use our Klansmen to escort White salesmen into Harlem and other parts of New York City that are suffering from the black plague.

I will expect you to supply my Klansmen with police pistols (so they won't have to carry their own pistols). They will also require machine guns, riot guns, tear gas and big clubs. They will especially want some big sticks with iron inside the wood so they can crack hard nigger skulls. Niggers have thicker skulls and smaller skulls than we Whites. In your police uniforms, my Klansmen will teach New York niggers to respect White Christian policemen. I will send my Christian Knights to your rescue as soon as you call for them.

Do you want to keep these plans secret or make them public? If we give publicity to these plans, the yellow-livered, cowardly darkies would probably start shaking in their shoes and showing proper respect for White people before the arrival of the Ku Klux Klan. Please advise.

In case you decide to keep our plans secret, remember that the secret might leak out. In case of a leak, strongly deny that you have called for the support of the Christian Knights of the Ku Klux Klan. I want you to jump up and down and scream when telling the newspapermen that we are not working together, in case our plans leak out. That will keep them from saying anything.

Tell you superiors to take their choice. You can either accept our support and have White Supremacy in your giant city; or, you can retreat and abandon New York City to Elijah Muhammad, his Muslims and black supremacy.

I know we will enjoy working together to roll back the black locusts. Together, my dear friend, we will save New York City for the White Race, the race that built civilization.

In the Christian bond of White racial brotherhood, I remain

Yours for Christ, Race and Country

J. B. Stoner

Imperial Wizard of the Christian Knights of the Ku Klux Klan
P.O. Box 48, Atlanta, Georgia
and
Archleader of The Christian Party
P.O. Box 48
Atlanta, Georgia

As a sign of his deep appreciation of Ma's support, Malcolm gave her this cer-
tificate he received from the Rector of El Azhar University. It was another first
for him and is one of the reasons he is honored by the American Muslim Coun-
cil in Washington under his Muslim name El-Hajj Malik El-Shabazz.

Office of the Supreme
Imam
Sheikh Al-Azhar.
10/9/1964

In the Name of Allah, the Merciful, the Compassionate. Thanks
to the Almighty, Who has sent His Messenger with guidance and
the True Religion in order that it may Prevail over all other
religions.

Prayers and peace be upon our great prophet Muhammad who
guides to the Truth and to a straight path.

We have received in our office at Al-Azhar Mr. Malkulm X
who is known now by the name: Malik El-Shabazz, an American
citizen who declared his faith and conversion to Islam and he
confessed the two Islamic articles saying "I confess that there is
no God but Allah and that Mohammad is His Prophet, and Jesus
is His servant and Messenger. I ceased to believe in any other
religion that contradicts Islam."

After seeing the certificate of the Islamic foundation in New
York dated 9/4/1964, and what the Head of the Great court of
Islamic law at Jeddah decided in this respect, Mr. Malik's
declaration of Islam has been assured to us.

Mr. Malik El-Shabazz (Malkulm X) with his true and correct
faith is one of the Muslim community, with their rights and
obligations and it is his duty to propagate Islam and offer every
available assistance and facilities to those who wish conversion to
Islam. This is a certificate to whom it may concern.

May God, Almighty, guide him and enlighten his heart by Islam
and direct him to the right path.

God's prayers and blessings be upon his prophet Mohammad,
his family and his companions.

The Rector of Al-Azhar
(Hassan Maa'moun)

An African student, Henry Odeyo Avaga, sent this letter to the OAAU office in New York City. It shows why white supremacists, colonialists, and others who believe that people of European descent have a divine right to rule the world were concerned about Malcolm's appeal to many students in the African and Islamic worlds (date unknown).

The late Mr. Malcolm X has been stigmatized by both whites and some lopsided blacks as racist, militant, and irrational. This is just a matter of opinion. History reveals that other races (yellow, brown, black) have experienced shameful and inhumane maltreatments. But especially so is the black. So, who is not a racist? Let his prosecutors answer that. Militancy in pursuit of overdue freedom and identity, to my honest conviction, is no vice. And who has not employed force to secure his freedom? Again his critics will refer to the world wars and answer this accordingly. Irrationality, like capitalism and communism, is a two-edged word. It all depends on which side you favour. His antagonists should not forget this.

Whatever he has said and done has been intended for the short-run or long-run interests of the so-long-underprivileged African race. All that he has been demanding is equality and identity for the blacks. As such we should not try to judge him by the means he employed in seeking this, but by the objective itself. Both force and peace have been used together in seeking man's objectives. The use of one does not necessarily obliterate the use of the other. "Fighting" with words should not be substituted for actual bullet-fist-operations. Those who are responsible for his death have achieved little, if not nothing at all. What he stood for, and what the black mass has been demanding, has never been accomplished. The only way to defeat him would have been to attain our demands. But so long as we are unsuccessful, he remains alive— alive in our hearts for therein we sincerely and honestly know and believe that what he said of us was true; that what he demanded for us was legitimate; and that what he said of the black oppressors was not untrue.

We therefore have to give him a place in our history. We have incurred a great loss at our own expense, because of our short-sightedness and folly. At this time we can hardly afford losing any leader among us. We are short of them and pure power-ambition should not lead us to work against our cause. I believe, therefore,

that the Society of African Descendants will try to synthesize
Mr. X's late ideals, and try to promote them where ever possible.

To Mrs. X are sent my deepest and heartfelt grief at the loss of
her dear husband. It is my hope that all men of goodwill will do
all they can to ensure you a comfortable living with your children
for the remainder of your life.

Very Fraternally yours,
Henry Odeyo Avaga

*In today's usage Ma's response to the following impertinent letter was the
equivalent of I Don't Think So!*

January 29, 1968

Mrs. Ella Collins
486 Massachusetts Avenue
Boston, Massachusetts

Dear Mrs. Collins:

Your signature and ours at the end of her will confirm our
following agreement regarding our right to portray you in our
motion picture tentatively entitled "MALCOLM X" (herein called
"The Photoplay"):

1. You hereby grant to us and our successors, assigns,
   distributees and licensees, in perpetuity, and throughout
   the world, and irrevocable and unconditional right and
   license to use, simulate and portray (herein referred to
   collectively as ("portray") you and your life in, and in
   connection with, The Photoplay.

2. (A) Our right to portray you shall include the right to
   portray (factually and/or) fictionally, and to such extent an
   in such manner as we in our sole discretion may elect,
   your likeness, personality, life, activities and career, under
   your name or under any other name selected by us in or
   connection with The Photoplay and to exhibit, distribute
   and otherwise exploit The Photoplay by any and all media,
   devices and places now known or hereafter devised.

(B) Our right herein granted shall also include the right to utilize any and all information obtained from discussions or communications with you concerning the subject matter of this motion picture.

3. Our right to portray you shall also extend to any and all reissues, remarks and sequels of The Photoplay; and, to any and all publicity, advertising and exploitation of The Photoplay, in any and all media now known or herein after devised, including but not limited to radio, television, synopses, adaptations, and publications.

4. You hereby covenant and agree that you will never bring or maintain any action or suit, at law or in equity, against us, or successors, assigns, distributees and licensees, or any thereof, or then respective officers, employees, directors or agents, based upon or arising our of any such use which we may make of your names, likeness, personality, life, activities and/or career, regardless of the manner in which, or the extent to which, we in our sole discretion portray the same.

5. You warrant that you have not been included or persuaded to enter into this Agreement by any representation or assurance made by us or in our behalf relative to the manner in which, or the extent to which, any of the rights or licenses granted hereunder may be exercised. You agree that we, our successors, assigns, distributees and licensees are under no obligation whatsoever to exercise any of the rights or licenses granted hereunder. The determination to do so or not shall be made by us in our sole discretion.

6. In full consideration of the rights herein granted by us, we shall pay to you the following:

(a) The sum of Two Thousand Five Hundred Dollars ($2,500) upon execution of this agreement and the delivery thereof to our Legal Department at 10201 West Pico Boulevard, Los Angeles, California.

(b) The additional sum of Twenty-two Thousand Five Hundred if we portray you in The Photoplay as herein provided for, payable upon the commencement of principal photography of The Photoplay.

(c) If you portray yourself in said Photoplay, the terms and conditions of your employment therein shall be negotiated.

If the foregoing is in accordance with your understanding and agreement, please so indicate by affirming your signature under the words "Accepted and Agreed To" at the end thereof.

Very Truly Yours
Twentieth Century-Fox Film Corporation

ACCEPTED AND AGREED TO:

_____

Ella Collins

Ma's lawyers wrote these two letters to Louis Lomax and Henry Klinger of Twentieth Century–Fox during early negotiations about a film on the life of Malcolm. Her insistence on their adhering to what she wanted in point one probably guaranteed that the film wouldn't be done, especially the demand that the film must show Malcolm's "great continuing influence throughout the world following his murder."

February 7, 1968

Mr. Louis Lomax
10201 West Pice Boulevard
Twentieth Century-Fox File Corporation
Los Angeles, California 90213

Dear Mr. Lomax:

I am sorry that I did not send this letter to you any earlier, but it was necessary that I communicate with my client as well as write this letter.

In accordance with our telephone conversation, this is to confirm that my client is interested in the following points:

1. That any motion picture concerning the life of Malcolm X will under no circumstances glorify the Muslim movement, but will, in fact, show the breach or split when he left their movement, and his great continuing influence throughout the world, following his murder.

2. Your paragraph (a) should not include the words, "fictionally, and to such extent and in such manner as we in our sole discretion may elect." In that manner, it would give greater meaning and sense to paragraph 2 (b).

3. The right of Twentieth-Century Fox Film Corporation to portray my client shall be limited to this picture.

4. By eliminating the words in paragraph "4" starting with the word regardless etc. it would give more credence to the words contained in paragraphs 2 (a) and (b).

5. Paragraph 6B should include an outside date of one year from the signing of this agreement by my client for the commencement of actual production.

6. My client desires to be seriously considered for the role of herself in the said picture.

7. You did agree to reimburse my client for her expenses and disbursements. Does this have be included in a contract or is out of petty cash?

I am sending a copy of this letter to Mrs. Collins.

I would appreciate hearing from you as soon as possible after receipt of this letter.

Cordially,

SJE/fe
Copy to Mrs. Ella Collins

March 13, 1968

Mr. Henry Klinger
Twentieth Century-Fox Film Corporation
444 West 56th Street
New York, N. Y.

Re: Malcolm X Picture
Mrs. Ella Collins

Dear Mr. Klinger:

As I told you in your office, at our meeting, I have already spoken to my client, Mrs. Ella Collins, and I have explained to her the whys and wherefores of our conversation together.

She has agreed to your verbal assurance that any motion picture concerning the life of Malcolm X will not attempt to glorify the Muslim movement, but will try to depict his life and continuing influence throughout the world as much as is possible in any motion picture. She has, similarly, accepted that no motion picture firm, and particularly yours, would depict anyone in a libelous manner, but that you did reserve the right to make a realistic but, if necessary, a somewhat fictional depiction of his life.

As we agreed, please include a paragraph in the contract that the right to portray my client shall be limited to this picture.

Mrs. Collins also told me that while no one but the motion picture company can set the policy, nevertheless, she would be seriously considered for the role of herself in the pictures.

I do not know what her petty expenses were, but when she sends me a list I will take it up with you. I do not believe it was more than $50.00

Mrs. Collins has also asked that her check be made payable to Organization of Afro-American Unity, Inc.

Awaiting a copy of the contract in accordance with the above, as well as the basic contract, I remain

Cordially,

SJE/

⟡

In this letter 20th Century–Fox decides to "temporarily" suspend negotiations on the film in response to the assassination of Martin Luther King Jr. on April 4, 1968.

Sidney J. Ettman
Attorney at Law
55 Liberty Street
New York, N. Y. 10005

April 11, 1968

Mrs. Ella Collins
486 Massachusetts Avenue
Boston, Massachusetts

Dear Mrs. Collins:

Mr. Henry Klinger of Twentieth Century-Fox Film Corporation called me early yesterday to advise me that due to the unfortunate tragedy of this past week, Twentieth Century-Fox has decided to temporarily suspend all negotiations concerning the motion picture of Malcolm X.

He made it especially clear that this does not mean that they have permanently shelved the picture, but rather that they have merely delayed any ideas, pro or con, relating to it for a few months.

As soon as I will hear anything relating to the photoplay, I will immediately get in touch with you.

With nothing further for the moment, I remain

Sincerely,
SIDNEY J. ETTMAN

SJE/

∽

In this letter and document Malcolm X Week is declared in Omaha, Nebraska, Malcolm's birthplace. Because of the efforts of my mother and Ms. Moore, the site was later designated a historical landmark.

CITY OF OMAHA

MAYOR'S CABINET		MAYOR'S CABINET
ALDEN AUST		P. RAYMOND NIELSON
PLANNING		PERSONNEL
	EUGENE A. LEAHY	
HERBERT FITLE	MAYOR	ALFRED PATTAVINA
LEGAL		PUBLIC SAFETY
EDWIN HEWITT		ROGER W. SAYERS
FINANCE		HUMAN RELATIONS
GENE E. JORDAN		CLARENCE E. SHAFER
PUBLIC WORKS		PARKS & RECREATION

September 24, 1971

Miss Ella Collins, President
Organization of Afro-American Unity, Inc.
224 West 139th Street
New York, N. Y. 10030

Dear Miss Collins:
Your letter to the president of the City Council has been referred
to me for action.

I am enclosing a copy of the proclamation signed by the
Mayor for the City of Oklahoma regarding the designation of
the period from May 16th through 22nd as Malcolm X Week. To
my knowledge, there has not been any bill or resolution creating a
marker for the birthplace of Malcolm X, however, this resolution
is not far off.

The person that you would want to contact regarding further
information of designating Malcolm's birthplace at 3448 Pinkney
Street, is Mrs. Rowena Moore, 2019 North 20th Street, Omaha,
Nebraska. Mrs. Moore is also the owner of the property on which
Malcolm was born.

I am sure this is the information that you are looking for.
If there are any further questions, please do not hesitate to
contact me.

Sincerely yours,
Roger W. Sayers, Director
Human Relations Department

41/14
Enc.

SELECT BIBLIOGRAPHY

Bancroft, Frederic. *Slave Trading in the Old South.* Columbia, S.C.: University of South Carolina Press, 1996.

Carson, Clayborne. *Malcolm X, The FBI Files.* New York: Carroll & Graf, 1991.

Childs, Essie Jones. *They Tarried in Taylor (A Georgia County).* Central Georgia Genealogical Society, 1992.

Clarke, John Henrik, ed. *Malcolm X: The Man and His Times.* New York: Macmillan, 1969.

Cruse, Harold. *Plural but Equal.* New York: William Morrow, 1987.

David Walker's Appeal. Baltimore: Black Classic Press, 1993.

Davidson, William H. *A Rockaway in Talbot: Travels in an Old Georgia County.* West Point, Ga.: Hester Printing, 1985.

Diop, Cheikh Anta. *The Cultural Unity of Black Africa.* Chicago: Third World Press, 1978.

Equiano, Olaudah. *The Interesting Narrative of the Life of Olaudah Equiano.* New York: Praeger, 1967.

Essien-Udum. Essien Udosen. *Black Nationalism: A Search for Identity in America.* New York: Dell Publishing Co., 1969.

Evanzz, Karl. *The Judas Factor: The Plot to Kill Malcolm X.* New York: Thunder's Mouth Press, 1992.

Fitzpatrick, Sandra, and Maria R. Goodwin. *The Guide to Black Washington.* New York: Hippocrene Books, 1990.

Garvey, Amy Jacques, ed. *The Philosophy and Opinions of Marcus Garvey.* London: Frank Cass & Co., 1967.

Gates, Henry Louis, Jr., "Malcolm Little's Big Sister." *New Yorker,* January 1995.

Gatewood, Willard B. *Aristocrats of Color.* Indianapolis, Ind.: Indiana University Press, 1990.

Giammanco, Roberto. *Potere Negro.* Bari, Italy: Laterza & Figli SPA, 1967.

Gillings, Richard J. *Mathematics in the Time of the Pharaohs.* Cambridge, Mass.: M.I.T. Press, 1972.

Ginzburg, Ralph, ed. *100 Years of Lynchings.* New York: Lancer Books, 1962.

Haley, Alex. *Roots.* Garden City, N.Y.: Doubleday, 1976.

Jackson, Dr. Kennell. *America Is Me.* New York: HarperCollins, 1996.

Jones, D. Norrece T., Jr. *Born a Child of Freedom, Yet a Slave.* Hanover and London: Wesleyan University Press, University Press of New England, 1990.

King, Martin Luther, Jr. *Where Do We Go From Here: Community or Chaos?* New York, Evanston, and London: Harper & Row, 1967.

Kondo, Baba Zak A. *Conspiracys: Unravelling the Assassination of Malcolm X.* Washington, D.C.: Nubia Press, 1993.

Litwack, Leon, and August Meier, eds. *Black Leaders of the Nineteenth Century.* Illinois: University of Illinois Press, 1988.

Lomax, Louis E. *To Kill a Black Man.* Los Angeles: Holloway House, 1968.

———. *When the Word Is Given.* Los Angeles: World Publishing, 1963.

Malcolm X on Afro-American History. New York: Pathfinder Press, 1970.

Mr. Muhammad Speaks, vol. 1, no. 4, December 1960.

"Negro Veterans Lynched for Refusing to Doff Uniform," *Chicago Defender,* April, 1919.

Nkrumah, Kwame. *Axioms of Kwame Nkrumah.* New York: International Publishers, 1967.

Powell, Adam Clayton, Jr. *Adam by Adam: The Autobiography of Adam Clayton Powell, Jr.* New York: Dial Press, 1971.

Rashad, Adib. *Islam, Black Nationalism and Slavery.* Beltsville, Md.: Writers Inc. International, 1995.

Senna, Carl. *The Black Press and the Struggle for Civil Rights.* New York: Franklin Watts, 1993.

Strickland, William. *Malcolm X Makes It Plain.* Oral histories selected and edited by Cheryll Y. Greene. New York: Viking Penguin, 1994.

Van Sertima, Ivan. *They Came Before Columbus; The African Presence in Ancient America.* New York: Random House, 1977.

We Charge Genocide. New York: Civil Rights Congress, 1951.

West, Dorothy. *The Living Is Easy.* Stratford, N.H.: Ayer Publishers, 1970

X, Malcolm, "We Arose From the Dead," *Muslim World and the U.S.A.,* August–September, 1956.

X., Malcolm, and Alex Haley. *The Autobiography of Malcolm X.* New York: Grove Press, 1991.

Young, Andrew. *An Easy Burden.* New York: HarperCollins, 1996.

INDEX